Chester W. Hartman

# HOUSING
# and
# SOCIAL
# POLICY

prentice-hall, inc.
englewood cliffs, new jersey

*Library of Congress Cataloging in Publication Data*

HARTMAN, CHESTER W
  Housing and social policy.

  (Prentice-Hall series in social policy)
  Includes bibliographies.
  1. Housing—United States. I. Title.
HD7293.H34      301.5'4'0973      74-16438
ISBN  0-13-394999-0

**PRENTICE-HALL SERIES IN SOCIAL POLICY**

*Howard E. Freeman, Editor*

© 1975 by Prentice-Hall, Inc.
Englewood Cliffs, N.J.

10   9   8   7   6   5   4   3   2   1

Printed in the United States of America

*Prentice-Hall International, Inc., London*
*Prentice-Hall of Australia, Pty. Ltd., Sydney*
*Prentice-Hall of Canada, Ltd., Toronto*
*Prentice-Hall of India Private Limited, New Delhi*
*Prentice-Hall of Japan, Inc., Tokyo*

# CONTENTS

# ACKNOWLEDGMENTS

When writing a book about so diverse a subject as housing policy, one is particularly dependent on the specialized knowledge and competence of persons expert in individual sub-areas. I am therefore most appreciative of the helpful commentary given on earlier drafts of separate sections by Richard Bolan, Fred Bosselman, Anthony Downs, Herbert Franklin, Bernard Frieden, Frank Grad, Marshall Kaplan, Langley Keyes, Myron Moskovitz, Dick Netzer, George Rucker, and George Sternlieb. My especial gratitude goes to Emily Achtenberg, Herbert Gans, Jill Hamburg, Paul Niebanck, and Jon Pynoos who read an earlier draft of the manuscript as a whole and offered extremely useful guidelines for revision. Leslie Crane provided excellent research assistance. Audrey David, Coleen Davison, Nancy Jones, Mary Logan, and Brian Yamada at various points bravely managed the typing of some barely legible draft material. The Institute of Urban and Regional Development and the National Housing and Economic Development Law Project at the University of California, Berkeley, provided a most supportive and informed atmosphere for completing the manuscript. And finally, although it is not customary to acknowledge debts to places, the several retreats I took at both ends of the country, first in Massachusetts at the Brigham house in Menemsha and the Hershfangs' in the South End, later in Pine Grove, California, at the Ballachey house, provided the kind of writing atmosphere that permitted me to draft and redraft the major portion of the book, a fact which may require modification of my long-standing criticism of the physical determinist school of planning.

# INTRODUCTION

This book begins with a premise: that all Americans have the *right* to decent housing, in decent surroundings of their own choosing, at rents or prices they can afford. This right has not yet achieved constitutional or legal status,[1] although our economy and society have the means to support it. We lack only sufficient political impetus to demand its fulfillment.

*Housing and Social Policy* is intended as an overview of the housing system for those looking into this complex field for the first time. In the course of a necessarily brief volume, I have tried to delineate the nature and dimensions of the housing problem, the barriers to increased and lower-priced housing production, the difficulties in maintaining decent occupancy conditions in the existing housing stock, and the successes and failures of government intervention in the housing market over the past four decades. For those who wish to investigate specific areas in greater detail, references to the more useful academic and popular studies are sprinkled liberally throughout the text.

This work was completed at a time of considerable crisis and confusion on the United States housing scene. General inflation in the economy is particularly hard on the housing sector, because mortgage money, (the life-blood of housing production and consumption) dries up, interest rates soar, and land prices and other elements rise steeply. In turn,

---

1. See Frank I. Michelman, "The Right to Housing," in Norman Dorsen, ed., *The Rights of Americans—What They Are—What They Should Be* (New York: Pantheon, 1971), pp. 43–64.

housing production falls, and the prices and rents of new as well as
existing housing rise to levels beyond the means of most families. In early
1973, the administration declared a moratorium on all federally funded
housing and community development programs, pending a reevaluation
of the government's role in the housing area.[2] And later that year, the
administration announced its intention of ending most of the existing
federal housing programs and substituting a housing allowance approach, although legislation to implement this new role may not be
forthcoming for a considerable time.[3] The Housing and Community
Development Act of 1974, signed into law by President Ford within weeks
after he took office, provides for a drastic reorganization of federal aid
to localities; it substitutes block grants for the former system of funding
specific programs and revises many of the federal housing programs. The
unprecedented crisis in American government during 1973 and 1974
diverted attention and energies from specific problem areas to basic
issues of survival and the administration's integrity and ability to govern.
What exact form national housing policy will take under the new administration remains to be seen, but it is not likely to depart markedly from
previous policies. None of the events of the recent past suggests any
lessened need to provide more widespread understanding of the nation's
housing problem, why it exists, and what will and will not provide solu-
tions.

The overarching issue raised in this book is whether the right to
decent housing is compatible with the profit system. Does control of the
basic elements of housing (in particular, land and capital) by private
entrepreneurs, who are motivated by the principle of profit maximiza-
tion, preclude building enough housing, at a cost lower-income
households[4] can afford, in places where they want to live? And can such
entrepreneurial control create and maintain decent conditions of occupancy in the existing housing stock? Further, do the existing institutions
and governmental relationships within our housing system hinder the
average citizen's attainment of decent housing? These economic and
political interests that shape the housing system are the fundamental
social policy issue addressed by this volume.

2. See Chester W. Hartman and W. Dennis Keating, "Housing: A Poor Man's Home is
*His* Problem," in Alan Gartner, Colin Greer, and Frank Riessman, eds., *What Nixon Is Doing
to Us* (New York: Harper and Row, 1973), pp. 42–57.

3. See John Herbers, "President Urges U.S. Allowances to Spur Housing," New York
*Times*, September 20, 1973.

4. As used in this book, the term *low-income* will refer to households with annual incomes
less than $4500–5000 for a family of four ($3000 for one- and two-person households, and
$6000–7000 for large families); *moderate-income* refers to households between these upper
figures and the income levels at which decent housing is available on the private market
without subsidy—around $8000–9000 for a family of four, lower for small households,
higher for large households. These distinctions are rough and somewhat arbitrary, but they
will give the reader a general idea of the groups being described. The term *lower income* will
refer to the entire group in need of subsidization.

# Chapter 1

# AN OVERVIEW OF THE HOUSING PROBLEM

## Why Housing Matters

Traditionally, notions of housing needs and concern about housing conditions have centered around issues of health and safety: poor housing conditions caused a variety of diseases, illnesses, and accidents; therefore such conditions had to be improved or eliminated, out of concern for the residents themselves or because of the threat these conditions, particularly fire and pestilence, presented to those whose homes surrounded the slums. Improved housing would reduce the incidence of such pathologies and dangers. Logic and data were available to demonstrate this relationship: rates of tuberculosis, dysentery, skin disease, and childhood infections were higher among slum dwellers, and the etiology of such diseases indicated that they could reliably be ascribed to poor ventilation, sanitary conditions, or kitchen equipment.

As housing conditions objectively improved, however, it became more difficult to demonstrate such relationships convincingly. In a major controlled longitudinal experiment in Baltimore in the late 1950s, Daniel Wilner and his associates found little correlation between the disease rates of an experimental group that moved from the slums to a public housing project and those of a control group that remained in the slums. It is noteworthy that the improved housing to which the experimental

1

group moved was public housing projects. Despite the generally good physical condition of these developments, they have severe social deficiencies (see chapter 4, "Dissatisfactions with Public Housing"). The absence of better results among those who moved may demonstrate that the concept of housing conditions today embodies a range of social as well as of physical attributes, and that improvement in only one aspect may not be perceived or experienced as improvement in overall living conditions.

This is not to say that housing conditions, even for the poor, no longer present any danger to the physical health and safety of inhabitants. Among the more notable hazards of slum living are a higher incidence of fires, related to poor heating equipment and wiring; higher rates of home accidents, from broken stairs and other structural defects; rat bites (it has been estimated that 14,000 Americans, mostly children, suffer rat bites each year, and that far more bites occur than are reported); and hazards to personal safety resulting from poor lighting, inadequate locks, and the like. For example, a recent Department of Health, Education and Welfare study showed that as many as 2.5 million Americans may be risking severe illness or death from carbon monoxide poisoning because of faulty heaters. One of the clearest instances of damage directly caused by housing is that some 400,000 children—virtually all of them residents of slum areas—may suffer from lead poisoning as a consequence of ingesting lead-based paint on walls and woodwork in older apartments. Interior use of lead-based paint was outlawed decades ago, but surveys in several cities indicate that in certain slum areas—the so-called lead belts—the interiors of 40 to 80 percent of the units are covered with this highly toxic material. Each year about 200 children from one to six years of age die from lead poisoning, and 800 suffer brain damage. Recently developed screening tests have found dangerously high levels of lead in the blood of 5 to 10 percent of all slum area children tested. If lead paint surfaces were eliminated or properly recovered, it would save lives and lower illness rates. But even though there is a considerable residue of housing that is demonstrably injurious to physical health and safety, it is improbable that the housing conditions of the vast majority of today's ill-housed are detrimental in this respect.

Recently the notion of housing-related pathologies has been expanded to include such aspects of social and personal life as juvenile delinquency, job and school performance, and family disorganization. The "social pathology case" for eliminating poor housing conditions is even more difficult to make. It may be a foolish and dangerous simplification to regard housing conditions, rather than broader aspects of the way the economy and society are organized, as the root cause for so-called social pathologies. While good housing can provide a supportive environment for change, it is unlikely that basic problems of employment, education, and crime will be swept away by moving into a good home in a nice neighborhood. Furthermore, many definitions of pathology derive from the biased perspective of the white middle-class majority. The country's serious need for improved housing cannot rest exclusively on arguments of health and safety or social pathology.

A sufficient basis for concern and action with regard to housing is that most people feel that their living conditions are central to their lives, and millions of American families deem their current living conditions as onerous and unacceptable in view of what the society offers to the rest of its people. Such an attitude is backed by data relating to standards society has promulgated concerning accepted norms. Not only are the living conditions of the ill-housed objectively deficient, they are also deprived in comparison with what others have, what they see and know about in other parts of the community, and what they know is possible under a different set of social priorities.

Most surveys of the poor show that housing is the first or second most important problem they face. For example, the 1966 Kraft survey of Harlem reports that "whatever way the problems are examined, housing keeps coming up as 'number one,' and by wide margins." The urban "riots" of the 1960s may legitimately be regarded as an extreme form of discontent and rebellion against general conditions of life, but it is instructive to note that, according to the official report on the 1967 Newark riots, ". . . Negroes cited 'bad housing conditions' most often when they were asked to choose among fifteen possible underlying causes of the 1967 disorders." Housing conditions should be understood to include not only the physical condition of the dwelling unit and structure but also control over living conditions, the cost of housing in relation to perceived value and ability to afford these costs, the conditions of the surrounding neighborhood, social life, and accessibility to community facilities and employment. There are signs that the housing issue is shifting from exclusive focus on the physical facility to what the facility produces in the way of residential services for the occupant, both within the home and on a neighborhood and community level.[1]

It is easy to understand why housing is so important to all households, and perhaps more important to the poor than to the non-poor. Many people—particularly housewives, children, and the elderly—spend more time in the home than in any other single place, and so the nature of the space is an important determinant of personal and family satisfaction. This is also true of the immediate neighborhood: unattrac-

1. See Morton L. Isler, "The Goals of Housing Subsidy Programs," pp. 415–38; and Henry J. Aaron, *Shelter and Subsidies: Who Benefits From Federal Housing Policies?* pp. 4–6.

tive, dirty, uncared for, depressing surroundings can contribute to great personal dissatisfaction and apathy. A neighborhood is usually a powerful determinant of social life—of the extent to which one socializes, of the kinds of people one socializes with, and of the nature and quality of this interaction. For most people housing and neighborhood are also the most accurate and evident indices of socioeconomic standing. Where and how one lives is an inward and outward sign of one's place in the society, an irrefutable label to one's self, one's friends, and the world. To live in poor housing, in a poor neighborhood—to be a "slum dweller"—is to be on the bottom of the heap. Finally, the location of a person's house with respect to schools, medical facilities, jobs, shopping, and transportation crucially influences the benefits that a person can derive from the society.

For most families housing ranks first or second in the household budget; thus expenses for housing consumption as they relate to ability to pay may be looked at as a distinct housing issue. It is a matter that becomes increasingly important as housing costs rise faster than income, in many areas and for many groups almost irrespective of whether there is an adequate level of housing services. The traditional yardstick for housing costs is the so-called rent-income ratio. Standards in this area are somewhat vague, however, and have little rational basis. The numbers most frequently put forth as the proper portion to devote to housing are 20 or 25 percent of family income, though it is somewhat higher for the elderly, who tend to spend less for food, clothing, transportation, and most other daily expenses and more for things like medical care. A Department of Labor study entitled "Housing the Poor and the Shelter-to-Income Ratio" concludes, however, that "the ratio of shelter cost to income for subsidized housing for the poor and near-poor family with children will work out to be well below 20 percent."

Because housing expenditures are a relatively fixed budget item—unlike food expenditures, for example, which can be adjusted immediately by consuming less, changing the composition of meals, or buying inferior products—families of lower income seek, albeit with little success, to keep housing expenditures to a reasonable portion of their income. Payments of 30, 35, 40 and more percent of houshold income for housing can lead to effects on health and well-being that are far more deleterious than those that come from overcrowded and substandard physical housing conditions. Among poorer families there is also the feeling or knowledge that the housing services they purchase are in many ways highly unsatisfactory and overpriced (see "The Ill-Housed," this chapter). Large families tend to allocate less for housing, since they need more for food, clothing, and other necessities, which creates a double bind, since they also need more housing space. Particularly in slum areas and for minority groups, failure to pay rent or utility charges at the stipulated time can and usually does result in immediate legal action or curtailment of service, as well as additional financial costs—moving, possibly higher rents, court payments, service resumption charges—and the nonfinancial costs of disrupted life patterns.

A family of four with annual income of $3000 really cannot "afford" to pay anything for housing, because they require their entire income simply to eat properly, clothe themselves adequately, receive decent medical care, and pay other necessary expenditures. An expenditure of 25, 20, or even 10 percent of this meager income for housing means depriving the family of necessities in other key areas.

Another issue relates to control of living conditions. A key aspect of slum rental housing—and the majority of the ill-housed in urban areas are renters—is the lack of control over one's life, and subservience to the landlord and others who exert effective control over the family's living conditions. Since the landlord-tenant relationship in law and economic reality overwhelmingly favors the landlord, the family living in poor housing rarely has any effective control over such basic matters as acceptance for tenancy, eviction, rent levels, maintenance, and repairs. This powerlessness extends to the residential surroundings and the quality of municipal services in the neighborhood. Poor housing thus mirrors the pervasive sense of impotence many poor families feel about their environment and about their lives. Such a global perspective gives demands for housing improvement far greater significance and many more dimensions than those associated with traditional arguments based on physical and social pathologies.

## Measuring Housing Conditions

If we can describe housing needs as a multidimensional package, it then follows that information by which to assess housing conditions and the scope of housing goals and programs ought to be equally comprehensive. In both areas, however, reality falls woefully short of the ideal. Available data on housing conditions, even notions of the kinds of data that are important, are but a small part of what we need to guide social policy. Moreover, the quality and reporting frequency for those items that are surveyed are extremely inadequate. A precise, reliable description of the nature and magnitude of the U.S. housing problem is not possible, and ideas based on the data that are available significantly understate the housing problem.

The sole source of data for the nation as a whole is the decennial housing census, which was begun in 1940. There have been four housing censuses to date (and occasional interim surveys). The infrequency with which comprehensive data are collected makes it difficult to gauge the magnitude of the housing problem and directional trends accurately, and equally difficult to formulate sound programs and policies. In the latter part of the decade the census data become increasingly less reliable, because the housing stock is in constant flux. We need more frequent censuses, possibly through sampling techniques, or a constant national or state monitoring system, based on local construction and demolition statistics and on-site checks to gauge the upgrading and deterioration of the existing housing stock, as indicators of emerging problems and as guides to remedial action. (A new Annual Housing Survey, based on a small national sample, was begun in 1973 to provide a regular indicator of housing changes.) It is a telling commentary on the nation's unwillingness to face its housing problem squarely that adequate data are not even assembled.

Other problems have to do with measurement techniques and what is measured—which to an extent determine and are determined by the way the housing problem is defined. Up through the 1960 Census, housing conditions were assessed by census enumerators, through visual inspection and interviewee responses. The tens of thousands who were hired for several months as census enumerators received cursory training and were unable to assess accurately many of structural and environmental conditions that should be examined, or to distinguish between superficial appearance and underlying reality. Census reliability in this area was so low that housing condition ratings were deleted entirely from the 1970 Census, and all that remains, apart from some wholly unreliable estimating procedures, is ratings of plumbing facilities and overcrowding. Many important aspects of living conditions that have to do with health and safety—faulty wiring, weaknesses in the building foundation, and defective heating equipment—cannot be determined on the basis of casual visual inspection, and indeed the Census makes no attempt to include these defects.

Census ratings are a minimal statement of the housing problem. Local housing codes, which in most urban areas set the legal minimum standard for residential occupancy, contain a far more detailed and comprehensive catalogue of standards and critical defects. The Massachusetts State Sanitary Code, for example, sets statewide mandatory minimum local standards for the following: kitchen and bathroom facilities, water supply, hot water and heating facilities, lighting and electrical facilities, ventilation, space and space usage, exits, insect and rodent infestation, garbage and rubbish storage and disposal, and sewage disposal. Millions of additional substandard units would have to be acknowledged if housing conditions were measured nationally by prevailing code standards. One startling glimmer of the magnitudes that may be involved is provided by data from so-called concentrated code enforcement areas (see chapter 3, "Housing Codes"). Under the terms of federal granting procedures these areas cannot be severely blighted or slum areas, yet in twelve such areas a total of 31,000 buildings received detailed inspection, and 72 percent were in violation of the local code. In five areas the percentage of buildings in violation was at least 85 percent, and in one area it was 98 percent! The National Commission on Urban Problems (the Douglas Commission), which collected and reported these data, noted that "the percentage of buildings which would be found in violation of the housing code, or the number and severity of code violations, or both, would be much higher in the poorer sections of these cities than in the sections inspected and reported upon." In large areas of our cities virtually every building may be in violation of the local code. The Washington Planning and Housing Association in its January 1968 newsletter reported that during 1965–66 of 115,913 dwellings inspected, 114,060 were not in compliance with the District housing code. As Oscar Sutermeister writes:

> It is readily apparent that even the most conscientious user of Census data ... would arrive at a total "substandard" housing figure which grossly underestimated the number of dwelling units having serious housing code violations. To use a total thus arrived at as a figure for substandard housing is grossly inaccurate and misleading, because it flies in the face of extensive consideration given by health experts, building officials, model code drafting organizations, and the local, state, and federal court system to what have become over a period of many years, the socially, politically, and legally accepted minimum standard for housing of human beings in the United States. ... Even if public and private efforts eliminate all housing which is substandard under most current federal definitions, there will still be millions of dwelling units below code standard.

Overcrowding, another important aspect of substandard housing, is not a property of housing quality per se, but rather of the "fit" between the size of the unit and the number of occupants. There is reason to believe that the effects of overcrowding on mental health and family life may be more severe than the effects of physically substandard conditions, and that we ought to devote more effort to ameliorating the housing plight of families overcrowded in physically adequate units. Among the more serious effects of overcrowding are increased stress, poor development of a sense of individuality, sexual conflict, intrafamilial tensions, and lack of adequate sleep, which contributes to poor work and school performance. Our measuring standards in this area are also crude and so probably understate the magnitude of the problem. The Census uses a ratio of 1.01 or more persons per room (not including bathrooms, hallways, and porches) as the point at which people in a household are living in overcrowded conditions. A ratio of 1.51 or more is severe overcrowding. The measure takes no account of family composition—age, sex, relationships—or the nature of the dwelling unit—layout, quality, and size of rooms. Greenfield and Lewis used a more sophisticated measure of overcrowding on a random sample of households and found an 11.6 percent overcrowding rate, compared to the 1.3 percent rate measured by Census Bureau criteria.[2] This measure of adequate space standards, which exceeds the traditional Census standard by a factor of nine, suggests that, as with physical conditions, our accepted measuring rods may sharply understate the magnitude of existing housing deficiencies.

With respect to the residential environment, as opposed to the dwelling unit itself, there is a virtual vacuum of standards or data. The concern of housing policy has been broadened in recent years to encompass the full range of residential services, but no meaningful and usable standards have been developed or applied to evaluate the neighborhood environment in which the individual housing unit is located. Nor are data on the residential environment collected on a large-scale or reliable basis to assess housing needs and gaps. Observation and informed opinion, however, offer convincing evidence that a great many neighborhoods in no sense provide decent living environments for their inhabitants, regardless of the condition of individual structures within the neighborhood.

Housing need or deprivation may thus be measured along a number of dimensions: the physical quality of the dwelling unit, extent of overcrowding, the burden of housing costs, and the quality of the social and physical environment. But our standards, measuring tools, and comprehension of the problem are severely limited, and there is good reason to believe that the nation's housing problem is far more serious than even the most "realistic" data sources and estimates indicate.

### The Ill-Housed

All these caveats about inadequate data and poorly developed standards notwithstanding, it is nonetheless necessary to turn to the available information to get at least a minimal picture of the nation's housing problems. According to the 1970 Census there were 68.6 million housing units in the U.S., 63.4 million of which were occupied. Of the 5.2 million vacant units, many are seasonal or designed to house migrant

2. The standard applied was: a married couple may share a room; no more than two children of the same sex may share a room past the age of twelve; no more than two children of the opposite sex may share a room past the age of three; all others must have individual sleeping rooms; and there must be two additional rooms, for food preparation and for general living purposes. See R. J. Greenfield and J. F. Lewis, "An Alternative to a Density Function Definition of Overcrowding."

laborers. Many of the year-round units are awaiting occupancy, are used occasionally by the owners, or are otherwise not on the market. Vacancy rates are meaningful only when broken down by metropolitan areas or counties, location within these local markets, price or rent, size, availability for rent or for sale, and other characteristics. An available, year-round vacancy rate of 3–5 percent in the local housing market is usually considered the minimum to permit necessary mobility, choice, and renewal of the housing supply. Vacancy rates furthermore are highly ephemeral and tend to be self-limiting, since new construction generally is not undertaken in a slack market.

Since the 1970 Census did not include structural ratings, we lack important information about the housing stock and can only make limited comparisons with 1960 data. There were 4.7 million year-round units without adequate plumbing facilities in the 1970 Census, 7 percent of the housing stock; in 1960, 15.2 million units, or 26 percent of the housing stock, either lacked adequate plumbing facilities or were structurally deteriorating or dilapidated.[3] Eight percent of all households, 5.2 million families, had a density ratio of 1.01 or higher in 1970, and 1.3 million families had a ratio higher than 1.5. In 1960 the corresponding figures were 11.5 percent of all households, 6.1 million families, and 1.9 million families. Of the 5.2 million overcrowded households in 1970, 4.4 million were living in units that had adequate plumbing facilities. If we use only non-overlapping Census criteria of inadequate plumbing and overcrowding, 9.1 million U.S. households, or one out of seven families, are living in substandard housing conditions.

Of the units without adequate plumbing, about one-third are located in Standard Metropolitan Statistical Areas (SMSAs), two-thirds in rural areas; within the SMSAs, slightly less than half the deficient units are in the central cities. (SMSAs consist of cities or "twin cities" with 50,000 or more inhabitants, plus contiguous areas that, according to stipulated criteria, are socially and economically integrated with the central city; as of 1970, there were 243 SMSAs, which together contained 69 percent of the nation's population.) For overcrowded units, the distribution is reversed: two-thirds are located in SMSAs, one-third in rural areas. The incidence of substandard housing conditions is disproportionately large among renter households.

A substantial portion of the nation's households thus are still living in substandard conditions, even by this most inadequate of measures,

3. The 1960 Census rated all units as either "sound" (no defects, or only the slight defects that are normally corrected during the course of regular maintenance), "deteriorating" (needing more repair than would be provided in the course of regular maintenance), or "dilapidated" (not providing safe and adequate shelter). "All plumbing facilities" means hot and cold piped water inside the structure, a flush toilet, and bathtub or shower inside the structure for exclusive use of the occupants of the unit.

although, taken together with information from the 1940, 1950, and 1960 Censuses, there would seem to be little doubt that on an aggregate basis the housing of the American people has steadily improved. Once one moves from the aggregate to specific subgroups and submarkets, the picture becomes somewhat different, particularly when housing costs are also brought into the picture. Based on scattered data and observations, it would appear that for the poor, the elderly, individual householders, racial minorities, large families, and in some rural areas and large cities, housing conditions are still extremely severe and may be getting worse.

A special Census Bureau survey of East and South Los Angeles taken immediately following the Watts riots of 1965 showed that since 1960 the proportion of substandard housing in these two areas had risen from 25 percent to 35 percent and from 18 percent to 33 percent, respectively, and that during the same period median rents had risen from $63 to $75 and from $69 to $77. A task force established by Mayor John Lindsay and headed by the late Charles Abrams found that between 1960 and 1965 the number of unsound units in New York City increased from 420,000 to 525,000, while the median rent:income ratio rose from 18.4 percent to 20.4 percent. In 1969 the number of unsound units in New York was estimated to be 800,000. In Boston, according to a study by the Boston Redevelopment Authority, "between 1960 and 1965 'deteriorating and dilapidated' housing in the city increased by 5 percent, from 21 percent in 1960 to 26 percent in 1965." As housing economist William Grigsby and his associates conclude, "mounting evidence strongly suggests that at some time during the past four or five years the long-term upward trend in housing conditions in major metropolitan areas has suddenly levelled off and reversed itself. Shelter problems for lower-income families in these areas are becoming worse."

Housing in rural areas, though improving, shows a disproportionate incidence of deterioration and dilapidation, as indicated above. There is especially a lack of adequate plumbing facilities: according to the 1970 Census nine out of ten units without a flush toilet or running water are rural. Lower incomes in rural areas are one reason for the greater incidence of poor housing conditions, but even at given income levels more rural families than urban families live in substandard housing: among families earning less than $3000 per year, the 1960 incidence of substandard housing was 45 percent in rural areas and small towns, 23 percent in urban areas. Studies by Cochran and Rucker of rural areas in Arkansas and South Carolina indicate no improvement or actual decline in housing conditions. The most ill-housed rural group of all, according to Sternberg and Bishop, are Indians on reservations: 67 percent were living in substandard or overcrowded conditions in 1970. Apart from income differentials, rural housing has lagged because of the shortage of credit in rural areas, more effective racial discrimination, widespread absence of building and housing codes, low levels of new construction, and competition of farm business for the family's housing dollar.

Perhaps the most serious form of deterioration of housing conditions in the last decade is the rapid rise in the cost of housing of any kind, as the Watts Area and New York City studies suggest. Good studies of changing rent levels are infrequent, but a 1970 study of the Boston area by the MIT-Harvard Joint Center for Urban Studies is probably indicative of what has been happening in almost all large urban areas. The survey showed that from 1960 to 1970 median rents have risen 66 percent, from $78 a month, including heat and utilities, to $130. At the same time there was only a 33 percent rise in median family income and a 27 percent rise in the cost-of-living index (which includes rent) for the Boston area. One out of every three Boston families now pays more than 30 percent of its income for housing, including nine out of every ten families with annual incomes of less than $3000. The survey found that "the majority of people who have incomes under $6000 per year cannot find suitable housing in Boston that will cost them less than 30 percent of their incomes." Those paying high rents and high proportions of their income for housing were frequently families living in small units and in the most deteriorating parts of the city. In San Francisco, according to 1970 Census data, fully 47 percent of all renters pay 25 percent or more of their income for housing. The same Census revealed that 8.1 million American renter families pay 25 percent or more of their income for rent, and 5.2 million pay more than 35 percent. (Data on housing costs as a percentage of income are not collected for homeowners.)

The people who suffer most from rising housing costs are those on fixed incomes, most notably the elderly. According to a recent study by a U.S. Senate Special Committee on Aging:

> Millions of older Americans—whether they live in congested cities or sparsely populated rural areas—now find themselves in a "no-man's land" with regard to housing. Hundreds of thousands are being driven from their homes because of prohibitive property taxes and maintenance costs. . . . Yet, it is becoming increasingly difficult to locate suitable alternative quarters at rents they can afford.

A high proportion of these older persons own their homes clear of mortgage debt, but rapidly rising property taxes (ironically, to pay primarily for educational services they no longer use) take substantial parts of their incomes. The Senate study revealed that more than 8000 aged Wisconsin homeowners who live on less than $1000 a year paid 30 percent of their incomes for property taxes alone.

The housing problems of low-income persons are compounded by the market reality that "the poor pay more," and also get less. If the poor are nonwhite, the gap is even greater. A report by Cicarelli and Landers on Portland, Oregon, shows that on a square foot basis average monthly rents in poor areas of the city were 18 percent higher than average monthly rents in nonpoor areas. A Department of Labor study of six cities showed that "homes occupied by low-income families were much more likely to be of lower quality, with respect to each of the specific character-istics studied, than were those occupied by families with higher incomes even when they paid the same rent." Among families paying $40 to $60 rent, 38 percent of families with under $3000 income were living in slum areas, compared with 21 percent of families with over $6000 income, while at this same rent level only 68 percent of the former were living in sound housing, compared with 87 percent of the latter. *Blacks Pay More for Less,* a recent report of the Department of Housing and Urban Development (HUD) based on 51 cities, showed that

> blacks living in low-income areas of major cities pay on the average more for shelter than whites living in the same areas [$95 median monthly housing expense for blacks, compared with $79 for whites]; a higher proportion of blacks than of whites must devote an inordinate amount of income to housing expense [a fifth of black families pay at least 25 percent of income for housing, compared with 14 percent of white families]; and yet a much higher proportion of blacks than whites [twice as high] live in overcrowded housing.

In some cities the differences are staggering: median monthly housing expenses in Chicago's low-income areas are $123 for black families, $88 for white families, or nearly 40 percent higher. These findings hold for Mexican-Americans as well, as a major study of this group by Leo Grebler and his associates has shown:

> The frequency of substandard housing among the Mexican-American population is not solely a function of income. The rate of substandard housing among Spanish-speaking households was perceptibly higher than for Anglos or all other households at every level of family income. . . . For example, the chances that a Spanish-speaking household in Los Angeles in the $7,000 to $10,000 income class will occupy a substandard housing unit were four and a half times the chances of an Anglo household having the same income.

Overall housing conditions for black families are markedly worse than for white families. In 1970 20 percent of all black households were overcrowded, compared with 8 percent of all households. Fourteen percent of all black households had either no running water or no hot water, compared with 5 percent of all households. Only 42 percent of all black families own their own homes, compared with 65 percent of all white families. A Gallup poll taken in late 1971 indicated that while 77 percent of all whites were satisfied with their housing situation, a substantial rise since 1949, only 51 percent of all blacks were satisfied with their housing situation, and that dissatisfaction among blacks had markedly increased during this period. Since by objective standards housing conditions for nonwhites improved tremendously during this period, the more important issues seem to be rising expectations and the gap between nonwhite and white housing conditions.

The available data make it clear that these differences in housing conditions among black and white households are not due solely to lower incomes or larger household size. Rather, they are attributable to the workings of a discriminatory housing market. In most localities there are two separate housing submarkets at all rent and price levels: a highly restricted market for racial minorities, and an open, free-choice market for the white majority. This "two-market" phenomenon is in large part a product of historical patterns and social preferences, particularly on the part of the white majority, but it is strongly undergirded with institutional supports. According to a 1972 government report entitled *Freedom of Choice in Housing:*

> A web of institutional discrimination exists that reduces the "effective" supply, especially for nonwhite minorities. The institutional web, comprised of many interrelated components, ranges from the services of realtors, mortgage lenders, government regulations, and administrative and political behavior of government officials; to patterns and practices related to employment, schools, transportation, and community services.

A long legacy of racially restrictive covenants or deed restrictions, no longer legally enforceable but still operant and embraced until the late 1940s by even the Federal Housing Administration, ensured sharply segregated neighborhoods. The real estate fraternity—brokers, rental agents, and property managers—still plays a strong role in determining who shall live where in cities and suburbs.[4] This influence and control is not used strictly to maintain apartheid, for there is great profit to be made in the carefully managed racial transformation of neighborhoods, a prac-

4. On the real estate industry, see William H. Brown, Jr., "Access to Housing: The Role of the Real Estate Industry"; Rose Helper, *Racial Policies and Practices of Real Estate Brokers;* and John H. Denton, *Apartheid American Style,* which discusses the role of the National Association of Real Estate Boards in the Proposition 14 campaign in California to nullify the state's open housing legislation. Elsewhere Denton argues that brokers manipulate racial patterns in the real estate market in order to keep the amount of direct dealing between buyers and sellers to a minimum. See National Committee Against Discrimination in Housing and Department of Housing and Urban Development, *Urban Renewal Demonstration Project.* A discussion of "fair housing" groups, the attempt at a countervailing force, is contained in Julia Z. Saltman, *Open Housing as a Social Movement.*

tice known as *blockbusting.* Introduction of nonwhite families, desperately in need of improved housing because of restrictions on their choice, will often cause white families to flee, selling their homes at "panic" prices to brokers, who then sell the homes at sharply inflated prices to incoming nonwhite families who are forced to pay this "race tax" because of limited options. (Among the more malodorous techniques that have been used by real estate agents to induce panic selling among whites are hiring a black woman to walk through residential streets wheeling a baby carriage, employing black real estate salesmen to go door to door and ask residents if they are thinking of selling, and sending postcards inviting people to a gathering to meet a fictitious new neighbor with a Spanish surname.)

The nation's housing problem thus is still immense, although it seems to focus on several clearly defined groups and areas. A recent study by David Birch and others at the M.I.T.-Harvard Joint Center for Urban Studies indicates that in 1970 13.1 million households (21 percent of all households) suffered from one or more forms of housing deprivation: a physically substandard unit, overcrowded living conditions, or high rent burden. Were we to measure physical inadequacy by local housing code standards; employ a less conservative measure of overcrowding (the study counted as overcrowded only households of three or more persons living at density ratios of 1.5 or more); include homeowners as well as renters paying an excessive portion of their incomes for housing; and add households living in inadequate neighborhoods and environments—it is likely that well over a third of the population is now in need of some form of housing assistance. In the three decades since the end of World War II the private market has been able to provide for tens of millions of families and effect a marked upgrading in the country's housing standards. Most of those still living in substandard conditions are persons whom the private market cannot serve; if they are to be housed decently, substantial subsidies and major institutional changes will be required.

## The Nation's Housing Goals

Nearly 25 years ago, in its preamble to the 1949 Housing Act, the Congress promulgated as the National Housing Goal "a decent home and a suitable living environment for every American family." Unfortunately, there was virtually no consideration given to implementing this goal—no quantification, no plan, no timetable. It is not uncharitable to describe the 1949 statement as little more than rhetoric. In the 1968 Housing Act Congress reaffirmed the 1949 goal, acknowledged that "this goal has not been fully realized for many of the nation's lower income families" and determined "that it can be substantially achieved within the next decade by the construction or rehabilitation of 26 million housing units, 6 million of these for low- and moderate-income families." These figures were a rough average of the estimates of need derived by the U.S. Department of Housing and Urban Development (HUD), the President's Committee on Urban Housing (which actually spoke of a need for "6 to 8 million units for the poor"), the National Commission on Urban Problems, and the National Commission on Civil Disorders. The Housing Act establishes a ten-year target date—June 30, 1978—for attainment of the goals, and makes provision for annual production goals. Significantly, the only specific attributes of the national goal are number of dwelling units and the approximate income class of the future occupants. There was no attempt to implement the "suitable living environment" half of the goal, and no guidance with respect to locational attributes.

The sheer number of units is impressive, particularly in view of the past record of the housing industry (which averaged only 1.4 million units during the 1960s and only approached 2 million units in one year—1950, with its postwar backlog) but it is important to recognize that even this goal falls short of the need. In arriving at these figures, units in the Census category "deteriorating" were not considered substandard if they had adequate plumbing facilities, there was no provision for dealing with overcrowding, and neither environmental features nor local code standards were taken into account. As Oscar Sutermeister observes:

> When President Johnson signed the Housing Act of 1968, he stated that the bill promised the elimination of substandard housing in the United States within the next decade. If the old definition of substandard housing is used in attempting to achieve this promise, the results will be a mockery to the ghetto residents of our nation who will still be living with uncounted millions of housing code violations.

Nor were subsidies projected for families living in decent housing but paying too high a proportion of their income for housing.

After a very slow start, largely because of inflation and the shortage of housing credit in 1969–70, production rates have picked up considerably. Few knowledgeable observers of the American housing scene feel, however, there is much chance of reaching the 1978 goal. Anthony Downs, a member of National Commission on Urban Problems, has written "I do not believe the nation will reach the official housing targets by 1980. This conclusion seems to me an inescapable result of any thorough and realistic assessment of the true probabilities that all of the key actors will behave in the ways necessary to carry out [these targets]"[5] The annual presidential reports on national housing goals for 1969 through 1972 support this conclusion. In 1969, only 1.6 million conventional units (plus 400,000 mobile homes) were produced, and in 1970 production fell to 1.4 million units (1.8 million, counting mobile homes). In 1971 and 1972 production rates climbed to an all-time high—2.2 million and 2.6 million, respectively, 1.7 million and 2.0 million not counting mobile homes. An end to the earlier "tight money" period and a sharp rise in production under two new interest-subsidy programs for moderate-income families introduced in the 1968 Housing Act, Secs. 235 and 236 (see chapter 5, "Subsidized Home Ownership," and "Interest Subsidies and Tax Benefits for Rental Housing") occasioned this upsurge. Since then, however, soaring interest rates and an administration moratorium on federal housing programs—followed by a policy decision to virtually abandon existing approaches to subsidized housing—have reversed the bullish trends in the housing market. Housing starts fell sharply during 1973 and early 1974; the average monthly rate of private housing starts in the four-month period from November 1973 through February 1974 was 34 percent below that of the same period in 1972 to 1973.

The most serious barrier to attaining the National Housing Goal is the sharply rising cost of housing production. The costs of new housing have risen to the point that four-fifths of all U.S. households can no longer afford to purchase a conventional unsubsidized new single-family house. Only 7 percent of New York City's population can afford the new privately financed housing being constructed there. According to National Association of Home Builders estimates, each $100 increase in the cost of housing prices 14,000 families out of the market.

One response of the homebuilding industry has been to give the consumer less in land, location, construction quality, space, and amenities, which means that these dollar figures understate the impact of rising costs. As Herbert Franklin observes, "that old, comforting notion that the housing supply will 'filter down' is being replaced by a new understanding: housing problems are filtering up." There is little doubt that with respect to costs the housing problem has become a problem for middle-income families as well as low- and moderate-income families.

5. Anthony Downs, "Moving Toward Realistic Housing Goals," p. 127. For a more roseate prospect, see *A Decent Home*, pp. 124–205, where the case is systematically presented that each of the necessary resources—credit, land, industrial capacity, labor, and materials —is available in sufficient supply. For the view that the goal of 26 million units exaggerates the level of need and may be harmful to the housing industry, see George Cline Smith, "Housing in the Seventies: Realism vs. Euphoria."

Responsibility for the increasing cost of housing lies almost exclusively with the costs of land and capital. According to Elsie Eaves and others, the cost of constructing the house itself—materials, labor, and the like—has been increasing at a rate less than the general cost of living, as measured by the Consumer Price Index. In fact, although wage rates for the construction trades have been rapidly rising, the portion of housing cost attributable to on-site labor has dropped over the past twenty years from 33 percent to 18 percent.[6] From 1949 to 1969, however, land costs on all new single-family homes built rose 319 percent. In 1949 land costs were 11 percent of the sales price, and in 1969 they were 24 percent of sales price. Land costs now are rising at the rate of 12 to 15 percent annually. Land speculation is a central and sacred activity in our economic system, and land investment is particularly popular as a hedge against inflation. Recently corporations and realty trusts have been investing in land. Nearly 150 of the country's major corporations are actively participating in real estate as an added source of income, and their combined holdings (in excess of their own production and service needs) may be as high as $9 billion. It is clear that land speculation and reduction of housing costs are contradictory ends and that spiralling land prices may rule out the possibility of low- and moderate-income housing altogether in some areas. The section in the Third Annual Housing Report on National Housing Goals that is devoted to land is all of eight lines and begins with the understatement, "the one major element in housing costs that federal policy has not addressed effectively to date is the cost of land." The Fourth Annual Report contains nothing on the problem of land costs. Most treatments of this problem glide over the basic causes for land price increases and call for vague remedies like "more efficient use of land." But if the National Housing Goal is to be reached, more fundamental intervention in the land market will be needed to reduce land and housing costs by curtailing land speculation or eliminating it altogether.

The price of capital is the other major element responsible for the increase in housing costs. For the builder this affects construction financing; for homeowner or renter it affects the cost of the mortgage, and hence monthly payments and rents. Construction financing rose 324

6. See the statement of Dr. Michael Sumichrast, Chief Economist, National Association of Home Builders, before the Joint Economic Committee, U.S. Congress, on *The Federal Budget, Inflation, and Full Employment, 1970–1975,* October 9, 1969. See also Sara Behman and Donald Codella, "Wage Rates and Housing Prices." The contrary view—that spiralling wage rates in construction industry are the principal roadblock to adequate housing—is found in Gilbert Burck, "The Building Trades Versus The People." In its December 1968 issue, *Fortune* solemnly declared that "the most powerful oligopoly in the American economy today is the loose confederation of craft unions known as the building trades."

percent from 1949 to 1969, from an average of $675 for all single family houses to $2860. As a percentage of selling price, it rose over this period from 5 percent to 11 percent. In recent years residential mortgage interest levels have been in the 8 to 9 percent range and sometimes higher. These rates are a far cry from the 4.5 to 5 percent levels of the mid-1950s, and it is likely that these newer levels are a permanent feature of the economy, at least for the foreseeable future. Debt service—interest and repayment of principal—was responsible for 59 percent of the monthly housing costs paid by the owner of a new FHA home in 1966. Renters do not pay financing costs directly, but absorb these costs in high rents. The government has taken some steps to increase the supply of mortgage money, but it has done little to reduce the onerous role of financing costs in the total housing cost picture. The President's annual housing reports go into great detail regarding the availability of an adequate supply of housing credit, but pay almost no attention to the cost picture from the consumer's viewpoint. It is notable that the various wage and price controls and other anti-inflationary measures instituted by the administration in 1971 and 1972 did not include control of mortgage interest rates. The current picture is the irony of relatively high, but fluctuating, construction output at the same time that cost factors are causing a housing crisis for middle- as well as low-income families.

It is almost a certainty that the 1978 goals will not be reached, particularly with respect to subsidized housing. It is important to understand why this will not occur—why the nature of the housing system is such an insurmountable barrier to even inadequate and incomplete goals of this sort. It is also important to understand the workings of the housing system as it affects the existing stock of housing and its occupants. The housing issue is emerging as a major test of the society and its economic system: whether the nation is willing and able to pay the costs and the social, institutional, and monetary changes required to provide all its people with decent homes and suitable living environments.

### References

AARON, HENRY J.
   1972 *Shelter and Subsidies: Who Benefits from Federal Housing Policies?*
        Washington, D.C.: The Brookings Institution, pp. 4–6.
ABRAMS, CHARLES
   1955 *Forbidden Neighbors: A Study of Prejudice in America.* New York:
        Harper & Row, Publishers.

ADVISORY COMMITTEE TO THE DEPARTMENT OF HOUSING AND URBAN
DEVELOPMENT, NATIONAL ACADEMY OF SCIENCES, AND NATIONAL
ACADEMY OF ENGINEERING
1972 *Freedom of Choice in Housing: Opportunity and Constraints.* Washington D.C.: U.S. Government Printing Office, p. 20.

ALDRICH, GRAHAME H., AND ASSOCIATES
1971 *Report on Real Estate Activities among Major Corporations.* Chicago: Society of Real Estate Appraisers.

ASSOCIATION OF BAY AREA GOVERNMENTS
"Estimates of Housing Needs: San Francisco Bay Area, 1970." Unpublished report.

BARNES, BART
1971 "Lead Poisoning Found in 10 Percent of Tests." Washington *Post* (May 28).

BEHMAN, SARA, AND DONALD CODELLA
1971 "Wage Rates and Housing Prices." *Industrial Relations* 10 (February), 86–104.

BIRCH, DAVID, ET AL.
1973 *America's Housing Needs: 1970 to 1980.* Cambridge, Mass.: Joint Center for Urban Studies of the Massachusetts Institute of Technology and Harvard University (December).

BOSTON REDEVELOPMENT AUTHORITY, PLANNING DEPARTMENT
1969 "A Study of Factors Bearing on Residential Rents in the City of Boston" (January).

BROWN, WILLIAM H., JR.
1972 "Access to Housing: The Role of the Real Estate Industry." *Economic Geography* 48, No. 1 (January), 66–78.

BURCK, GILBERT
1970 "The Building Trades Versus the People." *Fortune* (October), pp. 94–97ff.

CICARELLI, JAMES, AND CLIFFORD LANDERS
1972 "The Cost of Housing the Poor: A Case Study." *Land Economics* 48 (February), 53–57.

COCHRAN, CLAY, AND GEORGE RUCKER
1973 "Every American Family: Housing Needs and Nonresponse," in Donald J. Reeb and James T. Kirk, Jr., eds., *Housing the Poor.* New York: Praeger Publishers, pp. 149–79.

DENTON, JOHN H.
1967 *Apartheid American Style.* Berkeley, Calif.: Diablo Press.

DOWNS, ANTHONY
1970 "Moving Toward Realistic Housing Goals," in *Urban Problems and Prospects.* Chicago: Markham Publishing Co., p. 127.

EAVES, ELSIE
 1969 *How the Many Costs of Housing Fit Together.* Research Report No. 16, National Commission on Urban Problems.

FISHER, MARTHA
 1970 "Lead Poisoning in Children." *Journal of Housing* (February), 71–75.

FRANKLIN, HERBERT M.
 1969 "The New Federalism and Lower Income Housing: A Proposal for Consolidation and Reform." Washington, D.C.: The Urban Coalition (November 5), draft.

FRIEDEN, BERNARD J.
 1967 "Housing and National Urban Goals: Old Policies and New Realities," in James Q. Wilson, ed., *The Metropolitan Enigma.* Washington, D.C.: U.S. Chamber of Commerce, pp. 148–91.

GOLD, NEIL N., AND PAUL DAVIDOFF
 1968 "The Supply and Availability of Land for Housing for Low- and Moderate-Income Families," in *Technical Studies, Report of the President's Committee on Urban Housing,* II. Washington, D.C.: U.S. Government Printing Office.

GOVERNOR'S SELECT COMMISSION ON CIVIL DISORDER, STATE OF NEW JERSEY
 1968 *Report for Action* (February), p. 55.

GREBLER, LEO, JOAN W. MOORE, AND RALPH C. GUZMAN
 1970 *The Mexican-American People: The Nation's Second Largest Minority.* New York: The Free Press, p. 261.

GREENFIELD, R. J., AND J. F. LEWIS
 1969 "An Alternative to a Density Function Definition of Overcrowding." *Land Economics* 45 (May), 282–85. Reprinted in Jon Pynoos, Robert Schafer, and Chester W. Hartman, eds., *Housing Urban America.* Chicago: Aldine, 1973, pp. 166–70.

GRIGSBY, WILLIAM G., MICHAEL A. STEGMAN, LOUIS ROSENBERG, AND GORDON LIECHTY
 1970 "Housing and Poverty in Baltimore, Maryland." Ms., prepared for the Housing, Real Estate and Urban Land Studies Program, Graduate School of Business Administration, Univ. of Calif., Los Angeles. Revised form soon to be published.

HAWLEY, AMOS H., AND VINCENT P. ROCK
 1973 *Segregation in Residential Areas.* Washington, D.C.: National Academy of Sciences.

HELPER, ROSE
    1969 *Racial Policies and Practices of Real Estate Brokers.* Minneapolis: University of Minnesota Press.

ISLER, MORTON L.
    1971 "The Goals of Housing Subsidy Programs," in *Papers Submitted to the Subcommittee on Housing Panels,* U.S. House of Representatives Committee on Banking and Currency, Part 2 (June), pp. 415–38.

KRAFT, JOHN F., INC.
    1966 "The Report of a Survey of Attitudes of Harlem Residents Toward Housing, Rehabilitation, and Urban Renewal" (August).

NATIONAL ASSOCIATION OF HOME BUILDERS
    1970 *Economic News Notes* 16, No. 5 (May).

NATIONAL COMMISSION ON URBAN PROBLEMS
    1968 *Building the American City.* Washington, D.C.: U.S. Government Printing Office, p. 283 and Table 9.

NATIONAL COMMITTEE AGAINST DISCRIMINATION IN HOUSING
    1969 "Study and Report on the Listing Practices of Real Estate Agents," in Urban Renewal Demonstration Project, Part I (No. California D-8). Report prepared for U.S. Department of Housing and Urban Development.

NEWMAN, DOROTHY K.
    1971 "Housing the Poor and the Shelter to Income Ratio," in *Papers Submitted to the Subcommittee on Housing Panels,* U.S. House of Representatives Committee on Banking and Currency, Part 2 (June), p. 576.

PAZIANOS, JOYCE
    1972 "Housing: Clear Needs, Dim Prospects." *The American Federationist* (AFL-CIO) 79, No. 8 (August), 1–8.

RAPKIN, CHESTER
    1966 "Rent-Income Ratio," in William L. C. Wheaton, Grace Milgram, and Margie E. Meyerson, eds., *Urban Housing.* New York: The Free Press, pp. 168–75.

RENO, LEE P.
    1970 *Pieces and Scraps: Farm Labor Housing in the United States.* Washington, D.C.: Rural Housing Alliance.

ROTHMAN, JACK
    1961 "The Ghetto Makers." *The Nation* (October 7), 222–25. Reprinted in Jon Pynoos, Robert Schafer, and Chester W. Hart-

man, eds., *Housing Urban America.* Chicago: Aldine, 1973, pp. 274–78.

SALTMAN, JULIA Z.
   1971 *Open Housing as a Social Movement.* Lexington, Mass.: D. C. Heath & Company.

SCHMECK, HAROLD M., JR.
   1971 "Rise in Lead Poisoning Funds Is Urged." New York *Times* (July 5).

SCHORR, ALVIN
   1963 *Slums and Social Insecurity.* Social Security Administration. Washington, D.C.: U.S. Government Printing Office.

SHIPLER, DAVID K.
   1971 "Shortage of Housing Here Expected to Grow Worse." New York *Times* (August 10).

SMITH, GEORGE CLINE
   1971 "Housing in the Seventies: Realism vs. Euphoria." *Real Estate Review* 1 (Spring), 34–39.

STERNBERG, ARNOLD C., AND CATHERINE M. BISHOP
   1972 "Indian Housing: 1961–1971, A Decade of Continuing Crisis." *North Dakota Law Review* 48, 593–616.

SURVEY RESEARCH PROGRAM, MIT-HARVARD JOINT CENTER FOR URBAN STUDIES
   1970 *How the People See Their City: Boston, 1969* (June).

SUTERMEISTER, OSCAR
   1969 "Inadequacies and Inconsistencies in the Definition of Substandard Housing," in *Housing Code Standards: Three Critical Studies,* Research Report No. 19, National Commission on Urban Problems, pp. 83, 102.

U.S. BUREAU OF THE CENSUS
   1970 *Census of Housing: 1970, Detailed Housing Characteristics.* Final Report HC(1)-A1 and HC(1)-B1, U.S. Summary.

———
   1967 *Measuring the Quality of Housing, An Appraisal of Census Statistics and Methods.* Working Paper 25.

———
   1966 *Special Census Survey of the South and East Los Angeles Areas: November, 1965.* Series P-23, No. 17 (March 23).

U.S., CONGRESS, HOUSE
   1969 *First Annual Report on National Housing Goals* (January 23). House Document 91–63, 91st Congress, 1st Session.

———
    1970 *Second Annual Report on National Housing Goals* (April 2). House Document 91–292, 91st Congress, 2nd Session.

———
    1971 *Third Annual Report on National Housing Goals* (June 29). House Document 92–136, 92nd Congress, 1st Session.

———
    1972 *Fourth Annual Report on National Housing Goals* (June 29). House Document 92–319, 92nd Congress, 2nd Session.

U.S., CONGRESS, SENATE, SPECIAL COMMITTEE ON AGING
    1970 *Economics of Aging: Toward a Full Share in Abundance.* U.S. Senate Report No. 91–1548 (December 31), pp. 25–29, 44–47, 176–92.

U.S. DEPARTMENT OF AGRICULTURE
    1970 *Rural Housing: Trends and Prospects.* Agricultural Economic Report No. 193 (September).

U.S. DEPARTMENT OF COMMERCE
    1974 *Construction Reports: Housing Starts,* C20-74-2 (February).

U.S. DEPARTMENT OF HOUSING AND URBAN DEVELOPMENT, ASSISTANT SECRETARY FOR EQUAL OPPORTUNITY
    1972 *Blacks Pay More for Less* (November).

U.S. DEPARTMENT OF HOUSING AND URBAN DEVELOPMENT
    1970 *FHA Techniques of Housing Market Analysis* (January).

U.S. DEPARTMENT OF LABOR, BUREAU OF LABOR STATISTICS
    1966 "Differences in the Characteristics of Rental Housing Occupied by Families in Three Income Ranges Paying Approximately the Same in Six Cities" (September).

U.S. PRESIDENT'S COMMITTEE ON URBAN HOUSING
    1968 *A Decent Home.* Washington, D.C.: U.S. Government Printing Office, pp. 40, 45, 124–205.

U.S. PRESIDENT'S NATIONAL ADVISORY COMMISSION ON RURAL POVERTY
    1967 *The People Left Behind.* Washington, D.C.: U.S. Government Printing Office.

WALLIN, PETER L.
    1972 "Homeownership Problems of the Elderly." *Clearinghouse Review* 6, Nos. 4–5 (August–September), 227–32.

WILNER, DANIEL, ROSABELLE WALKLEY, THOMAS PINKERTON, AND MATHEW TAYBACK.
    1962 *The Housing Environment and Family Life.* Baltimore, Md.: The Johns Hopkins Press.

"U.S. Warning on Faulty Heaters"
    1973 San Francisco *Chronicle* (November 8).

# Chapter 2

# NEW HOUSING

The nation's ability to house all of its citizens decently depends in large part on its ability to produce substantial amounts of new dwellings for newly forming households and for those that now are ill housed. The need for housing exists in central cities, suburbs, small towns, and rural areas. The nature and performance of the housing industry are thus crucial to the amount, kind, location, and cost of the housing produced —that is, who gets housing and under what conditions. (An important subsidiary issue is the effect of various production processes on the wages and working conditions of the several million persons who earn their livelihood in the housing industry.)

A threshold question is money. Housing is very expensive: the median sales price of new single-family homes sold in 1972 was $25,900 (nearly $31,000 in the Northeast). The industry needs vast amounts of capital in order to function. Builders require short-term construction loans to pay for land, building materials, labor, and other costs. Those who purchase housing require long-term loans. The sources and amount of capital, the costs of borrowing, and the impact of these costs on housing consumers thus become key issues.

The "housing industry" is itself a huge and multi-faceted complex of production and distribution elements, embracing the acquisition and preparation of building sites, the manufacture and distribution of build-

ing materials, the construction process itself, sales and rental arrangements, and, once the building is completed, maintenance and
management. A multitude of actors are involved: lawyers, architects,
engineers, brokers, surveyors, local zoning and building code officials,
financing specialists, contractors and subcontractors, craftsmen and
union officials, industrial workers and managers in the building supply
field (which ranges from lumber to refrigerators to asbestos to doork-
nobs), insurance agents, repairmen, tax assessors, and many others.[1]

Because of tradition and the localized nature of housing construction, industrialization has not proceeded very rapidly in the housing field,
compared with, say, automobile production. Most housing in the United
States is still assembled on site by skilled and semiskilled workers who put
the final product together from a melange of components, some of which
have been manufactured elsewhere and brought to the site for assembly.
Automobile production, by contrast, involves manufacture of the final
product in its entirety inside a series of plants, after which the finished
product is delivered to the consumer. Given the expense and complexity
of the production process, introduction of mass-produced, factory-built
housing could probably result in substantial savings. The growing mobile
home industry is a significant move in this direction.

The onsite nature of housing production and the fixed location of
housing have given local governments broad powers over the housing
industry. Municipal and country governments basically control the quality standards of all new housing through building codes and, through
zoning codes, the location and type of housing that is built. This amounts
to an extraordinary degree of local control over who lives where.

Building codes have an honorable history. They are society's attempt to ensure the housing consumer that he is buying or renting a good
product. Since the eventual occupant of the house could not reasonably
be expected to observe and supervise the construction process, and since
many defects of housing construction are not immediately obvious to a
potential occupant or may not manifest themselves immediately, the
presence of the state, in the form of a building inspector who enforces
minimum building code standards, has without doubt been a beneficial
social development. As with many laudable developments, however, people have made less praiseworthy uses of building code regulations over
the course of time. Building codes still serve the housing consumer, but

1. A graphic portrayal of the complexity of the housing industry is found in "An
Overview of the Housing Industry," p.115, *A Decent Home*, Report of the President's Committee on Urban Housing. For a more complete discussion see ibid., pp. 149–59; *Building
the American City*, pp. 431–50; and Sherman Maisel, *Housebuilding in Transition*. A useful
compendium of materials on housing technology, both in the U.S. and in foreign countries,
is contained in *Industrialized Housing*, Materials Compiled and Prepared for the Subcommittee on Urban Affairs of the Joint Economic Committee.

they also serve the self-interest of some parts of the housing industry by protecting certain traditional materials and work methods and by impeding technological innovation. And to the extent that high minimum standards raise the cost of housing, the overall interests of the housing consumer are sacrificed to the exclusionary instincts of a locality's present population.

The power to "zone" land is essentially the power of local government to decide how its land shall be used, by which action it largely determines the number and kinds of people it will allow to live within its borders. It is an awesome power, with even greater implications for housing production, metropolitan residential patterns, and individual choice. Among those who live in the areas that surround large cities there is widespread desire to limit growth and avoid drastic changes in the character of the locality.

Zoning restrictions can sharply inhibit housing production and prevent the movement of lower-income households, particularly racial minorities, out of the central city into areas of lower density with generally better housing conditions, lower taxes, better access to many employment opportunities, and better services like schools and recreational facilities (other public services, such as transportation and hospitals, may be inferior to those in the central city). Such restrictions are major perpetuators of the "black neck in a white noose" character of our metropolitan area whereby central cities are becoming the domain of the poor and nonwhite, while the white population and the jobs they control move from the city to the outlying areas. This spatial separation of our population by race and income is widely regarded as a central factor in the deterioration of our cities, our suburbs (in more subtle ways), and the social fabric of the nation.

### Money Matters

The cost of housing is enormous—usually several times the average family's annual income. For almost all families, it is the most expensive consumer good they will ever own or rent. Because of this high cost, housing is highly dependent on credit, or borrowed capital. Builders and buyers of both old and new housing (because of rising values and inflation, old housing can be almost as expensive as new housing, and it is invariably more expensive than the cost of its original construction) create an enormous demand for capital, yet capital is raised and allocated primarily so as to maximize opportunities for profit, with little concern for social needs. (Michael E. Stone, in an unpublished paper entitled "Reconstructing American Housing," has proposed that the mortgage system be eliminated entirely, and that the capital costs of new housing and rehabilitation be financed through direct public capital grants.)

Housing production and consumption have been plagued with the twin problems of an inadequate supply of credit and the high cost of that which is available. The housing industry and housing consumers find it hard to compete with other major users of capital, notably corporations and the government, both of which often borrow regardless of the cost. Other industries usually operate on investments that are of a shorter duration and so can accommodate more readily to changes in the price of money, particularly through tax credits allowed for capital investment, but in housing production and consumption are postponable. In some industries capital requirements exercise relatively little influence on the ultimate price the consumer pays for the product, but increased capital costs directly produce markedly higher housing costs. The 1966 "credit crunch" demonstrates the vulnerability of the housing industry. When the amount of money flowing into new mortgages fell from $19.8 billion in 1965 to $12.7 billion in 1966, the number of housing starts dropped from 1,488,000 to 1,173,000. This decline was not the result of a decrease in the nation's total use of credit, which fell less than $1 billion during the period, but to competition for capital; in 1965 applicants for residential mortgages were able to secure 29 percent of the total funds available, but in 1966 they secured only 19 percent. Business and government borrowing, much of which was related to the war on Southeast Asia and the inflationary effects of that spending, prevailed over the housing sector, which is particularly dependent on outside financing because of the small size of most producers (see "The 'Housing Industry,' " this chapter). The problem is that during a time of inflation, when consumers have money available, the housing industry is unable to secure adequate amounts of capital, and high interest rates discourage consumers and producers. Conversely, credit is available and relatively cheap during those times the housing consumer has least money to spend on housing. As John Heimann has observed, "repeated experience has shown us . . . that this financial system [undergirding the housing industry] ceases to function effectively when it is most needed."

Government intervention in the housing finance area has a long and only partially successful history. The economic collapse of the 1930s was particularly hard on the housing sector: savings institutions folded, credit sources dried up, and owners were unable to meet mortgage payments. This self-reinforcing cycle led in 1934 to the establishment of a vast federal apparatus designed to increase and stabilize the sources of capital available to producers and consumers of housing. The primary agency of this new system was the Federal Housing Administration, established to insure mortgage lenders against default and thus take the risk out of certain classes of home loans. (A similar mortgage guarantee by the Veterans Administration was added in 1944.) Through promulgation of minimum property standards for all FHA-insured loans and the institution of an insurance system via a premium of one-half of one percent of the remaining unpaid balance, the FHA was able to restore lender confidence in mortgage loans. It also radically reshaped the mortgage instrument itself: FHA intervention converted short-term (five- to ten-year amortization period) loans of 50 to 60 percent of the value of the property into thirty- to forty-year loans of 80 to 90 percent and more of the total property value. It also served to lower interest rates, by virtually eliminating risk to the lender through the insurance feature. A system of level monthly interest and amortization payments throughout the life of the mortgage was also introduced to replace the "balloon mortgage," for which the borrower paid only interest payments until the note came due, when he had to repay the entire principal or arrange refinancing. (The FHA still plays an important role in the nation's housing picture, but, in recent years, cheaper, more efficient private mortgage insurance companies have been replacing the federal insuring agency, particularly for middle- and higher-income housing. According to Carberry's article in the *Wall Street Journal,* a single company wrote more mortgage insurance in 1971 than the FHA did.)

One result of this federal intervention was to make homeownership financially possible for the vast majority of American families, since high loan-to-value ratios meant low downpayment requirements, and long amortization periods meant low monthly payments. Most of the post-World War II suburban boom was made possible by the FHA. But these changes also increased the total cost of owning a home and diluted the concept of ownership. Over the life of a 29-year mortgage of $26,500 at a 7.25 percent annual interest rate, the homeowner will pay $60,552–$34,052, or 128 percent, more than borrowed. During the first few years of mortgage repayment virtually all payments go for interest; the "owner" does not begin to build up substantial equity in his property until many years have passed. Indebtedness to the lender over so long a period also increases the homeowner's vulnerability, since the lending institution may be regarded as the real owner of the home. An important result of federal intervention in the mortgage market has been to enhance the position and influence of those who control capital over the housing market.

About three-fourths of all money for residential mortgages comes from three institutional sources: savings and loan associations, mutual savings banks, and commercial banks. These institutions aggregate the savings of depositors and use this capital to provide credit in the most profitable way possible, consistent with government regulations that limit their investment options. The total resources of commercial banks are nearly twice the combined resources of the mutual banks and savings and loan associations, but the s & ls are by far the most important single source of mortgage money, because nearly all of their investments must by law go into residential mortgages. Almost half of all long-term housing mortgages acquired in 1970 and 1971 were acquired by savings and loan associations. Other sources of mortgage funds include insurance companies (which have been declining in importance in the housing field over the past few years); pension and retirement funds; federal, state, and local governments; and more recently the securities market, which has been encouraged to invest in mortgages through the development of federally guaranteed pools of mortgage-backed securities, marketed by the Government National Mortgage Association.[2]

To back up the primary mortgage market, the federal government has a byzantine array of agencies and programs, many of which date from the collapse of the housing credit system in the 1930s. These include the Federal Home Loan Bank Board and its twelve regional banks, a central banking system for home-loan banks analogous to the Federal Reserve System for commercial banks; insurance agencies, the Federal Deposit Insurance Corporation and the Federal Savings and Loan Insurance Corporation, to protect depositors in various types of savings institutions; and a secondary mortgage market, which permits mortgage investors to sell mortgages in their portfolios or convert them into securities acceptable to other segments of the investing public. There were small-scale private secondary mortgage companies to redistribute mortgage loans regionally and to permit individual lending institutions to increase their liquidity prior to the 1930s, but creation by the Federal Housing Administration of a standardized and secure mortgage instrument made establishment of a large-scale national secondary mortgage market possible and desirable. In 1938 Congress created the Federal National Mortgage Association (known colloquially as *Fannie Mae*). The FNMA assists the mortgage lending industry not only by providing added liquidity and hence more available mortgage funds but also by permitting lenders to continue servicing the loans they sold to FNMA and thereby earn substantial fees. Several other so-called special assistance functions were later added to its mandate, programs of direct government housing subsidies, (most notably Section 221(d)(3) direct loans, see chapter 5, "Interest Subsidies and Tax Benefits for Rental Housing") that had little to do with secondary mortgage functions. Fannie Mae became so profitable

2. For a discussion of these mortgage-backed securities see Bartke, "Fannie Mae and the Secondary Mortgage Market." The National Corporation for Housing Partnerships, another effort to attract private capital into the housing field, is described in Friedberg, "The NHP—An Invitation to Housing Partnership."

that in the 1968 Housing Act the special assistance functions were spun off to a new agency, the Government National Mortgage Association (known as *Ginnie Mae*), and the FNMA became a private corporation. Michael Stone says of this transition:

> This sequence of events is one of the clearest examples of the intermeshing of the state and private business under modern capitalism. A national facility, greatly needed and desired by private business to reduce its risks and assure it of ready markets for its products, is first created and nurtured at public expense. Once it becomes established and begins to repay its costs, the facility is turned over to private interests to that its success can produce profits for them.

In 1970 a new secondary mortgage agency, the Federal Home Loan Mortgage Corporation, was created specifically to serve the needs of the savings and loan associations.

Despite the plethora of assistance programs and regulatory agencies, money still is at the root of most housing problems. The absence of a supply of credit large and stable enough to finance the 1968–1978 National Housing Goal and the high interest rates charged for the capital that is available put decent housing out of the reach of a substantial portion of the nation's households. Within the housing sector, the demand for credit to build new housing must compete with the demand for credit to purchase existing homes. In 1971, only $27 billion of $69 billion worth of long-term residential mortgages was for new properties. Lenders who are naturally eager to protect the value of their existing mortgage loans may be reluctant to support a high volume of new construction activity for fear that too great an increase in the supply of housing could deflate the value of the existing stock, which is based to a large degree on scarcity.

Because of the generally high demand for credit, lending institutions have devised numerous ways to increase their profits, disguise high interest rates and evade interest rate ceilings on FHA and VA loans. Since the Korean War and the inflation it unleashed, a common practice among lending institutions has been to charge discount "points" as part of their loan, so as to reduce the amount actually loaned below the face value of the loan and thus increase the effective interest rate. These practices were introduced in response to the legal interest ceiling on FHA and VA loans: when the prevailing interest rate rises above this ceiling, lenders maintain their profits by making FHA-insured and VA-guaranteed loans only at a discount, sometimes of considerable magnitude. These surcharges are passed on to the purchaser in the form of higher prices, because the seller, who must by law pay these "points," adjusts his asking price so as to receive the desired amount after the loan is discounted. This practice hit particularly hard at the new FHA Section 235 and 236 interest-subsidy programs in the 1968 Housing Act. Mortgages were unavailable under these programs because the maximum legal interest rate was well below the market rate, and lending agencies were charging discounts of 8 to 10 percent for such loans. In order to limit the level of discounts and maintain the illusion of low FHA and VA interest rates, in late 1971 HUD introduced a so-called tandem plan. This plan is a complex double subsidization scheme whereby the Government National Mortgage Association commits itself to purchase FHA and VA mortgages at 95 to 96 percent of the mortgage value regardless of the prevailing price in the private secondary mortgage market. Then the GNMA sells the commitments back to the loan originator, to the FNMA, or to another lender at the going market price and absorbs the loss out of its own (government) funds. This appears to be a reduction in discount points, but it actually is carried out at public expense through hidden government subsidy. The tandem plan plus avoids confronting the basic problem which is the inadequate supply of money for the housing sector, and keeps real interest rates hidden from public view.

Another recent practice of lenders has been to demand equity participation in income-producing buildings over and above interest charges as a hedge against inflation. Also, as Payne points out, so-called closing costs—credit reports on the borrower, legal fees, surveys, title examination and insurance, appraisals, and "origination fees"—amount to a substantial sum, in some cases more than the down payment, and can provide considerable profit for lending institutions.

In 1973 the influential Committee for Economic Development published a report that had as its central recommendation the adoption of variable rate mortgages. Variable interest mortgages would be a major change in the mortgage instrument, because they would protect lending institutions in an era of steadily rising interest rates from having long-term mortgage money tied up, through the workings of a contract interest rate that would vary with economic conditions instead of remaining constant throughout its term. The purpose of such variable rate mortgages is to shift the risk of rate fluctuation from the financer to the borrower and to improve the position of thrift institutions in times of rising interest rates. Savings and loan associations, the central element in the housing finance picture, suffer from the inherent weakness that they "borrow short" and "lend long"—that is, their funds derive from deposit accounts that can be withdrawn on demand or on short notice, whereas their investments are fixed in long-term mortgages (few of which are held to maturity, the average being ten to twelve years). In times of inflation and rising interest rates government regulations and the realities of their investments limit the ability of the s & ls to attract new money or retain their existing accounts, and savers invest elsewhere to obtain higher returns. The ability to adjust the return on outstanding loan commitments to current interest rates would enhance the position of savings and loan institutions at the expense of the borrower, particularly in view of the long-term upward trend in interest rates. The effect on the borrower could take the form either of increased monthly payments or an extended repayment period. Higher monthly payments cause financial hardship or default for many borrowers. The effect of an extended payment period, which offers little flexibility in any case, would be to defer equity buildup, which has been shown to correlate with higher default rates. Variable rate mortgages would disadvantage borrowers greatly. They would also increase the power of lending institutions, would probably reduce home ownership, and would certainly cause lenders to become more restrictive in their underwriting practices, particularly with respect to racial minorities and working-class families who might not have the economic mobility to sustain future higher interest rates.

Solving the money problem is a prerequisite for solving the housing problem. Whether it is done by increasing the supply of credit or by channeling a larger portion of the credit available to the housing sector, greater planning and management of the economy will be required to attain the National Housing Goal. The present system of free competition for capital funds does not and cannot make for an adequate housing program. Congressman Wright Patman has proposed a national development bank, to make below market-rate housing loans to families with incomes lower than the median. Capital for the bank would come from reserve funds of commercial banks, which would be directed by the Federal Reserve Board to make such investments, and from private pension funds, which also would be required to invest a certain percentage of their assets in the housing bank as a *quid pro quo* for the tax exemption they enjoy. (In 1972 private pension funds had $117 billion in assets, of which only $4 billion was invested in mortgage loans.) Congress shelved this proposal as a consequence of strong opposition from the Nixon Administration and from banking interests on the grounds that it was an unwarranted interference in the free enterprise system. The idea of direct government loans—that is, of using the tax system to support massive public lending—appears to have even less of a chance, even though it would be far less expensive and might be the only way to make an adequate supply of housing capital available at a cost that does not necessitate rents and prices out of the reach of the vast majority of Americans.

The present system provides enormous profits for lenders and middlemen. Virtually all the programs and mechanisms that have been devised over the past forty years have been designed to support institutions that supply credit rather than to provide benefits for people who need housing. The FHA insures the lender against loss; the borrower, who pays the premium, is insured against nothing. As Michael Stone has aptly described the situation:

> The crucial decisions in the housing sector—as in most major areas of this society—are not made primarily on the basis of human needs. Instead, the important decisions revolve around the flow of investment capital into housing, and these decisions of course are made on the basis of opportunities for profit . . . Mortgage-lending institutions are the dominant force in the housing sector and contribute directly to the existence and maintenance of the housing problem.

## The "Housing Industry"

Virtually all housing in this country, including government-sponsored units, is built by the private sector, and the characteristics of the industry's organization, labor force, financial resources, entrepreneurs, and technology largely determine the success or failure of housing activity, public or private. Most homebuilding in the United States is a highly localized, nonindustrialized process, and most homebuilders produce a small volume of homes, usually under fifty units per year. Comparison with the auto industry is instructive. In the housing industry over 300,000 firms produce 1.5 to 2 million units annually; in the auto industry four major corporations produce 8 million cars annually. In 1967 the largest merchant builder produced only 5100 homes, the largest factory-based home manufacturer produced 11,500 units, and the largest mobile home manufacturer produced 18,000 units. Almost all homes in the U.S. are built by bringing materials to the site and assembling them there, as opposed to a system whereby the entire home or major elements thereof—rooms, kitchen and bathroom units, service systems, walls, and panels—are fabricated in a plant and then transported to the site for installation or assembly. (The distinction is not an absolute one: smaller prefabricated components such as prehung doors and roof trusses are widely used by onsite builders, and even a highly industrialized housing system requires considerable onsite work to prepare the site and foundation, make necessary utility connections, and assemble the components.)

The reasons for this have something of a chicken-and-egg quality. Size and the relative immobility of homes are responsible for the tradition of onsite housing construction. Since the onsite building process requires little capital, builders tend to be small, and people move in and out of the construction industry easily and rapidly. The homebuilder frequently is little more than the captain of a pickup team consisting of a variety of craftsmen and subcontractors assembled for a particular job. The structure of local craft unions protects this fractionalized process, and the network of municipal building and zoning regulations is adapted to and fosters a local approach. The practice of financing most home construction and purchase through local savings institutions that can evaluate and service mortgage loans also supports this mode of operation. The nature of the product originally dictated a particular style of production, and related practices and regulations developed around it that now serve to maintain the status quo.

Some developments have occurred toward the manufacture of homes, apart from mobile homes, which we shall discuss later in the chapter. Data assembled by the Douglas Commission suggest that 15 to 20 percent of all nonfarm housing starts in 1967 were manufactured to some degree by the nation's 4000 home manufacturers and producers of preassembled components, although this proportion did not represent an increase over previous years. Few manufacturers produce more than a few hundred units annually, and in many instances no significant cost savings occur, either because of their insufficient scale of operation or their failure or inability to use more advanced technologies. No one has attempted factory production of housing on a large enough scale or with a sufficient degree of freedom in the use of new materials and techniques to produce true economies, mainly because of the restrictions of local building and zoning codes. The poor track record of home manufacturers to date and the success of many large conventional homebuilders have led to a prevailing skepticism about the potential of industrialization. Probably the most successful examples of volume building in this country are the various Levitt developments, constructed through highly sophisticated and efficient use of conventional onsite construction techniques.

Indoor, mass-produced, assembly-line production of housing has several obvious advantages. Interference and delays from inclement weather are averted. Large savings on building materials can be achieved through mass purchasing and direct ordering from manufacturers and wholesalers, because this eliminates the substantial dealers' profit, which can add 15 to 20 percent to the cost of materials; large and regular orders also make possible development and custom manufacture of new materials. Assembly-line production and the use of heavy machinery permit greater specialization of labor and the use of less skilled workers, increasing labor output and reducing labor costs per unit. Guaranteed work will reduce hourly wages to a level lower than the very high rates that craftsmen now demand, in part to compensate for the irregularity of their work. The crafts unions are now caught in the bind of very high hourly wages but only moderate annual incomes, and they tend to price themselves out of the market and reduce total construction demand. The indoor manufacturing process also means vast savings in production time: some of the more advanced systems of component building can produce a home in a few days, as opposed to the several months that onsite construction ordinarily takes. This is a critical factor if housing production is to double over the next ten years. Faster construction time also means more efficient use of scarce and costly capital and a consequent reduction in the per unit cost of construction financing. The growth of large housing producers might also generate new sources of capital, through reinvestment of corporate profits and sale of public stock issues.

Any saving in production costs can have a substantial multiplier effect, by reducing many related costs that are based on production costs. A case study presented by the Douglas Commission, based on cost estimates for Toledo, Ohio, indicated that a $1600 saving in production costs for a single-family home, using total prefabrication through a sectionalized building system instead of conventional construction, could translate into a $3300 difference in final sales price when related savings on interim financing, sales commission, closing costs, builder's profit, and mortgage financing are added up. On the negative side are the high capital costs of industrializing housing production and the added costs and marketing limitations imposed by the need to transport bulky units or components by road or rail.

## Mobile Homes

In terms of housing costs, housing standards and building technology, probably the most important recent development in the housing industry is the phenomenal rise of the so-called mobile home. More than 600,000 were produced in 1973, compared with 90,000 in 1961. Mobile home production now amounts to about one-third the number of conventional homes built annually, and two-thirds of all single-family homes costing less than $20,000.

Unlike their ancestor the trailer, most mobile homes are not intended to be moved frequently. Rather, their mobility refers (1) to the fact that each of these fully equipped and furnished homes, which average 60 feet in length and 12 feet in width, is moved as a unit from the factory where it is produced to the site where it is installed to utility connections; and (2) to the fact that each is capable of being moved from site to site. But because of the costs of such a move—done by professionals at the cost of over $1 a mile—a family wishing to move any distance may be more likely to sell its old mobile home and purchase another. (On the other hand, the knowledge that the home can be moved may be important to many persons; the term "relocatable home" might be more accurate.)

Because mobile homes are entirely prefabricated, they benefit from uninterrupted production, mechanization, and greater use of unskilled labor, and they are free of many of the restrictive local codes and building practices that hamper and increase the cost of traditional onsite construction. These advantages are responsible for the markedly lower cost of mobile homes. The average cost of a fully furnished mobile home was $6950 in mid-1973. (The more luxurious, better-equipped mobile homes may run as high as $20,000.)

There are several important qualifications that need to be made to this comparison. The first has to do with space. The average mobile home contains less than 700 square feet of indoor space, while the average floor area of one-family homes produced in 1971 was 1555 square feet, and only 11 percent of these homes had less than 1000 square feet. Still, through efficient use of space, the mobile home manufacturer is providing what the consumer regards as a complete home, and so square foot comparisons must be qualified as well. The enormous rise in mobile home sales suggests that consumers are willing to accept compact (or cramped) quarters in exchange for a lower price, but the most frequent complaints of mobile home owners have to do with limited living area and lack of storage space. "Double" mobile home units, which give twice the space, but at twice the price, are increasing in popularity.

The purchase price of the mobile home does not include a place on which to set the unit down, so space rental ($40–60 or more a month in mobile home parks and rising because of site shortages due largely to zoning impediments) or the price of a lot must be added. Another important difference in price to the consumer lies in the methods of financing. Long-term mortgages permit payments for conventional homes to be spread over twenty to forty years and result in relatively small monthly payments for principal and interest, but such mortgages are rarely available for the purchase of mobile homes, because their mobility and presumed short life make most mortgage-granting institutions reluctant to issue this kind of loan for a mobile home. Most mobile homes are purchased under what is called a *conditional sales agreement,* which is the type of loan used for automobile purchases. This is a short-term loan (usually for five to seven years, sometimes as long as twelve years), of the so-called *add on* type: installment payments are computed by adding on interest for the entire amount of the loan for the full length of the amortization period (with a mortgage loan interest is based on the outstanding principal alone, and that amount is constantly declining over the life of the mortgage). This makes the effective interest rate almost twice as high as the stated rate. These installment loans are very attractive to lenders, and some mobile home dealers price their units very low and earn their profits by making and servicing loans. The conditional sales contract also gives the borrower far less protection against default. Failure to meet payments can result in total loss of the asset, whereas under mortgage agreements the borrower can recover a portion of the principal he has repaid following the foreclosure sale to repay the mortgagee.

This financing device results in monthly financing costs that are not very different from the costs of purchasing a more expensive home under a mortgage agreement. Monthly financing costs, using average terms, for a $6000 mobile home are only $6 less than those for a $16,000 single-family home built and financed in the conventional manner (though furniture is included in the mobile home loan, but not ordinarily in the mortgage). The buyer will own the mobile home outright in a far shorter time than will the buyer of a conventional home, but the economic and physical depreciation of the mobile home is more rapid and tends to cancel out this advantage. And while the value of the mobile home inevitably depreciates, a conventional home and the land it sits on will usually appreciate in value. The 1969 Housing Act permits FHA to insure personal installment loans for mobile homes with very low downpayment requirements, but the tight money market and restrictive FHA terms have led most savings institutions to avoid this program. If the government were able to create longer-term, higher loan-to-value loans through its insurance system at prevailing mortgage interest rates, the monthly costs of purchasing and maintaining a mobile home could be substantially cut.

Mobile homes are particularly popular in rural and depressed areas, where there is little housebuilding capacity; as vacation homes; for households subject to periodic transfer (servicemen and skilled workers on long-term construction projects, for example); and in areas where a population boom has produced a severe housing deficit, such as around space installations or military bases. As one might expect from the description of space standards, retired couples and families without children are among the principal buyers of mobile homes.[3]

The mobile-home park has been an important addition to the country's physical and social landscape—there are about 25,000 of them in the U.S. They tend to be located in outlying areas where land costs are low, and they offer a range of community facilities: laundries, lounges, swimming pools, even churches. These developments, as Johnson points out, are in essence small, socially homogeneous communities. Many do not

3. The first large-scale census of the mobile home population was a recent Census Bureau study done for the Department of Housing and Urban Development entitled "Housing Surveys Parts 1 and 2. Occupants of New Housing Units: Mobile Homes and the Housing Supply" (Washington, D.C.: U.S. Government Printing Office, 1969). Information on mobile homes and their occupants generally comes from popular journals and from industry sources and their trade group, the Mobile Home Manufacturers Association in Chicago. Most official bodies and academic researchers ignore this segment of the housing market. One of the few good studies is Drury, *Mobile Homes.* Another useful treatment is Morris and Woods, eds., *Housing Crisis and Response.*

allow children, or are limited to one- or two-child families. Pets are often barred. Management is quite stringent, and it is usually easy to evict any incompatible residents because few parks offer leases. (Mobile home owners are just beginning to organize to oppose oppressive practices by park owners, such as "exit fees," limitations on the resale of the home, and requirements that the resident purchase his home from the park owner as a condition for renting space, or that he purchase equipment such as awnings and "skirting" from the park operator or from a dealer approved by him.) Needless to say, these residence parks are not the outposts of racially integrated living. These mini-suburbs are a reaction to and an escape from the many features of city life, a retreat to a safe, peaceful, comfortable environment. Like many other special forms of residential environments—for the elderly, young marrieds, would-be young marrieds—mobile home developments will doubtless continue to increase in popularity in coming years.

Mobile homes are now being used in public programs as well. Urban renewal, highway and other land-taking agencies are using mobile homes for temporary relocation purposes. Emergency housing needs, such as those created by floods, have also been met through mobile homes. The low-rent public housing program has begun to use mobile homes, too, particularly in areas where land costs are low and in parts of the country where mobile homes are generally popular. One clear advantage is the capability of creating a housing development in a few weeks or months. Local housing authorities can also benefit from full construction cost economies, since they can pay for the units outright; and if they buy in large quantities they can secure price reductions and have units manufactured to their own specifications. The mobile home industry also shows signs of moving a (short) step over into production of modular homes. In several cities mobile home manufacturers have constructed small modular home projects—one- to three-story town houses and row houses mainly. The same efficiently produced rectangles, if stacked and grouped (with necessary changes in load-bearing walls), can be used as modular components of multi-family developments in urban areas. Mobile homes have also been used for schools, temporary commercial buildings, churches, motels, and dormitories.

The phenomenal rise of the mobile home is a response to the spiralling costs of conventional home construction. Some of the industry's achievements are clearly praiseworthy. It has demonstrated the potential of offsite housing fabrication. On the other hand, markedly lowered standards of space and durability generally characterize the mobile home, and this is a disturbing development on the American housing scene. Mobile homes tend to be vulnerable to hurricanes and high winds, and many are not fire resistant. Jack Anderson reports that the poor construction quality and safety defects of many mobile homes are under investigation by the Center for Auto Safety, a Ralph Nader-founded group. If government housing policy turns to mobile homes as a "bargain" solution to the housing problems of lower-income groups, as the administration has suggested, the effects of this shift would be profound with respect to American housing standards and metropolitan residential patterns.

## Building Codes

Building codes regulate the construction of new buildings and the substantial rehabilitation of existing ones. They are designed to insure that adequate standards are met with respect to durability, to prevent the development of unsanitary and unhealthy conditions, and to protect against fire, collapse, and other hazards. Promulgation and enforcement of building codes are an exercise of the state police power that has traditionally been delegated to local governments (including counties). Local code enforcement inspectors are responsible for issuing building permits, inspecting and approving building and renovation plans, and inspecting and approving work when it has been completed.

Nearly half of all local governments have building codes. Manvel points out that within SMSAs 82 percent with populations over 5000 and 98 percent with populations of 50,000 and above have such codes. Not all places have comprehensive building codes; some merely have codes to cover specific elements of construction, such as electrical and plumbing systems.

Building codes are the subject of widespread and largely justified criticism, primarily because they make homebuilding more difficult and more expensive. Key defects are the lack of uniformity of code provisions among different localities and the inflexible and archaic nature of the code provisions themselves. The building code system presupposes a plethora of small builders, each operating with onsite construction methods, few of whom operate across municipal boundaries often enough to be bothered by the existence of different regulations in different cities and towns. As many as several hundred local building codes may be operant within a single metropolitan area. So long as the traditional systems of construction and of industry organization prevailed this lack of uniformity was not terribly irksome. But with the growth of and potential for large-scale builders who operate over an entire metropolitan area and in several different metropolitan areas, lack of uniformity becomes costly because it reduces opportunities for mass production by preventing standardization of plans, materials, and building operations. Construction plans must be reviewed and approved in each locality and modifications made to satisfy the local code, which all too often is administered by incompetent local officials who are sometimes corrupt as well. (See Shipler's articles in the New York *Times.*) Local inspectors tend to be conservative, trusting to the "tried and true" and afraid of the consequences of mistakenly approving some new material or procedure.

Regional variations in construction standards such as heating and insulation specifications and snowload factor are to some extent justifiable, and special standards are needed for unique situations such as localities subject to earthquakes and tremors; but by and large there is no reason for not having a single, uniform code, based on engineering and health considerations, throughout a region. What is safe in one area is equally safe in nearby areas. The reasons the current building code system continues to exist are local autonomy, tradition, the power of building material manufacturers and the crafts unions, and intentional economic exclusion of lower socioeconomic groups (higher building standards mean higher home prices, which mean higher income residents). One of the more recent exculsionary uses of building codes in both urban and rural areas has been to keep out communes and other countercultural attempts to construct alternative living arrangements and life styles (housing and zoning codes are often used for the same purpose). For a graphic description of one clash between the counterculture and local building codes, see John van der Zee's *Canyon.*

Some progress has been made in recent years in achieving greater uniformity. The major forces for change are the so-called model codes, of which there are now four. These model codes are generally of high quality and sufficient flexibility. Each has gained popularity in a particular region of the country, which enhances their usefulness. National electrical and plumbing codes also exist. Slightly over half of the local government units surveyed by the Census Bureau for the Douglas Commission had a code that "substantially incorporates" a national or regional model code. However, most localities fail to follow the periodic updating of the national codes, and the commission concluded that "only about 15 percent of all the municipalities and townships above 5000 in population had in effect a national model building code which was reasonably up-to-date; about 85 percent of the units either had no code, did not use a model code, or failed to keep the code up to date." Even in communities that use model codes, builders find that local officials interpret these codes in an inconsistent manner. To be effective, uniform model codes require uniform and competent administration. A survey of building code inspection practices by the International City Managers' Association reported a multiplicity of code enforcement agencies, the results of which were inefficiency, poor coordination, a lack of qualified personnel, and inadequate salaries and administrative budgets.

At an intermediate level in the struggle for uniformity, several states have recently promulgated statewide building codes. In a few cases these are mandatory, although the mandatory code generally excludes substantial parts of the housing stock, usually one-, two-, and sometimes three-family homes. Some states attempt to induce localities to adopt the statewide code voluntarily through a series of "sweeteners." The state of New York, for example, offers to localities that adopt its code services relating to code administration and centralized certification and testing facilities for new materials and practices. Four-fifths of the communities in New York have adopted its uniform code. Some states have mandatory minimum codes, but permit localities to adopt stricter codes; this vitiates the benefits of uniformity and allows perpetuation of exclusionary practices.

Another problem is the way and the extent to which existing building codes thwart reasonable innovation in materials and fabrication procedures. Building codes have generally retarded technological progress, often by employing what are known as specification standards (identifying specific permissible materials and procedures), as opposed to performance standards (identifying a minimum level of performance, for example, ability to withstand a given amount of pressure per square inch before a structural member will collapse or establishment of instrumentally measured noise or heat levels for acceptable insulation). New materials cannot be introduced under specification standards without modifying the building code or convincing a series of local officials of their acceptability. Prefabrication (offsite) construction processes are greatly hampered by a system that relies on onsite inspection; stories abound of prefabricated walls with built-in wiring having to be dismembered at the site in order to convince an inspector that local standards have been met. (California now has a statewide code for factory-built homes that substitutes state inspection in the factory for local codes and onsite inspection; local governments still control the "tie-down" process—plumbing, electrical, and other connections—and still exercise zoning controls over factory-built housing.) Delays in gaining approval are costly, approvals are not always given, and procedures for appeals are generally ineffectual. Without question, the current building code system is incompatible with any move toward large-scale production and innovative technology and the cost reductions that might thereby be attained.

To illustrate some of the specific impediments to technological progress and cost reduction inherent in the current code system, the Douglas Commission queried localities about a group of products and practices that most frequently are the butt of builders' complaints. Plastic pipe for waste systems and drainage is considered one of the most important new products in the building industry; it is as durable as metal but lighter and less expensive. Yet nearly two-thirds of all governments with building codes and three-fourths of all municipalities in SMSAs with populations over 50,000 prohibit its use in drainage systems. Almost half of all governments with building codes prohibit preassembled electrical and plumbing units, despite their economic advantages and their high quality of performance. The total impact of these restrictions on housing costs was revealed in a commission survey of manufacturers of prefabricated housing, who are most adversely affected by these codes because of their offsite production process and their potential for a large marketing area. The survey indicated that if these manufacturers want to market their homes in twenty states they must meet 21 major code requirements in excess of model codes or FHA minimum property standards. As a result, a total of $1800 would be added to the cost of a 1000 square foot home that could cost $12,000 (without land) under model code or FHA standards—in other words, a 15 percent "surcharge" is attributable to the present building code system. This alone prices hundreds of thousands of families out of the market. The astronomical growth of mobile home production, which generally is not subject to local building code regulations, highlights the difficulties faced by homebuilders, particularly builders of low-priced units.

Criticism of local building codes has been rife for decades. (Over fifty years ago a Senate committee wrote: "The building codes of the country . . . are not uniform in principle and in many instances involve an additional cost of construction without assuring more useful or more durable buildings.") Remedies are near at hand, but require abrogating that sacred American principle called local determination. Uniform mandatory statewide codes would go a long way toward meeting the need for uniformity and flexibility, particularly if states adopted one of the four uniform national codes. A more useful approach might be for the federal government to promulgate a national building code with built-in allowance for regional variations and special local circumstances and induce local governments to adopt it by offering benefits and services or making adoption of the code a precondition for receipt of certain types of federal aid or both. The federal government currently requires that all FHA-insured housing meet FHA minimum property standards. At the least, building standards might be made uniform for all federally-assisted housing. It is important, however, that any uniform code set standards only at the level necessary for the safety and health of the occupants. Standards above this level only serve to raise the price of housing and exclude large segments of the population from the market for new and rehabilitated housing. Development of uniform and flexible codes will not in itself satisfy the need for immediate, large-scale innovation in the building industry, but elimination of this harmful manifestation of localism will break down one important barrier to a large-scale low-cost housing program.

## Zoning

Zoning laws are an exercise of the state police power to regulate various aspects of land use. They are usually administered by local governments, under state enabling legislation. Zoning grew from the common law "nuisance doctrine," which placed limits on an owner's use of his property by reason of the deleterious effects complete freedom of use might have on neighboring properties. The country's first zoning ordinance (Los Angeles) dates from 1909. Approximately 10,000 communities now exercise zoning powers.

The principal aspects of land use regulated by zoning ordinances are: how land is to be used (for example, residence, commerce, industry, open space); population density (by stipulating minimum lot sizes for residential development); and structural bulk (by stipulating minimum side yards, setback from the street, building height, and the proportion of a lot that can be covered by the building). Other matters sometimes regulated by local zoning ordinances are landscaping and appearance, signs, provision of off-street parking, and minimum house size.

The principal impact of zoning on housing relates to the production and location of housing in undeveloped and underdeveloped areas. In central cities and built-up parts of the suburbs, zoning generally has less impact, and the effects of the zoning ordinance are more complex. Liberalizing the zoning in a given neighborhood or block can permit an increase in the overall housing supply, but usually for a different group of users. Often developers want to replace single- and two-family residences with denser apartment house developments, a change that because of locational advantages and the costs of purchasing and demolishing existing residences usually results in a shift from lower- and lower-middle-income family occupancy to occupancy by childless couples and individuals with higher incomes who can pay higher rents. In such cases "downzoning" or retention of more restrictive zoning classifications will protect lower income groups. In outlying areas the purpose of zoning is to control the rate and type of change at the neighborhood and community level and to protect property values and at the same time, given the prevailing reliance on the property tax, to secure sufficient real estate tax revenue to provide necessary municipal services. (See chapter 3, "Reforming the Property Tax.") Generally, only those residential uses that "pay their own way" are welcomed. As Williams and Wacks note, "the present system of land use controls . . . actually puts a premium on kicking the poor around." The most common valid criticism of local zoning regulations is that they (often intentionally) restrict sharply the construction of lower-priced and multifamily housing in outlying areas and so hinder solution of the housing problems of low- and moderate-income families. The power of those who arrived first to control future use of local land functions effectively to prevent change and growth.

The zoning mechanism produces an exclusionary effect through such devices as large-lot zoning, prohibition of multiple dwellings, minimum floor area, subdivision regulations, prohibition of mobile homes and mobile home parks, and administrative barriers.

### LARGE-LOT ZONING

If the zoning ordinance requires a house lot to be a minimum of one-quarter acre, one-half acre, a full acre, or larger (zoning ordinances in some towns require three- or four-acre minimum lot sizes), this reduces the total amount of housing that can be built and effectively increases the price of the home, not only by the price of the additional land, but often by increasing the quality and size of the house as well, since many developers vary the price of the homes they build according to the size and price of the lot. (The increase in land prices when more intensive development is permitted tends somewhat to offset this effect.) With land costs a substantial and growing part of total house costs, the addition of every quarter acre to the minimum lot size prices thousands of families in a metropolitan area out of the market. A survey done for the National Commission on Urban Problems showed that one-fourth of all metropolitan area municipalities with at least 5000 population do not permit construction on lots of less than one-half acre,[4] and this practice appears to be spreading rapidly (though many communities use large-lot zoning as a "holding" classification, and grant rezoning to higher density classifications on a case-by-case basis).

### PROHIBITION OF MULTIPLE DWELLINGS

Many suburban areas forbid multifamily rental housing entirely or assign only a tiny percentage of the community's buildable acreage to this use. According to Harold Finger, assistant secretary for Research and Technology, HUD, over 99 percent of the country's undeveloped land

4. See *Building the American City,* p. 214; see also Gold and Davidoff, "The Supply and Availability of Land for Housing for Low- and Moderate-Income Families."

zoned for residential use is restricted to single-family homes. (Where zoning is not so restrictive, however, suburban garden apartment construction has proceeded. The increasing cost of single-family homes, financing difficulties for home purchasers, and consumer preference for the convenience and facilities offered by renting an apartment are responsible for this trend. New suburban apartment construction is almost exclusively in the middle- and upper-rent ranges.)

### MINIMUM FLOOR AREA REQUIREMENTS (HOUSE SIZE)

Zoning provisions that require a house to be at least a certain number of square feet are not so common as minimum acreage restrictions, but they have a much clearer effect on housing costs and who can live on the land. Arguments have been made and upheld by the courts that such regulations are in the interests of public health and safety, but the more extreme of this type of regulation are motivated strictly by fiscal and social considerations.[5] The zoning ordinance of one Minneapolis suburb requires a 1700 square foot minimum house, which effectively bars any new home buyer below the upper middle-income range.

### SUBDIVISION REGULATIONS

Most localities also have a separate type of regulation that governs such preparations of undeveloped land for homebuilding as installation of sewers and water lines, laying out of streets and sidewalks, and the like. The standards imposed on builders in laying out subdivisions also have substantial impact on the cost of the final product. Requirements that there be one or one-and-a-half parking spaces for each unit (usually part of zoning ordinances, rather than subdivision regulations) also add considerably to the final cost, a somewhat ironic feature for lower-income and elderly families who may not own a car.

### PROHIBITION OF MOBILE HOMES AND MOBILE HOME PARKS

Local zoning ordinances severely limit the location of mobile home developments, and some communities ban them altogether, both of which hamper the industry's growth and create difficulties in providing low-priced housing, as Bair points out. This derives in part from older

5. For a good discussion of the issues raised by zoning by minimum house size see Haar, "Zoning for Minimum Standards: The Wayne Township Case"; Nolan and Horack, "How Small a House?—Zoning for Minimum Space Requirements"; Haar, "Wayne Township: Zoning for Whom—In Brief Reply;" and Williams and Wacks, "Segregation of Residential Areas along Economic Lines." Zoning ordinances that openly stipulate a minimum construction cost or house value have been consistently struck down by the courts.

prejudices about "trailer camps" and the kinds of people supposed to inhabit such places, but it also has to do with aesthetic objections and fear of large numbers of newcomers and the troubles and expenses they will cause. Financial concerns are perhaps paramount. Since in most jurisdictions mobile homes are not considered real property, they do not contribute to regular property tax assessments (though they may come under personal property tax assessment). The site is taxed as real property, and site rent in mobile home parks reflects these taxes, but local residents and officials feel that the costs of servicing mobile home populations will far exceed the tax revenues they bring in. Mobile home advocates, on the other hand, argue that these newcomers have few children of school age, that many services, such as garbage collection, are provided by the park owner, not the municipality, that the indirect benefits to the community (purchasing power, for example) are considerable, and that the kind of people who now move into mobile home parks cause few difficulties to the municipality. (See Altschuler and Betts.) No definitive cost-benefit studies have been done of this population, however.

ADMINISTRATIVE BARRIERS

Apart from the content of the zoning ordinance, Anderson tells how local administration of zoning frequently presents additional barriers to potential housing developers. The trend in zoning is toward more flexible controls, to allow local administrators to approve or disapprove a given development on an ad hoc basis. This practice may permit better planning, but it also has the potential for preventing unwanted development. In smaller cities and towns, zoning administration frequently is not only incompetent, but possibilities for intentional and costly delay and harassment are legion, as many a developer can attest to. Court battles, while occasionally successful, cost much time and money.

In short, the zoning tool, apart from its use to protect and enhance the municipal tax base, is used by many suburban areas primarily to keep out "incompatible uses"—not only the glue factory and tannery, but low- and moderate-income families and racial minorities. While this is not a new use of zoning ordinances,[6] the veneer of "proper land use planning"

6. Some of the earlier uses of the zoning power, from less genteel times, are instructive. "Zoning ordinances that exclude classes of persons from a specified area are not unknown in the United States. In particular, the possibility of physically separating whites from blacks and orientals suggested itself to various city fathers early in the development of land use control. . . . Racially exclusive zoning provisions have been struck down by the courts consistently, at least when recognized as such." (Sager, "Tight Little Islands: Exclusionary Zoning, Equal Protection, and the Indigent," p. 780.) There is a history of attempts at racially exclusionary zoning in Williams, "Planning Law and Democratic Living." For further zoning history, see Delafons, Land Use Controls in the United States, and Babcock, The Zoning Game.

has become more transparent, and the social purposes of zoning restrictions have become more widely acknowledged. The words *incompatible* and *undesirable,* so frequently heard among zoning advocates, must be candidly recognized as referring primarily to people and social class and racial groupings, and only secondarily to structures and uses.

The fundamentally local character of zoning prevents a metropolitan approach to solving the housing problem. Within most metropolitan areas there are dozens of communities, each with its own zoning restrictions and administrative powers. In the San Francisco Bay Area there are over 100 separate zoning jurisdictions; in the New York region there are over 500. Given the enormous potential and need for housing development outside the central city, any one community that "lets down its guard" runs the risk of being flooded with lower-income housing developments. Only by inducing or coercing a large number of outlying communities simultaneously to relax their restrictions as part of a comprehensive metropolitan plan could any one community be confident that it would not be overwhelmed with new development. (A plan worked out among cities and towns in the five-county Dayton metropolitan area—which unfortunately fell apart before it could be implemented—called for building 14,000 units of low- and moderate-income housing, with each locality's share based upon a formula that took into account the population, available land, and existing low- and moderate-income housing in each community. See Miami Valley Regional Planning Commission, *A Housing Plan for the Miami Valley Region.*)

To the extent that these land-use restrictions and controls derive from fiscal considerations, it is all the more important to change the present property tax system and otherwise find a solution to the financial problems of local governments. The issue is extremely sensitive politically, but relaxation of these restrictions would appear to be a precondition to any large-scale housing development program.

Attacks on local restrictive zoning practices have been mounted through the courts in recent years. Courts in general have given zoning ordinances presumption of validity, and its 1974 decision upholding the right of a Long Island village to bar more than two persons unrelated by blood or marriage from occupying a single-family house was the Supreme Court's first zoning decision since the 1920s. Several suits filed in the federal courts by the National Committee Against Discrimination in Housing, the NAACP Legal Defense Fund, and Suburban Action challenge the right of local communities to exclude low-income residents as a denial of the Fourteenth Amendment guarantee of equal protection of the laws. (A recent zoning innovation, upheld by the New York Court of Appeals for the town of Ramapo, New York, is the "development timing" or "controlled growth" ordinance, which prevents any new residential development without "special permits," which in turn are coordinated with the locality's provision of community facilities.) One of the attacks on such exclusionary zoning practices is that they impede employment opportunities, since most new economic activity is located in areas where low-income and minority families find it difficult to secure housing. It will be some time before these suits are finally decided, but the impact of judicial restriction or of the abolition of local restrictive zoning could be immense.

Change of this type could be brought about by the states as well. Since municipalities exercise their zoning powers under state enabling legislation, states can modify or otherwise restrict these powers. A recent Massachusetts statute takes a gingerly step toward requiring suburban communities to accept lower-income housing. A public agency or a private nonprofit or limited-dividend developer of low- or moderate-income housing whose request for a building permit has been refused locally can appeal to a body established by the State Department of Community Affairs, which has the power to overrule the locality. As Sherer explains, however, exemptions can be granted for only a miniscule fraction of the locality's land, and the locality's remaining jurisdiction over design and planning standards may permit effective sabotage of the regional zoning action through imposition of excessive and costly standards or delay. In the few years it has been in effect the law has had little impact. A related development is creation of the New York State Urban Development Corporation, a state-wide renewal and housing agency with the power to override local zoning and building codes, as described by Reilly and Schulman.

At the federal level, HUD's recent "Breakthrough" program is aimed primarily at local building code restrictions, but the principle it embodies—substitution of federal housing construction standards and guidelines for local determination—may have wider applicability. The President's Committee on Urban Housing recommended that "limited power be granted to the Secretary of HUD to pre-empt local zoning codes from application to federally subsidized low- or moderate-income housing projects." Many advocate a carrot rather than a stick—that is, giving certain kinds of federal aid only if the locality agrees to accept some amount of lower-income housing. A recent report by the President's Task Force on Urban Renewal recommends that "federal aids *of all sorts* be withheld from communities unless they undertake a program to expand the supply of low- and moderate-income housing within their boundaries." Not only has the administration completely ignored this recommendation, according to the New York *Times* story of July 23, 1970, the White House delayed release of the report for six months without explanation.

The tradition of local autonomy in the field of land-use regulation is extremely strong, so not many state legislatures are likely to act to force suburbs to accept development of lower-priced housing units and the persons who will occupy them, and the federal government in recent years has shown little inclination to impose itself on Middle America on behalf of Lower America.

## New Communities

In recent years new communities (sometimes called new towns) have been proposed with increasing frequency as a means of fostering large-scale housing production and freeing developers from restrictive building code and zoning ordinances. (Since they would be municipalities of their own, local controls in new towns could be shaped to the needs of the developers.) This proposal is to develop very large, relatively self-sufficient residential areas on raw sites, with supporting commercial and public facilities and substantial nearby employment opportunities for residents. New towns have a long and honorable history in England, Scandinavia, and other countries, where they generally have been introduced as an element of national urbanization and housing policy, in order to populate new areas and limit expansion of existing urban concentrations. In the United States, there have been relatively few recent attempts to establish new communities, largely because of a limited amount of government aid, in the form of loan guarantees. Most efforts have been made primarily because of the profit-making urges of developers. Federal legislation passed in 1966, 1968, and 1970 provided some assistance for new community development. Government loans are now available to cover interest payments for land acquisition and development during the initial operating period, in addition to mortgage insurance for site acquisition and preparation, public facilities grants, and some planning and technical assistance aid. But as Clapp points out, the level of government assistance available in this country is quite minimal compared to that in England. There, the Ministry of Housing and Local Government and local housing authorities can create ad hoc development corporations to undertake actual development of new towns: site selection and acquisition, planning and design, and building housing and community facilities.

Social as well as economic benefits are touted for new towns. The hope is that by "beginning over" the massive problems that characterize large cities can be avoided (however see Karmin on Columbia, Maryland), but it is likely that this is merely a euphemism for escaping those who live in large cities. According to the Eichler and Kaplan study of new communities in California, "the very things buyers in new communities hope to avoid is the inclusion of lower-income families," which also means racial minorities. Citing the findings of a parallel study of these same California developments by sociologist Carl Werthman and others, Eichler and Kaplan make the following perceptive, if depressing, observation:

> Planning turned out to have a very different meaning, albeit an important one, to buyers than to professionals, including community builders. To the buyers "planning" essentially means conditions or actions which minimize the risk that identifiable or unknown changes would present to their social image and their monetary investment. The change most feared by residents is the construction of markedly less expensive housing nearby.

Economic advantages are claimed through use of cheaper outlying land and mass-produced housing. Yet most housing in new communities is well beyond the reach of lower income families, and the costs of providing the facilities and infrastructure to support a community of 50 to 100 thousand people are astronomical. A primary source of profits for developers of new towns therefore has been ownership of the commercial and industrial sites in and near the community that derive their value from the proximity of the new population and offer the developer monopolistic profits. (The new towns idea, as originally put forth by Ebenezer Howard, called for community ownership of revenue-producing land.) It would appear that new towns offer little prospect for reduced housing costs.

## The Cost Dilemma

Substantial moves toward mass-produced, industrialized building in the United States could be brought about by making rational local building and zoning codes, because this would permit large-scale building in metropolitan areas for a wide spectrum of housing consumers; but it is important to realize the limitations of such changes alone and the other changes that are necessary if the building industry is to serve America's full housing needs. The costs of manufacturing the housing unit are only a proportion of total housing costs, and the benefits of rational production can easily be dissipated unless the broader housing system is taken into account. A case-study of a factory-built house reported by the Douglas Commission reveals these limitations:

> In the upper midwest, an all-weather, single-family dwelling unit of approximately 1,000 square feet can be built and delivered to the site for approxi-

mately $4,000, about $1,000 of which represents the margin to the manufacturer for profit, overhead, and selling cost. Freight is approximately $100. The costs at the site for foundation, painting, finish, carpentry, site improvements, electrical and plumbing subcontracts, permits, crane rental, etc., add about $11,500, exclusive of land. [p. 435]

Thus, in this example the basic production cost is only one-fourth of the final price to the consumer (excluding land costs). Roughly an equal amount comes from costs between the factory and final installation of the house at the site. The total cost is almost doubled as a result of profits, sales, advertising, marketing, and interest costs. These costs too would have to be drastically lowered if industrialized housing is to be available to the full range of housing consumers.

The costs of major production factors—most notably land and capital—are a large and continually rising portion of the final price of housing. Developed land, now 25 percent of the intitial cost of a conventional single-family home and 13 percent of the cost of an elevator apartment unit, is the fastest-rising element of all major housing costs. A serious program to produce 2.6 million units per year will exert markedly inflationary pressures on land prices, unless a system of controls over land disposition or public recapture of increased values is introduced (see chapter 3, "Reforming the Property Tax"). Debt retirement is now 53 percent of the monthly occupancy costs of a single-family home and 42 percent of the cost of occupying an elevator apartment unit (over half of which is for interest payments). Other occupancy costs—taxes, heat, utilities, and maintenance—also represent a substantial portion of the costs to the consumer of owning or occupying his residence. Local real estate taxes represent about one-fourth of total monthly housing costs (for single-family homes), and as service demands on local governments increase, so will the tax bill. Heat and utility costs account for about one-sixth of total occupancy costs. These are as much housing costs as are the costs of producing the housing unit, and all will have to be controlled, lowered, and made rational if decent housing is to be brought within the reach of everyone.

The savings that might be effected through industrializing the housing production process, moreover, are not likely to come about without creation of a large, secure market. Heavy capital investment in production facilities and materials necessitates large-scale and efficient production. But historically housing demand and housing production have been erratic because they are related to the fluctuating supply and cost of credit, the availability of existing housing stock as an alternative outlet for demand, and the lack of any serious national resource planning to achieve specified production goals. A large and predictable market would require adequate funding, in the form of both stable and reasonably priced credit and necessary government subsidies, and the removal of constraints on new technologies and metropolitan- and region-wide building imposed by local building and zoning codes.

One way these changes in the housing industry might come about is through expansion of some of the nation's large corporations into housing production. Of the twenty U.S. corporations with the largest sales, according to Keating five now build and sell houses themselves, and another five are involved in real estate investment and land development. The acquisition of some of the larger builders by corporate giants (such as the purchase of Levitt by International Telephone and Telegraph) may portend further development. ("Operation Breakthrough," a recent and much heralded HUD program, attempted to encourage and introduce cost saving technologies developed by large corporations. HUD gave development contracts to several of these corporate giants; the hope was that HUD certification of new building systems would satisfy local code requirements, and that state governments would amass public and private markets for this new housing on a metropolitan and regional basis. But uncertainties about funding, the quality of the new building systems, relaxation of local building and zoning codes, and the states' ability to aggregate a large enough market over a sufficiently long period of time combined to give the program very limited success.) The economic and political power of the nation's large corporations might be sufficient to bring about the necessary required regulatory changes at the local level and also to pry loose the government support needed to create national or regional production markets. But the dangers of such a development should also be noted. According to Baran and Sweezy, our knowledge of the oligopolistic behavior of corporate entities gives us ample reason to believe that production cost savings would not necessarily be passed on to the consumer and that product quality might decline. Industrialized housing produced by large corporations might well be characterized by controlled obsolescence designed to guarantee a permanently and predictably high level of demand.

An understanding of the trends and potential of the homebuilding industry suggests that there is no cheap or easy way out of the nation's housing problems. Technological advances will not markedly reduce the costs of providing all Americans with decent homes unless major institutional changes are made simultaneously, and the changes needed in both the private and public sectors to expand production and reduce the price drastically appear to be politically infeasible.

## References

ADVISORY COMMISSION ON INTERGOVERNMENTAL RELATIONS
 1966 *Building Codes: A Program for Intergovernmental Reform.* Washington, D.C.: U.S. Government Printing Office.

ALTSCHULER, KAREN B., AND ROBERT S. BETTS
 1970 *Mobile Homes: Evolution of the Market, Consumer Costs, Taxation and Controversy, Comparative Costs.* Berkeley, Calif.: University of California Center for Planning and Development Research, Working Paper 123 (January).

ANDERSON, JACK
 1973 "Mobile Home Industry Abuses." San Francisco *Chronicle* (March 7).

ANDERSON, ROBERT
 1969 *The American Law of Zoning.* Rochester, N.Y.: Lawyers Cooperative Publishing Company.

BABCOCK, RICHARD
 1966 *The Zoning Game.* Madison, Wis.: University of Wisconsin Press.

BAIR, FREDERICK Jr.
 1967 "Mobile Homes—A New Challenge." *Law and Contemporary Problems* (Spring), 286–304.

BARAN, PAUL, AND PAUL M. SWEEZY
 1966 *Monopoly Capital.* New York: Modern Reader Paperbacks.

BARTKE, RICHARD W.
 1971 "Fannie Mae and the Secondary Mortgage Market." *Northwestern Law Review* 66, 43–47.

———
 1972 "Home Financing at the Crossroads—A Study of the Federal Home Loan Mortgage Corporation." *Indiana Law Journal* 48, 1–42.

BRECKENFELD, GURNEY
 1971 *Columbia and the New Cities.* New York: Washburn.

CARBERRY, JAMES
 1972 "Bucking the Feds—Home Buyers, Lenders Cheer as Private Firms Insure More Mortgages." *Wall Street Journal* (August 10).

CLAPP, JAMES A.
 1971 *New Towns and Urban Policy: Planning Metropolitan Growth.* New York: Dunellen.

COMMITTEE FOR ECONOMIC DEVELOPMENT
  1973 *Financing the Nation's Housing Needs.* Washington, D.C.: Committee for Economic Development (April).

DELAFONS, JOHN
  1969 *Land Use Controls in the United States,* 2nd ed. Cambridge, Mass.: M.I.T. Press.

DERTHICK, MARTHA
  1972 *New Towns In Town: Why a Federal Program Failed.* Washington, D.C. The Urban Institute.

DRURY, MARGARET
  1972 *Mobile Homes: The Unrecognized Revolution in American Housing.* New York: Praeger Publishers.

EICHLER, EDWARD P., AND MARSHALL KAPLAN
  1967 *The Community Builders.* Berkeley, Calif.: University of California Press, pp. 172, 119.

FRIEDBERG, SIDNEY
  1971 "The NHP—An Invitation to Housing Partnership." *New York Law Journal* (November 11).

FUNNYE, CLARENCE
  1970 "Zoning: The New Battleground." *Architectural Forum* (May), 62–65.

GOLD, NEIL N., AND PAUL DAVIDOFF
  1968 "The Supply and Availability of Land for Housing for Low- and Moderate-Income Families," in *Technical Studies, Report of the President's Committee on Urban Housing,* II. Washington, D.C.: U.S. Government Printing Office.

HAAR, CHARLES
  1960 *Federal Credit and Private Housing: The Mass Financing Dilemma.* New York: McGraw-Hill Book Company.

_____
  1954 "Wayne Township: Zoning for Whom—In Brief Reply." *Harvard Law Review* 67, 986–93.

_____
  1953 "Zoning for Minimum Standards: The Wayne Township Case." *Harvard Law Review* 66, 1051–63.

HEIMANN, JOHN G.
  1967 *The Necessary Revolution in Housing Finance.* Washington, D.C.: Urban America.

HOOD, EDWIN T., AND JAMES A. KUSHNER
  1971 "Real Estate Finance: The Discount Point System and Its Effect on Federally Insured Home Loans." *University of Missouri-Kansas City Law Review* 40, 1–23.

HORSLEY, CARTER B.
1973 "Mobile Home Owners Battle for Rights." New York *Times* (October 14).

HOWARD, EBENEZER
1965 *Garden Cities of Tomorrow* (first published in 1898). Cambridge, Mass: M.I.T. Press.

INTERNATIONAL CITY MANAGERS' ASSOCIATION
1964 *Municipal Building Inspection Practices*, Management Information Report No. 241. Chicago.

JOHNSON, RICHARD J. H.
1969 "Low-Income Housing Exclusions in U.S. Assailed." New York *Times* (November 7).

JOHNSON, SHEILA K.
1971 *Idle Haven: Community Building among the Working Class Retired.* Berkeley, Calif.: University of California Press.

JONES, OLIVER, AND LEO GREBLER
1961 *The Secondary Mortgage Market: Its Purpose, Performance, and Potential.* Los Angeles: Real Estate Research Program, University of California.

KARMIN, MONROE W.
1971 "Columbia, Planned City, Finds It Shares Woes Facing Unplanned Cities." *Wall Street Journal* (July 14).

KEATING, WILLIAM DENNIS
1973 *Emerging Patterns of Corporate Entry into Housing.* Berkeley, Calif.: Center for Real Estate and Urban Economics and Institute of Urban and Regional Development, University of California.

MAISEL, SHERMAN
1953 *Housebuilding in Transition.* Berkeley, Calif.: University of California Press.

MANVEL, ALLEN D.
1968 *Local Land and Building Regulation.* Washington, D.C.: National Commission on Urban Problems, Research Report No. 6.

MEYERSON, MARTIN, BARBARA TERRETT, AND WILLIAM L. C. WHEATON
1962 *Housing, People, and Cities.* New York: McGraw-Hill Book Company, pp. 153–77.

MIAMI VALLEY REGIONAL PLANNING COMMISSION
1970 *A Housing Plan for the Miami Valley Region.* Dayton, Ohio: Miami Valley Regional Planning Commission (July).

MORRIS, EARL W., AND MARGARET E. WOODS, EDS.
1971 *Housing Crisis and Response: The Place of Mobile Homes in American*

*Life.* Ithaca, N.Y.: Department of Consumer Economics and Public Policy, Cornell University.

NATIONAL COMMISSION ON URBAN PROBLEMS
   1968 *Building the American City.* Washington, D.C.: U.S. Government Printing Office, pp. 214, 257, 431–50, 460–75.

NOLAN, VAL, JR., AND FRANK E. HORACK, JR.
   1954 "How Small a House?—Zoning for Minimum Space Requirements." *Harvard Law Review* 67, 967–86.

PAYNE, JOHN C.
   1970 "Ancillary Costs in the Purchase of Homes." *Missouri Law Review* 35, 455–514.

PERLOFF, HARVEY S.
   1966 "New Towns Intown," *Journal of the American Institute of Planners* (May), 155–59.

PERLOFF, HARVEY S., AND NEIL C. SANDBERG, EDS.
   1973 *New Towns: Why—and for Whom?* New York: Praeger Publishers.

REILLY, WILLIAM K., AND S. J. SCHULMAN
   1969 "The State Urban Development Corporation: New York's Innovation." *The Urban Lawyer* 1 (Summer), 129–46.

RODWIN, LLOYD
   1956 *The British New Towns Policy: Problems and Implications.* Cambridge, Mass.: Harvard University Press.

SAGER, LAWRENCE G.
   1969 "Tight Little Islands: Exclusionary Zoning, Equal Protection, and the Indigent." *Stanford Law Review* 21, 780.

SHERER, SAMUEL A.
   1970 "Snob Zoning Developments in Massachusetts and New Jersey." *Harvard Journal of Legislation* 7, No. 2 (January), 246–70.

SHIPLER, DAVID K.
   1972 "City Construction Grafters Face Few Legal Penalties." New York *Times* (June 27).

   _____

   1972 "Study Finds $25-Million Yearly in Bribes Is Paid by City's Construction Industry." New York *Times* (June 26).

SPOLAN, HARMON S.
   1971 "The Case for Variable Rate Mortgages." *Real Estate Review* 1 (Summer), 15–18.

STEIN, CLARENCE S.
   1957 *Toward New Towns for America.* New York: Reinhold Publishing
        Company.
STONE, MICHAEL E.
        "Federal Housing Policy: A Political-Economic Analysis," in Jon
        Pynoos, Robert Schafer, and Chester W. Hartman, eds., *Housing
        Urban America.* Chicago: Aldine, 1973, pp. 423, 432.

———
   1973 "Reconstructing American Housing." Unpublished article.
U.S., CONGRESS, HOUSE
   1969 *Congressional Record,* Remarks of Congressman Wright Pat-
        man, December 29, pp. E11068–E11071.

———
   1972 *Fourth Annual Report on National Housing Goals* (June 29).
        House Document 92–319, 92nd Congress, 2nd Session, pp.
        9–15, 52–92.
U.S., CONGRESS, JOINT ECONOMIC COMMITTEE, SUBCOMMITTEE ON
URBAN AFFAIRS
   1969 *Industrialized Housing,* Materials Compiled and Prepared for
        the Subcommittee on Urban Affairs of the Joint Economic
        Committee. Washington, D.C.: U.S. Government Printing
        Office (April).
U.S., CONGRESS, SENATE, COMMITTEE ON BANKING AND CURRENCY,
SUBCOMMITTEE ON HOUSING AND URBAN AFFAIRS
   1967 *Study of Mortgage Credit.* Washington, D.C.: U.S. Government
        Printing Office (May).
U.S., CONGRESS, SENATE, SELECT COMMITTEE ON RECONSTRUCTION
AND PRODUCTION
   1921 *Report No. 829,* 66th Congress, 3rd Session (March 2), p.
        2.
U.S. DEPARTMENT OF COMMERCE
   1973 *Construction Review* (February), pp. 4–8.
U.S. PRESIDENT'S COMMITTEE ON URBAN HOUSING
   1968 *A Decent Home.* Washington, D.C.: U.S. Government Printing
        Office, pp. 113–21, 143–44, 149–59.
U.S. PRESIDENT'S TASK FORCE ON URBAN RENEWAL
   1970 *Urban Renewal: One Tool among Many,* the Report of the Presi-
        dent's Task Force on Urban Renewal (May), p. 7.
VAN DER ZEE, JOHN
   1971 *Canyon.* New York: Harcourt Brace Jovanovich, Inc.

WETMORE, JOHN M.
    1971 "Variable Rate Mortgages." *The Mortgage Banker* (March), 16–26.

WILLIAMS, NORMAN
    1955 "Planning Law and Democratic Living." *Law and Contemporary Problems* 20, 317–50.

WILLIAMS, NORMAN, AND EDWARD WACKS
    1969 "Segregation of Residential Areas along Economic Lines: Lionshead Lake Revisited." *Wisconsin Law Review* 1969, 827–47.

"Comments on Proposed Amendments Relating to Variable Interest Rate Mortgage Loans"
    1972 Filed October 16 with the Federal Home Loan Bank Board (Washington, D.C.: Center for National Policy Review, Catholic University School of Law.)

*Controlling Urban Growth—But for Whom: The Social Implications of Development Timing Controls*
    1973 Washington: The Potomac Institute (March).

"It's Time to Take the Low-Price Market Back from the Mobiles"
    1971 *House & Home* (April), pp. 62–71.

# Chapter 3

# EXISTING HOUSING

We need vast amounts of new units to provide all Americans with decent housing, but we must also attend to the more than 70 million existing units. In any given year new production will only add about 2 percent to the total housing stock, so the maintenance and renewal of the existing stock must also be a prime concern of public policy.

In 1960 over 15 million housing units were either structurally unsound or in need of better plumbing facilities. As we noted earlier, the 1970 Housing Census abandoned structural ratings, so there is no reliable national figure of how many units currently are in need of repair. While the total number of substandard units has steadily been declining, in parts of most inner-city areas housing conditions and the real estate environment have markedly deteriorated over recent years. This has been especially true of absentee-owned rental units, where the conflict between the profit motives of owners and the capacities and demands of lower-income tenants has proved detrimental to all. In these areas migration patterns have caused wholesale turnovers of occupancy, often with one race or economic class rapidly replacing another. A substantial part of the housing stock is old and neglected, much of it beyond salvage, at a time when municipal governments that are financially hard hit are lowering service levels, and when property taxes, insurance costs, fuel bills, water charges, and labor costs are increasing. The result in these areas has been a failure to maintain and improve existing structures and the withdrawal of purchasers and lending institutions from certain parts of the market.

According to both Sternlieb and Stegman, some owners of inner-city residential property, particularly smaller, less-experienced landlords, are making little money, and many of them would like to sell their buildings. Problems of rent collection, turnover, vandalism, securing competent building managers and maintenance personnel, and rising costs make property ownership unattractive for many landlords. Personal ties and communication between landlord and tenant decrease as social, ethnic, and geographical distance between the two widens, and both take less care of the property.

Despite lack of profit in such properties, rents remain high, in large part because of the costs of financing. In low-income inner-city neighborhoods, standard sources of housing credit may be unavailable as a result of the "redlining" practices of lending institutions. Banks that will invest in inner-city areas give only short-term loans at high interest rates. In these "blighted areas," blighted all the more by the absence of housing investment funds, small mortgage companies and individual lenders, often charging near usurious rates, fill the gap, and purchase money mortgages are common, whereby the seller must take back a mortgage on his property because no alternative method exists for financing the sale.

Kessler explains that second and third mortgages are not uncommon as ways of minimizing the amount of cash equity the owner must put up. The family that purchases its own home in one of these areas may be forced to accept an "installment purchase contract" or a "land installment contract" instead of a mortgage. Unlike the mortgage instrument, where legal title rests with the mortgagor, these devices are usually proffered at high interest rates and inflated values and do not vest title in the new "owner" until the full amount of the loan is repaid. This means that if payment default occurs the occupant loses everything, rather than retaining the equity he has built up over time, as occurs with mortgage financing. Many of these installment contracts also authorize the speculator-owner—usually a real estate agent—to make repairs on the house in order to protect his investment, and to add these charges to the occupant's debt without his approval or permission. See Grigsby et al. for further details concerning such contracts.

The result of this complex and shaky financing structure is commitment to sharply inflated debt service. According to Johnson:

> The mortgagee is the silent partner in real estate speculation. He is the legally protected hidden investor who demands his payment before outlays are made for maintenance or repairs, even for the superintendent's salary

or for heating oil supplies. The small landlord is virtually the mortgage-holder's employee, fronting for him and operating the property.

Johnson goes on to argue that although the actual value of real estate declines with age, the real estate industry appropriates tremendous unearned speculative profits because of inflated rents and a scarcity-created market price produced by the housing shortage, and that mortgages and investments in existing buildings that create no new wealth are nothing more than speculation on the inflated rents that tenants are forced to pay.

When there is no hope of making a profit or selling the building, the owner may simply walk away from the property. Widespread building abandonment, often of sound structures, has occurred in many large cities. In New York City alone it is estimated that in the late 1960s and early 1970s 20,000 units were abandoned annually. Shipler describes the factors that led to abandonment of a building on New York's West Side:

> a changing neighborhood with an exodus of the white middle-class and an influx of the Negro and Puerto Rican poor, a quick sale with a high mort-gage, a short-term ownership characterized chiefly by neglect, a superinten-dent who sold narcotics and opened vacant apartments to his clients, an owner who apparently made a profit while the building degenerated.

Abandonment is frequently the end of a chain of quick profit-taking known as "milking" a building. Shipler's analysis of this same building showed that the owner made a $50,000 profit in three years by doing minimal repair work and not paying taxes (a strategy unscrupulous own-ers can get away with in many cities, since statutes often provide that several years must elapse before the city can foreclose on the property even though a lien is placed on a tax delinquent building). Owners also take a business tax loss on abandoned buildings, which can be another source of profit. Many abandonments are by decent but desperate own-ers, some of whom have come into property through the accident of inheritance.

The abandonment phenomenon, an indicator of deep malaise in the inner-city housing market, also presents immediate practical problems. Abandoned buildings are usually vandalized within days and soon become fire traps. The cancer can spread rapidly through a block or neighborhood, as block after block of empty buildings in the Bronx and Brooklyn testify. To prevent this, cities must have the power and funds to take control of property as soon as it is abandoned and commence speedy rehabilitation, perhaps through the local housing authority, or demolition. Franklin has proposed a federal land bank to acquire inner-city properties from owners who might otherwise abandon them. In the

*Washington Post,* Ronis writes of an approach introduced in Baltimore, Wilmington, and several other cities called *urban homesteading.* Abandoned and tax-foreclosed properties owned by the city are given to lower income families who agree to bring them up to code standards within a certain period. If the family effects this rehabilitation and continues to live in the property for a stipulated period, usually three to five years, title to the home is transferred to the family. This idea, though creative, has little likelihood of succeeding without easily available rehabilitation loans and development of a blockwide or neighborhoodwide approach.

Another contributing factor to poor building maintenance is the effects of the income tax system on investors in rental housing. Rapid "book" depreciation and the tax shelter it creates are at the heart of high profitability in real estate (see chapter 5, "Tax Shelters and People Shelters") and encourage rapid turnover of property. As Richard Slitor notes, the federal income tax structure

> creates a tax environment in which frequent turnover of large investment and business real estate is a normal investor adjustment to interrelated tax depreciation and financial leverage considerations, thus operating to increase instability of property tenure . . . The old fashioned motives of careful stewardship, conservation, and rational long-range management of investment are apparently subordinated in the tax shelter operation which often characterizes multi-unit rental housing development, luxury as well as slum.

These and other forces have prevented the traditional "trickle-down" or filtration theory of how lower-income groups improve their housing from working. New construction for upper- and middle-income households sets off a "chain of moves" that frequently results in a general upgrading of housing standards,[1] but there are many limitations and impediments to this process. High financing costs, taxes, and maintenance expenditures may prevent rents and prices in housing formerly occupied by upper-income groups from falling enough to come within the range of lower-income families, particularly in times of housing shortage. As housing filters down, maintenance expenditures often drop precipitously and housing quality sharply deteriorates, often to a level below code standards, another function of housing shortage and the economic and political impotence of low-income residents. Further, the dual housing market (see chapter 1, "The Ill-Housed") means that much of the filtered down housing will not be available to nonwhites. Normal market forces simply

---

1. A good review of the filtration literature is Grigsby, *Housing Markets and Public Policies,* pp. 84–110. See also Smith, *Housing: The Social and Economic Elements.* On the chain of moves, see Lansing, Clifton, and Morgan, *New Homes and Poor People: A Study of Chains of Moves,* and Kristof, "Housing Policy Goals and the Turnover of Housing."

do not provide decent housing for lower-income groups, so we need specific strategies to maintain and rehabilitate older housing and to produce new housing.

Maintenance and rehabilitation strategies for the existing housing stock must take into account the true nature of the housing market. Since landlords basically seek to maximize the profit from rental housing rather than to provide decent and satisfactory living conditions, the government must enforce housing standards, but without the tools to enable building owners to meet these standards such an enforcement apparatus is self-defeating. The realities of imbalanced legal and economic relationships between those who own and control property and those who consume housing must also be addressed, and the government must act to effect the market controls and changes in the law that are needed as temporary or permanent measures. Finally, those external factors that affect housing conditions and costs—for example, the property tax system that supports local government—must be reformed.

## Housing Codes

Housing codes regulate the occupancy conditions of residential units by governing the physical condition of the property and setting standards for maintenance and the density of occupancy. Although there were some housing regulations in the nineteenth century, widespread use of housing codes is a recent phenomenon. Most are a result of HUD's Workable Program requirement, established in 1954 to ensure that municipalities receiving federal housing and community development assistance were at least taking local steps to meet their housing problems. In the 1950s fewer than 200 communities in the United States had such ordinances; today there are over 5000 localities with a housing code. Many cities and towns do not yet have housing codes: Manvel reports that a 1968 Census Bureau survey showed that even within SMSA's 15 percent of cities larger than 50,000 had no such codes, and a 1965 Public Health Service survey showed that only 42 percent of the nation's population lived in areas covered by housing codes.

The housing code sets a standard that is considerably higher than conditions in that part of the housing stock that is old and deteriorating. The task of those who enforce the housing code is to bring such units up to the promulgated standard, in many cases for the first time, since the code is imposed on a housing stock that antedates the regulation by decades and was originally built to standards lower than those now deemed minimum levels of habitability. With respect to newer units, housing code standards are minimal compared with the building code standards that governed their construction (see chapter 2, "Building Codes"), and the purpose of the housing code is merely to prevent deterioration below that original standard. However, enforcement occurs in the context of economic and political realities that tend to keep older units and their occupants in substandard conditions. Code enforcement may therefore be seen as an effort to do by government regulation what the private sector and more constructive government programs have been unable to do: insure that all families are living in decent housing. The results are as might be expected: of 29 communities reviewed in a U.S. General Accounting Office study published in 1972, "28 did not have effective, citywide code enforcement, and HUD officials said that few communities in the nation had effective code enforcement."

Housing code enforcement is characterized by many subsidiary defects. A great many codes are of poor quality. In comparing standards contained in a cross-section of housing codes, the Douglas Commission found that

> there are wide variations among them; that they are often in conflict, that the variations are so great that by definition they could not be based on scientific or objective standards; that many provisions are couched in subjective language—"adequate," "in safe condition," "in good repair;" that many of the objective standards are based on a combination of tradition, rule of thumb, or personal experience; and that they differ in emphasis from structure to health, depending on the code adopted.

Many substantively acceptable codes contain totally inadequate enforcement provisions, and when adequate enforcement provisions exist, the administrative process may be defective. When there is more than one code applicable to minimum standards of habitability and more than one agency responsible for administration, the usual result is poor communication, poor coordination, and generally inefficient operations. A 1965 report of the Massachusetts legislature showed that among the state's 32 largest communities all but one had more than one code regulating conditions of human habitation (the modal number was five), and 23 of the 32 communities had at least four separate agencies responsible for code administration. There was an administrative reorganization in New York City several years ago, but before that residents had to contact one agency if they had no water, a second if they had no hot water, and a third if their water pipes were leaking. Since code enforcement depends heavily on complaints by residents, the existence of a bureaucratic maze presents a strong barrier to effective administration.

Code enforcement agencies are almost universally understaffed, their inspectors underpaid and poorly trained and equipped. The Massachusetts report referred to above showed that almost half the state's largest cities and towns did not even have one full-time inspector, and one-third reported they had no educational or training requirements for code enforcement personnel. Where the code enforcement process operates only on the basis of response to individual complaints, staffing shortages may not be so pronounced; but this is an inadequate method, because tenants may not initiate complaints for fear of landlord retaliation, ignorance of the law, or because they perceive difficulties in securing enforcement. A 1972 Cincinnati report indicated that "the ineffectiveness of the called-in complaint procedure for uniformly enforcing the code is brought out by the fact that 99 percent of the buildings in Operation CHANCE program [a systematic inspection program in a single neighborhood] were discovered to be in code violation at the outset." A superior system employs systematic and periodic inspections, on a neighborhood basis or over the entire city on the basis of ratings of each building in the city according to the number and type of deficiencies and concentrating first on the most defective structures. Such a system can be preventive rather than simply corrective and may also produce some amount of voluntary compliance, since owners know they will be inspected regularly. But systematic area inspection is very costly, and few cities are willing to undertake the expense.

In 1965 federal aid for local code enforcement was introduced, in the form of urban renewal projects consisting entirely of concentrated code enforcement. HUD paid two-thirds the cost (three-fourths in communities with populations of 50,000 or less) of administering the housing code systematically in a blighted neighborhood, using federal rehabilitation loans and grants (see "A Comprehensive Approach to Rehabilitation," this chapter), and furnishing certain municipal services, such as provision and repair of streets and sidewalks, street lighting, and tree planting. Nationally, through 1971 only 201 grants were made under this program. The 1965 Housing Act also introduced a program of federal aid for demolition of hazardous structures. Only 156 grants were made under this program through 1971.

No matter the system, there is said to be a good deal of corruption in this area: landlords may consider a small bribe a regular cost of doing business, and poorly paid inspectors, demoralized by the situation in which they work, may be susceptible to such blandishments. (It has been suggested that local residents be trained as housing inspectors, in order to provide employment and "new careers" and to increase the quality and honesty of code administration, since local residents might have more stake in enforcing codes rigorously. The July 1969 *Journal of Housing* reports one such experimental program, in Paterson, New Jersey.)

Enforcement problems are immense even with good codes and adequate staff. The courts generally are of scant assistance in the enforcement process. According to Carlson, Landfield, and Loken, "when present judicial remedies are surveyed, one is impressed by the degree to which the judicial process hinders adequate code enforcement. The courts seem unable to process violations efficiently." Few judges take housing violations as seriously as they take other types of cases, nor do they have sufficient background in housing or knowledge of the particular defendant and his patterns of operation to make a sound judgment. The involvement of lawyers and judges in the real estate field has been widely suspected, and this may be another factor in lax judicial processes. This topic, however, has not yet been the subject of systematic study or of much published material. (Goodman's *The Tenant Survival Book* is one exception.) Information about repeated violators could be centralized in computerized records, but this is rarely done, and this lack of complete data hinders the adequate handling of housing cases. In some cities, such as Baltimore and Boston, special housing courts or housing sessions have been established so that judges can build up expertise and interest in housing, become familiar with specific violators and patterns, and operate in a framework wherein their judgement is not adulterated by intermittent contact with more serious and dramatic crimes. But by itself this innovation has not produced any significant improvement in the judicial process.

One economic incentive that could induce some degree of compliance is the system of fines for code violations, but this has completely broken down, largely as a result of an inadequate judiciary. A study of major violators in Chicago (persons who had been prosecuted in court at least fifty times) from 1950 to 1962 revealed an average fine per suit of only $32. A Boston study showed that of 4420 housing code violations, 400 went to court; of these, fines were levied in only 12 cases; of these, none was paid. Other figures showed that judges granted an average of eight continuances per case; in one instance the continuance was for 390 days. When the case has to do with substandard living conditions, justice delayed is justice denied (and since in most cases inspectors must be present at court hearings, delays and delaying tactics have the effect of reducing the available inspection force). Jail sentences are almost never imposed, although many codes provide for them. The same Boston report concluded that "judicial enforcement has consistently failed to uphold the rulings of the city inspection authorities" and made clear the effects of lack of judicial support on the entire enforcement process:

> Inspectors became demoralized because they have seen deplorable conditions and carried their duties out as charged under law, only to watch violators go unpunished. Landlords, perceiving that the courts will not deal harshly with them, are willing to disobey the inspector's notice to abate violations.

As we noted at the outset, the root problems of local code enforcement run much deeper than the foregoing catalogue of defects. The futility of most local housing code enforcement programs stems from failure to recognize the realities of the housing market, particularly for low-income families. Where there is a shortage of decent, low-rent housing, where tenants' rent-paying capacities are limited, and where landlords have little cash equity in their buildings, code enforcement is a two-edged sword, difficult to wield and capable of inflicting injury on those it is designed to aid. Since virtually all residential properties are privately owned, the aim of an enforcement program is to cajole or coerce the private owner into bringing his property into compliance. To do this his motivations and economic capabilities must be taken into account. To proceed oblivious of these factors is to risk forcing the owner to abandon the building, a phenomenon that is already occurring on a large scale in many cities without the inducement of code enforcement. Proposals to "put teeth" into the process—through vacate orders, municipal repair, demolition and receivership powers, denying federal income tax depreciation allowances to buildings in violation of the housing code, making the mortgagee party to enforcement actions—all run the risk that landlords will walk away from their properties rather than make the required repairs. Very few city governments are willing to assume direct responsibility for removing code violations and managing or disposing of buildings abandoned by their owners. (See related discussion of rent receivership programs in "Landlord Versus Tenant," this chapter.) What is "uneconomic" for a private owner is usually equally uneconomic for the government, and a combination of the general financial difficulties of local governments and the limited notion of municipal responsibility in the housing field have led to a hands-off policy regarding code enforcement in many blighted areas. In Frank Grad's words, "where there are no vacancies, a code enforcement agency has virtually no room to maneuver in, for even the most miserable shelter is better than none."

If the housing code is enforced, the results may be highly damaging to low-income residents, as Hartman, Kessler, and LeGates point out. The supply of low-rent housing may be reduced, through demolition or abandonment, or rents may be raised, which necessitates either a move to lower-priced, and probably substandard, quarters, or added costs that the family cannot afford without taking money away from other necessary budget items. (Families displaced under federally aided code enforcement are entitled to federally funded relocation assistance and payments under the 1970 Uniform Relocation Act, but such aid is not usually available to families displaced by purely local code enforcement activity, which is by far the more common type of enforcement.) A Sacramento study by Scott and Rabin showed that in the 1963–1970 period over 1100 units in low-income neighborhoods were lost through repair or demolish orders, and a 1970 HUD report on Chicago showed that in 1969–1971 61 percent of all units planned for removal from the housing supply through public action would be lost through the municipal housing code enforcement program. Rent increases occasioned by code enforcement are also common, because wherever possible owners will pass on to tenants the costs of making repairs required by code inspectors. A report prepared for the National Commission on Urban Problems documented code-enforcement-induced rent increases in several cities, and a 1968 feasibility study of a proposed federally assisted code enforcement project in a low-income area of San Francisco showed that even with low-interest (3 percent) rehabilitation loans monthly rent increases of $5 to $20 were likely in nearly half the units, and that "probably less than half [of the residents] can afford rent increases." Although tenants in such buildings would like better housing, they are not likely to favor getting it through a system that forces landlords to make expenditures he will pass on to the tenant in the form of higher rents. Such a system would in effect require current tenants to foot the bill for past neglect.

Those instances in which code enforcement has been successful have generally been in areas where serious violations were not dominant, where landlords were financially capable of making needed repairs but not willing to make them, and where tenants were willing and able to absorb additional costs. An "ideal" situation is where a few deteriorating buildings exist in a neighborhood of sound buildings. In such a situation a few landlords are taking advantage of the external benefits of the area, while surrounding owners suffer from the decreased value that a few parcels of blight cause to their properties. Where wholesale blight exists, there are strong disincentives for any single owner to improve his property, by virtue of these same externalities, and getting all owners in a neighborhood to upgrade their properties simultaneously is extremely difficult. If tenants cannot afford rent increases, upgrading will only result in conversion of an entire neighborhood from low-income to middle- or upper-income residency. (See Nash for examples.) As long as there are not enough subsidization funds to cover the inevitable rent increases, code enforcement will be of dubious benefit to low-income residents. The local government's legal requirement that all housing must meet minimum standards is not accompanied by a reciprocal government guarantee that owners and residents of substandard housing will be able to meet the costs incurred by enforcing these standards. Code enforcement is often looked upon as a magic wand: all we need to do to eliminate slums is promulgate minimum standards and then go out and enforce them. This can be useful in some situations, but it cannot be regarded as a serious answer to the problem of slums. Once we understand the processes by which slums are formed and perpetuated, it is clear that there is no magic here. Code enforcement can work only in tandem with low-interest loans and outright grants to financially weak owners, controls on rents of buildings improved with these aids, rent supplements to low-income tenants, full relocation aids and compensation where displacement is necessary, and a system for forcing improvement of the salvageable part of the housing stock that owners will not bring up to code standards, accompanied by all necessary changes in the management and ownership of such structures. In other words, housing codes will only work when they are part of a comprehensive program of housing rehabilitation.

## A Comprehensive Approach to Rehabilitation

All we now have in the way of information on which to base an overall rehabilitation strategy for urban housing is a series of case experiences with rehabilitation projects, each involving only a small number of units, many of limited generality. The "logic" of a strategy to rehabilitate wherever possible rather than to build new structures is compelling: it is cheaper and faster to salvage the good parts and replace or repair the bad than to tear down a structure and construct an entire new building. Displacement and relocation problems that characterize clearance and redevelopment can be avoided, community and neighboring ties sustained; and for low-income families in particular, living in rehabilitated housing can be psychologically and socially more desirable than living in new housing projects that serve to identify and isolate their residents.

Unfortunately, however attractive and compelling the theory of this logic, its application has frequently failed. A detailed explanation of the problems of rehabilitation is contained in the final report of the President's Committee on Urban Housing, *A Decent Home:*

A thorough-going rehabilitation effort may be more complicated and more time-consuming than new construction. Rehabilitation rarely lends itself to highly sophisticated management techniques. Few jobs can be planned beforehand in a central office. Decisions on what should be done will often depend on what is discovered when walls are stripped. The rehabilitation work itself must be postponed until after the expiration of existing tenant leases, the relocation of tenants, and the gutting of the existing structure. Financing arrangements are likely to be even more complicated than for new construction. The uncertainty inherent in rehabilitation work means that supply of materials and labor is hard to schedule. Uncertainty forces contractors to raise their bids in case the worst possible conditions exist. Construction operations are likely to be slow and painstaking because many materials have to be custom-cut to fit the existing structural frame. Since many *ad hoc* decisions must be made, and because the cutting and assembly work is often more exacting than it is in new construction, both laborers and their supervisors must be especially skilled. . . .

Rehabilitation rarely provides opportunities for significant economies of scale. Virtually every rehabilitation job is unique. Few structures have similar designs. If two structures were identical when originally built, they are likely to have been altered since. If still identical in design, it is unlikely that they have deteriorated in exactly the same manner, and thus they are likely to call for different types of rehabilitation work. . . . The fact that ownership of the slums tends to be highly atomized greatly inhibits the emergence of any substantial changes.

(The report further states that for seventeen projects in ten cities the per-unit rehabilitation costs ranged from $6500 to $19,800.) When rehabilitation is completed, basic space and environmental standards may still be below today's accepted minima because of substandard original construction (inadequate light and ventilation, room sizes too small) that no amount of renovation can overcome; and since in a tight market slum buildings can be highly profitable, the costs of acquiring properties for rehabilitation will not be cheap. Rehabilitation activity may still displace residents, if they have to move out for long periods during the renovation process or if resultant rent increases are more than they can afford.

A 1968 report on the rehabilitation of masonry row houses in Boston's South End arrived at the following conclusions:

Rehabilitation costs ranged from $9,600 to $13,900 per unit (compared with original estimates of $2,500 to $4,000), $11.20 to $14.50 per square foot, not significantly below new construction costs, and possibly higher than new construction costs when the shorter life of the rehabilitated structure is taken into account. Monthly rents for the rehabilitated units—even using three percent Section 221(d)(3) loans, a large number of tax foreclosed properties conveyed free by the city, and non-profit sponsorship—averaged $106 for a two-bedroom apartment, $143 for three- and four-bedroom apartments. Only by entering into leasing arrangements with the Boston Housing Authority could these units be made available to low-income families.

Virtually no opportunity was offered to introduce innovative cost-saving techniques, in part due to the small size of the project—50 units were completed in the first phase, an additional 42 in a second stage.

Difficulties in dealing with government red-tape at both the local and federal (FHA) level made the job considerably more difficult.

Highly skilled labor was required, and labor costs amounted to 40 percent of total construction costs. A program to train unskilled youths in rehabilitation skills proved a complete failure (possibly due to the low wages paid to trainees—$1.25 an hour).

One rehabilitation project that received national attention involved gutting the insides of old-law tenements in New York City and lowering prefabricated cores in with cranes. The effort was labeled the *instant rehabilitation* project because the entire process took a matter of days. Residents moved to a hotel and returned to a completed new unit inside the old shell. A 1968 evaluation report by the Institute of Public Administration showed that rehabilitation costs per usable square foot of space were a staggering $45—nearly twice as high as new construction. Furthermore, the report stated, "the livability and attractiveness of the reconstructed buildings were improved but remain considerably below standards under which such buildings were outlawed 66 years ago."

One of the largest federally sponsored rehabilitation projects, involving over 2000 units in Boston's Roxbury-North Dorchester section and inelegantly known as *BURP* (Boston Urban Rehabilitation Program), points up the many problems of even large-scale rehabilitation. The program was announced by HUD in the fall of 1967 as a "crash effort" to undertake massive rehabilitation in a minimum amount of time. The units were to be rehabilitated for low- and moderate-income families using FHA-guaranteed loans and rent supplements. The developers and contractors all had experience with FHA and rehabilitation work, and FHA processing was to be speeded up to avoid traditional red tape. As soon as the project was announced, it ran into numerous troubles, not all of which are unique to rehabilitation efforts. The community, largely black, objected that they had not been consulted about the project; several of the developers chosen were known slumlords; there was no viable provision for relocating the 1950 families living in the apartments to be renovated; there was no assurance that those displaced would have priority in occupying the rehabilitated units; and there was no attempt to provide economic benefit to the black community via the $27 million project by involving black contractors and workers in the effort.

Although some adjustments were made in the project to meet these objections, a study by a local advocacy planning group showed the following:[2]

> Cost-cutting measures by developers, including use of substandard materials, failure to provide competent supervision, incomplete work, and failure to fix roof and plumbing leaks, have led to accelerated deterioration of BURP apartments. As a result, serious defects exist in FHA-approved BURP units. FHA failed to monitor developers' work effectively.
>
> As a result of poor construction and agency supervision, heating and maintenance costs are excessively high, and tenants are being forced to foot the bill through FHA-approved rent increases.
>
> The buildings selected for rehabilitation included many which were least in need of rehabilitation—a phenomenon probably explainable by FHA's desire to have the program "succeed" and the developers' desire to avoid the financial uncertainties of extensive rehabilitation.
>
> FHA paid virtually no attention to the potential for community economic development and employment and training programs as part of the BURP project.

The above examples not only make it clear that rehabilitation is difficult but that a range of government aids and controls is required for successful rehabilitation of low-and moderate-income housing. Two federal programs designed to facilitate this type of rehabilitation were introduced in the mid-1960s. One, Section 312 of the 1964 Housing Act, was a program of direct 3 percent loans. The other, Section 115 of the 1965 Housing Act, was a program of outright grants. Both were limited to families of modest income living in urban renewal or concentrated code enforcement areas or in areas where such a program was planned for the near future. (The thrust of the Section 312 program was always ambiguous, with respect to its intended beneficiaries. Owners of property in urban renewal areas were eligible for such loans no matter what their incomes; 60 percent of the recipients had annual incomes over $6000. The program made no provision for rent limits, so the benefits of the subsidized interest rate were not necessarily passed on to the low- and moderate-income tenant.) In addition to rehabilitation costs the program also permitted building owners to refinance their existing mortgage under certain conditions. The ability to refinance existing mortgage indebtedness at favorable terms may be an extremely important element of a

---

2. See Urban Planning Aid, *An Evaluation of the Boston Rehabilitation Program.* The report was carried out at the request of a militant tenants group that had formed in the area in response to the rehabilitation plan. The project is described from a developer's viewpoint in Goldston, "BURP and Make Money." A middle-of-the-road position of the controversial project is offered in Keyes, *The Boston Rehabilitation Program: An Independent Analysis.* About two-thirds of the units rehabilitated under the program have fallen into default.

rehabilitation program. Rapkin, in his study of a Boston urban renewal area, found that more than 40 percent of the families in the project area would actually reduce their monthly payments after renovation if they refinanced the entire property, including renovation costs, with low-interest, long-term direct government loans, and that for another 24 percent monthly costs would remain substantially the same. The reason is that mortgages in blighted areas, particularly those populated by non-whites, are usually obtained at high interest rates and for a short term. But through 1971 there were only 25,000 Section 312 loans, covering 41,000 units. The Section 115 grant program was available to owner-occupants of buildings with one to four units and with annual incomes generally not in excess of $3000. The maximum limit of the grant was $3500 (increased from $3000 and $1500 in the 1969 and 1968 Housing Acts, respectively). Through 1971, only 35,000 grants had been made. Both these approaches could be highly useful rehabilitation tools if they were properly structured and funded.

There are a number of other federal aids to rehabilitation. The FHA Sections 235 and 236 interest-rate subsidy programs (see chapter 5, "Subsidized Home Ownership" and "Interest Subsidies and Tax Benefits for Rental Housing") are available for rehabilitation, as are rent supplements (see chapter 4, footnote 3). "Project Rehab," a program sponsored by HUD that involves over 20,000 units in ten cities, is modeled after the BURP program and uses a variety of these tools. The public housing program can also be used for rehabilitation: Taggart notes that units put under contract in fiscal 1969 resulted in an average saving of $5000 per unit (30 percent of the cost of new units), though it is difficult to quantify differences in durability and quality. Local housing authorities use the rehabilitation approach most commonly in conjunction with their leasing programs (see chapter 4, "Housing Projects and Beyond"); the long-term lease the housing authority can offer often induces landlords to upgrade their properties to code standards and can facilitate the necessary private financing.

A major federal incentive for rehabilitation through the income tax system was provided in the 1969 Tax Reform Act. Owners of low- and moderate-income rental housing who expend a minimum of $3000 per unit for rehabilitation can depreciate the entire expenditure, up to a maximum of $15,000 per unit, over a five-year period. This extraordinarily rapid allowable depreciation rate is designed to encourage rehabilitation because of the enormous benefit it provides for high-income investors, particularly if an FHA-insured high loan-to-value ratio loan is used, which permits considerable leverage. Benefits to an owner are explained thusly in *Analysis of the Tax Shelter:*

To illustrate, assume that the depreciable rehabilitation expenditures of a project total $500,000, of which 90 percent or $450,000 is supplied through an FHA-insured mortgage loan and $50,000 is paid by the owner in cash. During each of the first five years that the project is rented to low- and moderate-income families, the owner may claim $100,000 in tax deductions for depreciation. If the owner is in the 60 percent tax bracket, he will save in the first year (and, of course, in each succeeding year) $60,000 in federal income taxes. Thus, in five years he will recoup through tax savings a total of $300,000, all for a cash outlay of $50,000, which has been recovered within a year.

This should prove a huge windfall for investors, amounting over five years to an estimated $400 million in foregone tax revenues (that is, added income for taxpayers in the higher brackets), and one hopes it will improve housing conditions for low-and moderate-income families as well. As of this writing, there have been no analyses of the impact of this provision, although Congress provided that at the end of 1974 the effect of this rapid rehabilitation write-off would be evaluated and a decision made whether to terminate or continue it.

On the municipal level, a key form of assistance for rehabilitation is exemption of certain types of improvements and repairs from an increase in the building's assessed value, which can amount to a substantial subsidy. On a grander scale, in 1965 Philadelphia established the Philadelphia Housing Development Corporation, a quasipublic corporation with a $2 million revolving fund of city money to undertake low-rent rehabilitation. The corporation acquires run-down, vacant properties (mostly city-owned property acquired through tax foreclosure, but also property from owners seeking to abandon their properties and take any tax loss benefits they can secure) through purchase and donation and turns them over to developers for rehabilitation at pre-negotiated prices. The PHDC then offers the completed units to families with incomes just over the public housing eligibility limits and to the Housing Authority for use as public housing. It also attempts, as Fielding explains, to secure cooperation from city agencies regarding code enforcement and provision of municipal services to support its rehabilitation work. Cities can also establish rehabilitation loan funds. In response to HUD's curtailment of its Section 312 low-interest loan program in 1973, San Francisco and several other cities devised a subsitute program whereby large banks lend money directly to the city. This shelters the interest from federal income tax and therefore results in a considerably lower interest rate, and the city in turn loans the money at these lower rates to property owners who wish to undertake housing rehabilitation.

On the whole, government assistance for rehabilitation is of small magnitude; most federal and state aid stresses new construction. There is not yet sufficient information and experience to determine the extent to which housing policy can rely on the rehabilitation approach, but experience with government aids and rehabilitation pilot projects such as those described above makes it seem that a rehabilitation policy would have to contain at least the following elements to be successful:

1. Criteria for the kinds of houses to salvage, stated in terms of location, age, structural material, basic plans, and building type. Those buildings deemed unsalvageable would have to be replaced as soon as possible; if they represent a very large portion of the housing stock in a given area (for example, New York City's Old Law Tenements), intermediate, "holding action" renovation should be undertaken to remove the most serious violations and create a minimum level of amenities until such time as they can be replaced, even if this means a relatively uneconomic expenditure of funds. Any long-term housing program must take into account people's short-term, intermediate needs for better, even if not wholly satisfactory, housing.

2. Very large expenditures of public funds in the form of low-interest loans, property tax abatements, and outright grants to developers and owners and rent subsidies to low-income tenants which will bridge the remaining gap and eliminate the "financial bulldozer" that compels tenants to move because they cannot afford the higher rent caused by renovation.

3. Controls on private developers to limit rent increases and insure high-quality work.

4. A large-scale neighborhood approach to rehabilitation. Few owners will or can be expected to improve their properties in the absence of general improvement in the surrounding area; conversely, one or two blighted properties can have a cancerous effect on the surrounding buildings. Plans for comprehensive code enforcement and area-wide rehabilitation will be needed in conjunction with government financial aids. To be most effective, these programs should be planned and supervised on a decentralized basis by neighborhood groups and representatives.

5. Adequate provision for insurance. Insurance coverage, primarily against fire loss, is unavailable in many blighted areas "redlined" by carriers, and as Friedman points out, lending institutions will not grant repair loans for uninsured properties. The federal-state assigned risk FAIR Plan (Fair Access to Insurance Requirements) introduced in the 1968 Housing Act provides some relief, but under this plan insurers and their rates continue to be governed by weak, often "captive" state insurance regulatory agencies, and the defects have been monumental—rates double those charged in the voluntary market for similar risks, illegal cancellations, unwarranted fees and charges, short-term and inadequate coverage, and failure by the companies to inform the public of availability of the plan. George K. Bernstein, the Federal Insurance Commissioner, states:

There is little indication that the Plans are adequately striving for improvement or that they yet recognize the validity of many of the criticisms they receive. . . . A more basic question raised by these reports is whether the FAIR plan approach is really an adequate solution to the residual urban market problem. In a list of the inequities that appear in even the best-managed Plans . . . an affirmative answer is hard to justify. [cover letter to the "Report on FAIR Plan Operations 1971"]

Bernstein's recommendation is that all companies licensed to do business in a state be required to write all insurable applicants at the same rate, with high risk policies reinsured by a mandatory pool, a plan which would represent a return to the original insurance concept of spreading the risk. Given the importance of insurance to housing rehabilitation-maintenance and to the owner's security, and that coverage can be a substantial portion of ongoing housing expenses, the soundest approach may be nonprofit government provision of low-cost property insurance.

6. General environmental improvement. This will require a large public investment in such municipal facilities and services as tree planting, street paving and lighting, schools, garbage collection, and street cleaning.

7. A program for temporary relocation of families whose homes are being worked on. Even under an ideal rehabilitation system, tenants may have to move out of their apartments temporarily, either because the home is unlivable for a period or because the work cannot be done efficiently while the apartment is occupied. Most renovation is possible in as short a time as a few weeks. Temporary dwellings such as mobile homes could house neighborhood residents *seriatim* as their homes are remodeled, to minimize disruption in social patterns, schooling, and other neighborhood ties. Elimination of the dislocation effect may be one of the key advantages of rehabilitation.

8. A pool of rehabilitation specialists, entrepreneurs, and craftsmen. Any future advances in housing technology will be only minimally applicable to rehabilitation, save perhaps with respect to selected features, such as preassembled bathrooms and kitchens. Small builders who are displaced by any coming break-throughs into mass, factory-based housing construction may find rehabilitation work a logical and rewarding alternative. Cost reductions may be possible as builders and craftsmen develop substantial background in the problems and methods of housing rehabilitation. Employment of local workers and contractors will provide economic benefits to the community and can produce the social benefits generated when people are involved in planning and rebuilding their own neighborhoods.

A comprehensive rehabilitation program of this type can provide residents of blighted urban areas with the option of remaining in the inner city in decent conditions. If it is carried out without parallel efforts to increase options for movement to outlying urban and suburban areas, however, it runs the risk of functioning as a "containment" policy to keep the poor and racial minorities away from the white and middle-class areas. The need for new housing in diverse locations is as great as the need for a comprehensive housing rehabilitation program.

## Landlord Versus Tenant

Some 70 million Americans (23 million households) live in a home owned by someone else. Many strains are inherent in this situation, particularly since the landlord-tenant relationship is markedly one-sided in favor of the property owner, expecially for low- and moderate-income families, owing to the landlord's superior economic position and the state of the law. This is not intended to imply that all landlords are necessarily either incarnations of evil or recipients of handsome profits. Many small landlords are in a marginal economic position, and the high rate of building abandonment in many cities is evidence that owning residential property is not always profitable. But every landlord is seeking to make a profit, and in this quest he makes use of his superior legal, political, and economic power. The conflict between the profit motive and the tenant's basic need/desire/right to decent housing is the starting point for this discussion.

The acute shortage of decent low-rent housing and the even more constricted supply available to nonwhite, large, and welfare families has created a situation of extreme inequity. Landlords feel little compulsion to create and maintain conditions satisfactory to the tenant, and the tenant has little effective recourse except the "freedom" to move to another apartment where the same imbalance will probably prevail. According to the report of a federally sponsored National Conference on Legal Rights of Tenants, "in cities with a shortage of housing for low-income families, even the tenant's legal right to vacate and look for better housing elsewhere is ineffective in practice. He has no practical alternative but to take what is offered and pay what is asked." Rents often bear little relationship to the quality or quantity of housing offered: many low-income householders pay more per square foot of living space and get less for their housing dollar than do middle-income families, who have greater choice and bargaining power. Conditions of occupancy are at the landlord's will. Tenants who complain too much or who seek to have the housing code enforced can be evicted or have their rents raised. (There is statutory protection in more than a dozen states against "retaliatory eviction" or retaliatory rent increases to tenants who can demonstrate that the action is the result of their attempts to have the code enforced. Motivation, though, is difficult to prove, and Moskovitz points out that at the end of the statutory period—usually three to six months—the tenant is again exposed to retaliatory eviction, which vitiates most of the value of the protections.) Even when the tenant is successful in getting the landlord to make repairs, he can be and often is forced to pay for these repairs through a rent increase. Nothing compels a landlord to give a tenant a lease, and the majority of low-income residents do not have leases, which means that rents can be raised or eviction accomplished with thirty days' notice. (Except in cases of nonpayment of rent, many courts will grant a tenant who appeals an eviction notice a short stay of eviction where there are reasonable grounds for doing so.) Where leases do exist, they are usually written in so one-sided a manner that, except for the protection offered against rent increases during the leasing period, they provide little benefit to the tenant. (Not all tenants want leases; some are unwilling to be tied down, especially given the few benefits offered by most leases.) Most landlords use a model lease drawn up by the real estate board, so it is not surprising that leases are loaded in favor of the landlord. Under terms of the Chicago Real Estate Board's Model Lease (drafted in 1936), taking possession of the apartment is conclusive evidence that the tenant has received the premises in good order and acknowledgment that the landlord has made no promises to repair or redecorate; costs of vermin extermination must be borne by the tenant; tort liability for damages suffered as a result of defects in the building is all but excluded; and rights to service of notice of eviction and rent demands are waived. Many of the so-called exculpatory clauses that relieve landlords of certain obligations are patently illegal and have been so ruled by the courts, yet their continued presence in lease forms serves to intimidate and befuddle tenants. Apart from the poor housing conditions this situation produces, the lack of real economic or legal restraints on the landlord is a source of great bitterness and frustration among slum residents. Higher-income families tend to avoid this by owning their homes. (According to the 1970 Housing Census, 50 percent of families with under $4000 annual income are tenants, whereas 39 percent with incomes in the $7000–9999 are tenants. Only 19 percent of families with incomes over $15,000 are tenants.) When people with high incomes do rent, their greater resources give them the ability to move to other quarters if they are dissatisfied and make them far less vulnerable to exploitation by the landlord.

The law serves to back up the landlord's economic advantage. Landlord-tenant law still is rooted in its medieval origins, when conveyance of an interest in land was primarily for agricultural purposes. Buildings and improvements were rarely involved, leaseholds were long term, and it was legitimate to expect that the tenant would assume effective responsibility for the property once he had obtained the right to use it. Today, however, leases on urban residential property pertain to people's dwellings, involve spaces such as common indoor and outdoor areas that are not clearly part of the lessee's domain, and are generally short term. Failure to repair or improve a single property may affect many tenants. But the law has not yet developed a clear set of obligations for the landlord, and economic pressures in the market are not adequate to create them. A well-functioning system exists to enforce the obligations of tenants: if a tenant fails to pay his rent or otherwise behaves unsatisfactorily, the landlord has at his disposal the effective power of the courts to evict the tenant, and, except where rent strikes and rent withholding are legal, the reason for nonpayment of rent is irrelevant. In the words of a recent government report entitled *Tenants' Rights: Legal Tools for Better*

*Housing:* "The traditional legal interpretation of the tenant's obligation to pay rent as independent of the landlord's obligations means that no matter how badly the landlord fails in his obligations to the tenant, the tenant must continue to pay his full rent to the landlord on time, or be evicted."

In some states a bond of considerable size must be posted in order to appeal an eviction, which effectively deters the poor from pressing such challenges. The tenant's power to enforce the landlord's half of the bargain through housing codes and other administrative and judicial proceedings is severely constrained. Most of the landlord's obligations that have developed in the past few decades have come through building and housing codes, which establish property construction and maintenance standards. But these obligations are to the city or state and must be enforced by local officials; a tenant derives no rights from these codes that he can enforce himself. The inability of local administrators to use the codes to ensure the maintenance of decent, safe, and sanitary dwellings has been amply demonstrated. (See "Housing Codes," this chapter.)

Some jurisdictions have recently developed an expanded set of legal tools through statute and case law, to require adequate property maintenance. Garrity reviews tenant-initiated remedies that are enforceable by the court. Among the newer remedies available to tenants are rent withholding (or legalized rent strikes) and rent receivership, though so far only a few states authorize one or both approaches. Each attempts to buttress the only real economic leverage the tenant can directly exert: withholding rental income from the landlord. The legal machinery for rent withholding varies in different states. Under some statutes the tenant simply stops paying rent, and when the landlord brings summary process action the court will accept as a defense against eviction the existence of hazardous violations of the housing code. More often the tenant must petition the court for permission either to withhold his rent or to pay it into an escrow account (usually held by the court). Most statutes require that code violations be serious, that they not be tenant caused, and that the tenant not be behind in his rent. A New York statute (applicable in Buffalo and New York City) requires that the city's Building Department prepare a list of "rent-impairing violations" in order to avoid the necessity for judicial determination in each case of the severity of the violation and its eligibility to meet the general statutory language of the rent withholding law. Under most statutes the landlord receives his rent after he makes the necessary repairs, and sometimes the money in the escrow account will be turned over to him in order to permit him to make these repairs.

Rent strike statutes have not been widely used, partly because of administrative impediments, partly because the laws themselves frequently are drafted so as to discourage widespread use. Some states require a certified statement of violation by the local code enforcement agency as a precondition to court action, but often it has been the ineffectiveness of the enforcement agency that has been the impetus for passage of rent withholding legislation. The New York statute requires that six months must elapse after the violation has been recorded before rents can be withheld. The policy of those enforcing the laws is usually to give the landlord an extension so long as he promises to repair. While the tenant waits, in conditions which may endanger his health or well-being, the landlord may adopt one stalling device after another. Often he can stall until the tenant moves and the case is withdrawn, and thus avoid the repairs altogether. Lack of widespread knowledge about the existence of such laws, the reluctance of tenants to go to court, and the paucity of legal help have also held down the number of rent strikes.

Another application of the rent withholding principle is so-called receivership laws, which empower the court to appoint a receiver (a public agency, private organization, or individual) who will apply the rent monies directly to correct outstanding violations. This has the effect of temporarily removing both property and rental income from the landlord's control and theoretically at least makes available the money necessary for repairs. Receivership statutes have run into trouble in the courts because they interfere so fundamentally with the complex web of financial and property interrelationships in the housing field. In those jurisdictions where they have been available, they have either been minimally used or have proved unworkable. A critical weakness of the receivership approach is that in many instances the receiver must invest well beyond the capacity of current rent rolls in order to repair badly deteriorated buildings. Those buildings a landlord has badly neglected may be precisely those that cannot be economically salvaged. The receiver is faced with the choice of allowing serious conditions to go uncorrected, making inadequate repairs, or, where the statute establishes a revolving loan fund, spending money beyond current rent receipts. In addition, rents may have to be raised to cover the costs of repairs. Because of the underlying economics of the slum problem, the receiver may find himself in a situation only slightly different from that of the slumlord. The program may in fact encourage abandonments that the city is financially unwilling and unprepared to take on. If the receivership program is aggressively pursued, it will quickly go bankrupt, as happened in New York City. The single-building approach inherent in receivership programs is another weakness, inasmuch as the surrounding area is not improved at all. The receivership program may be useful in improving buildings that are not badly dilapidated and that the landlord is unwilling to improve, but at best it has limited applicability. Thus, rent withholding and rent receivership, which attempt to create effective economic leverage for the low-income tenant, have so far been of little value, except perhaps to grant short-term rent abatement and as a means of organizing tenants. There is the possibility that these laws have scared landlords into improving their properties in order to avoid legal action, but the demonstrated ineffectuality of these approaches scarcely makes them very potent means of intimidation.

Change in landlord-tenant law is gradually being wrought, primarily through the litigation efforts of Legal Services attorneys. (The *Clearinghouse Review,* published by the Northwestern University School of Law, regularly reports new developments in landlord-tenant case law.) One new approach is based on the legal theory that a landlord, in renting out premises, implies a warranty that the unit is fit for habitation. The case for extending the concept of consumer protection to housing rests on the public's interest in requiring safe and sanitary dwellings, the unequal power positions of buyer and seller, and the acknowledgment that repairs generally will not be made unless the landlord makes them. This theory makes code violations not solely as a matter for state action but gives the tenant a right of action as a third-party beneficiary.[3] Considerable difficulties are created for the courts in defining and applying standards of habitability, but promulgation of a well-articulated list of "warranty-impairing defects," analogous to that required under the New York statute described above, would ease their task. There is another theory outlined by Sax and Hiestand that is based on torts and damage suits. According to this theory landlords might be sued, possibly in class actions, for physical, emotional, and psychological damages attributable to slum living. A third approach involves creating by statute a uniform lease that assigns obligations equitably between landlord and tenant. And an ordinance recently passed in Ridgefield, New Jersey, requires landlords to place with the city security deposits, which can be used to make emergency repairs that the landlord refuses to carry out; this turnabout of the traditional practice of tenant security deposits, if broadly implemented, could be a major step toward eliminating hazardous living conditions in rental housing.

In 1972 the National Conference on Uniform State Laws adopted the Uniform Residential Landlord and Tenant Act. This act takes a significant step toward recognizing the warranty of habitability and protecting against retaliatory eviction, and attempts also to deal with other imbalances in the landlord-tenant relationship—and the Uniform Laws

3. This argument was first accepted by the District of Columbia Circuit Court of Appeals in *Javins* v. *First National Realty Corporation* (and has subsequently been accepted by other courts). The court stated: "in our judgment the old no-repair rule cannot coexist with the obligations imposed on the landlord by a typical modern housing code, and must be abandoned in favor of an implied warranty of habitability." See also Moskovitz, "Rent Withholding and the Implied Warranty of Habitability—Some New Breakthroughs."

Commission is obligated to introduce this act and to press for passage in every state legislature. The act itself is not terribly strong, and not so advanced as the statutes in some states, but for many states it does provide a substantially better set of landlord-tenant laws than they now have.

The impact of such changes in landlord-tenant law is a painfully slow way to bring about change. Court decisions are not binding outside their own jurisdictions, and within a jurisdiction it takes a great deal of time for decisions to filter through the lower courts and for practices to accord with case law. Basic economic and political conditions are rarely changed through law suits.

A different but perhaps complementary approach to the problem of tenants' impotence is political organization: the formation of tenant associations or unions. Absentee landlords, form leases, devices to hide the owner's identity, and realty companies that manage hundreds of buildings make it impossible for the individual tenant to bargain for advantageous living conditions. Just as industrial and crafts workers were able to improve their bargaining position with large companies and other employers and thus gain better working conditions, so groups of public housing tenants, tenants of a single building or a single landlord, or residents of a given neighborhood can use collective action to improve their bargaining position with landlords and gain better housing. There is potential for nationwide organization through the rapid growth of groups like the National Tenants Organization and statewide tenant groups in New Jersey and Massachusetts. The NTO includes tenant organizations in privately owned housing, but its principal focus is on public housing. The New Jersey Tenants Association, with 200,000 members at lower- and middle-income levels, endorses political candidates, lobbies for legislation, and supports rent strikes.

Tenant unions often employ traditional union techniques like picketing and attempt to pressure landlords into signing collective bargaining agreements. Some of the more sophisticated contracts establish the union as sole bargaining agent for all tenants in a given building or of a given landlord, institute the "shop steward" system, and deduct "dues checkoff" from the rent payment. The short-range objectives of these organizing efforts are usually to get landlords to make needed repairs, to obtain more equitable leases, and to regulate rents.

As Marcuse and Burghardt both show, the effectiveness of tenant unions to date has been mixed. In some college towns (notably Berkeley, Madison, and Ann Arbor) students have formed unions to combat the extremely high rents, but as Katz and Moskovitz both show, the transiency of the student population and prevalence of typical "town-gown" conflicts have limited their successs. Some of the most significant successes have come in public, rather than privately owned, housing, because "projects" in many ways offer the most natural constituency for organizing, and because the public authority is politically more vulnerable than a private landlord. Successful rent strikes have been organized against housing authorities in several cities; the most notable success was the nine-month 1969 St. Louis strike that resulted in a new, tenant-oriented housing authority, an elected tenant affairs board to advise on public housing policy and to arbitrate disputes between individual tenants and the housing authority, a revised rent schedule, and physical improvements in the city's various projects. (See chapter 4, "Dissatisfactions with Public Housing," for a discussion of the new public housing lease and grievance procedure, which resulted directly from organized tenant lobbying.) Tenant union organizing has had some successes, and has considerable potential for the future, but it has run into substantial problems. Apathy and high turnover rates among slum residents make organizing difficult, and the frequent reliance on outside organizing help often can result in a leadership vacuum. Moreover, when and if the tenant union movement really does begin to grow, many owners will probably seek to sell or abandon properties that have been "organized."

One possible result—perhaps even the intent—of tenant organization may be to make absentee slum ownership untenable and to force "distress sales" to local groups. But there is no magic in this approach: in view of the advanced deterioration of most slum buildings, full control or ownership of these properties might prove a white elephant. If this process is ultimately to benefit tenants, government subsidization programs to assist in rehabilitation and rent payments will be necessary. Unprofitable or troublesome experience with tenant management or ownership can be the quickest way to destroy a local organization. On the other hand, strategies for broader social change may be effected through tenant organizing, such as that Frances Piven and Richard Cloward advocated so as to disrupt the slum system at its root. They analyzed the failure of the 1963–64 rent strike movement in New York City in terms of excessive reliance on cumbersome and ineffective legal procedures, and one of their observations was that "slum profits have depended on collusion between city agencies and landlords; in return for nonenforcement of codes, the slumlord takes the blame for the slum and enables the city to evade the political ire of the ghetto." They suggest that next time slum tenants en masse go on "illegal" rent strike and pocket the rents instead of depositing them with the court. In their scenario landlords would be forced to abandon their buildings, and when the city came into possession of the abandoned buildings it would be constrained politically from evicting such a vast number of low-income persons. Once in possession of these buildings, the city would be compelled to act positively and seek federal aid to avoid becoming a major slumlord itself.

Another form of direct tenant action is "squatting," moving into vacant public or private buildings, often those owned by expanding institutions such as hospitals and universities. Squatting, though not widespread, has received a lot of attention in the media and elsewhere, particularly in New York but also in Boston, Chicago, Milwaukee, and other cities. Squatting actions have usually been well organized, with the dual purpose of obtaining needed housing and dramatizing housing shortages. New York's "Operation Move-In" in 1970 focused on the West Side urban renewal area and the depletion of low-rent units the project was causing. Some 200 families in need of living space occupied boarded-up buildings under the protection of community supporters (though arrest and eviction were as often the result as were negotiation and concessions by the city). Squatting is a very radical act because it directly challenges notions of legality and private property and asserts the primacy of human needs. It is a statement that the system is not going to give and that therefore people in need must take. Many organizers of the New York squatters movement felt that the central demand expressed by these direct actions was elimination of private profit from the housing market, extension of public ownership and tenant control to all housing, and assertion of the right to a decent place to live as paramount. No squatters movement, in New York or any other city, has yet won substantial material gains (though some individual housing needs have been met and a few specific buildings salvaged), but it is potentially a very powerful tool, one that inspires exhilaration in those who participate and panic among those who control property and govern cities.[4]

The inordinately weak position of tenants in the "housing system" is a critical defect in the process of obtaining and maintaining decent housing for the poor. The nature and extent of tenant power as it evolves over the coming years can have great impact on all aspects of the housing problem, not just in the area of landlord-tenant laws. If strong tenant unions come into being, they can work profound changes not only in the landlord-tenant relationship, but in the entire system of local and national housing priorities.

4. For a good discussion of squatting tactics and other aspects of tenant organizing, see Goodman, *The Tenant Survival Book*, pp. 63–111, 171–91, 193–210. Relevant treatments of squatting in other countries are found in Hollister, "The Politics of Housing: Squatters"; Abrams, *Man's Struggle for Shelter in an Urbanizing World;* and Turner, "Housing Priorities, Settlement Patterns and Urban Development in Modernizing Countries."

## Should Rents Be Controlled?

In several cities where the housing shortage is particularly acute, pressures are mounting to institute or expand public regulation of rents and rent increases. (During World War II rents were regulated nation-wide.) Few claim that rent control is a perfect tool or that by itself it can solve the housing problems of our cities, but it is an understandable and rational response to an increasingly untenable situation in many cities where rent increases are placing a near unbearable burden on low-income families, particularly the elderly and others who live on fixed incomes. Substantial parts of New York City's housing stock have been subject to rent control for decades. Massachusetts recently passed enabling legislation, following which four cities (Cambridge, Somerville, Brookline, and Lynn) enacted comprehensive local ordinances. In Berkeley, California, a strong rent control ordinance, placed on the ballot through the initiative process, was passed by the voters in 1972, but was subsequently struck down by the courts. Legal barriers to introducing rent control ordinances have hindered local efforts. In states where home rule charters do not permit municipalities to establish local rent control, special state enabling legislation, usually difficult to secure, is a prerequisite. Other cities have rent grievance boards and voluntary landlord controls, which often are a first step toward true rent control. As part of President Nixon's anti-inflationary measures, all rents in the nation were frozen for ninety days in late 1971, and were then subject for more than a year to guidelines and controls during Phase II of the administration's economic program.

The political and academic battles regarding rent control center around its immediate and long-range effects on the housing market and the political and economic philosophy it is presumed to embody. Rent control systems differ with respect to coverage and administration, but the basic function of rent control is to set administratively maximum allowable rents, rather than to let them be controlled by the market. Evictions, building conversions, and demolitions are usually controlled too, since these are common ways landlords will try to avoid controls and dilute the protection offered to the housing consumer. (The New York City statute even provides for relocation payments to displaced families when permission is given for eviction to allow upgrading of the property. This requirement—that private owners compensate tenants for costs incurred when the owner seeks to maximize his profit—is almost unique in American housing law.)

The extreme is Lawrence Frank's proposal to regulate the entire current and future stock of rental housing in the manner of a public utility, with rates (rents) set by a public body, and with a sinking fund, created by capturing the landlord's depreciation allowance, to maintain and eventually replace obsolete structures. Some categories of housing usually are exempted from controls to avoid presumed negative effects on the housing market and to neutralize potential political opposition. Among the most common exemptions are housing constructed after passage of the regulation (so as not to discourage new construction); high-rent housing (since upper-income families who occupy these units presumedly are not in need of this protection); government-subsidized housing and accommodations owned by certain institutions, such as schools; and rental units in small, owner-occupied structures (since owner-occupants are presumed to be less avaricious than absentee commercial landlords, and in order not to create a large class of voters opposed to rent control). Rent levels may be fixed as of the date of passage of the regulation or rolled back to a previous level, or they may be set through more complex procedures having to do with a maximum profit allowed to each landlord, based on actual cost and revenue figures. Rent adjustments, appeals, and ongoing supervision are usually handled through an elaborate administrative mechanism.

There are cogent arguments for and against rent control, backed by a certain amount of hard data. The negative case rests not so much on denial that a serious housing problem exists as on the argument (well articulated by Kain) that rent control is an inefficient and inequitable form of intervention in the housing market. Where the rent control ordinance does not cover the entire rental housing stock (as is the case in most existing and proposed systems), a controlled and uncontrolled stock is created. All occupants of the controlled stock, regardless of income—that is, regardless of their need for help—are aided, whereas needy families who do not happen to live in the controlled stock are denied assistance. If the demand for housing increases faster than the housing supply, rents in the uncontrolled stock can be expected to rise even higher than if there had been no rent control. Low- and moderate-income families unfortunate enough to be living in the uncontrolled stock may thus be damaged by rent control. Two classes of owners are also created, again with little discrimination between the kinds of landlords that are helped or hurt by this division. Upper-income owners with substantial resources may be the owners of uncontrolled buildings, while owners least able to afford the reduced income imposed by rent control may fall into the other category. Moreover, setting rent levels as of some arbitrary date may reward those landlords who have been rent gougers in the past by fixing their rents at these exorbitant levels and simultaneously penalize more lenient, humane landlords for having charged fair rentals. In short, both the benefits and costs of rent control are to an extent unjustly allocated. As Achtenberg (who is positively disposed toward rent control) succinctly describes it: "Rent control arbitrarily taxes owners of controlled housing and tenants of noncontrolled housing, to benefit owners of noncontrolled units and tenants in the controlled stock."

Opponents of rent control also argue that many landlords who make marginal or no profit will be forced to abandon their buildings; that adequate maintenance will become impossible; that the city will lose important tax revenues through underassessment caused by rent control; that new construction will be discouraged, since upper-income families will take advantage of the benefits of rent control rather than upgrade their housing standards; that there will be considerable corruption in enforcement of the law; that it will create a "black market" for housing; that administration will be costly and inefficient; that rent control will produce inefficient allocation of space, since persons will tend to remain in large, rent-controlled apartments after their children leave home; and that the system will increase tensions between landlord and tenant. And in addition to these practical considerations, there is also the philosophical question of whether in a generally free-market economy one segment ought to be singled out for price controls.

Proponents of rent control also argue their case both philosophically and pragmatically. They hold that during periods of severe housing shortage government intervention in the housing market is desirable to protect the interests of the poor and those on fixed incomes. They concede many of the defects cited by opponents, but they argue that many of these shortcomings characterize the housing market generally and are not caused by rent control, and that alternatives such as a huge low-rent housing program appear politically unfeasible. Rent control does not encourage good maintenance, but neither does the housing system generally (see "Housing Codes," this chapter), and maintenance is no better in cities without rent control; indeed, rent control may be a powerful tool to ensure compliance with housing codes, because under systems such as the one in New York the city is empowered to lower rents (down to $1 per month) until serious hazards are removed. Landlord-tenant relations are inherently poor and would be poorer if rents were higher and evictions easier. Landlords' profits, it is argued, are sufficiently high, as demonstrated by the fact that they continue to purchase, own, and operate property of their own free will; and many of the benefits of owning real estate are to be found, not in operating profits, but in the income tax structure (see chapter 5, "Tax Shelters and People Shelters").

The data from New York City indicate that rent control has not only benefited the poor, but large segments of the middle class as well—and these are the system's most vocal supporters. According to Rapkin, before the recent changes in New York's rent control system more than 90 percent of all households earning less than $4000 lived in controlled units (43 percent of all families earning over $15,000); and in the 1960–1965 period rents in controlled units rose only 8 percent, compared with a 21 percent rise in controlled units. But the New York City case also indicates that if rents are established at levels that low-income families can afford, without subsidies to increase their rent-paying abilities, one consequence can be severe undermaintenance and abandonment of buildings. (It should be noted, however, that while abandonments may be caused in part by rent control, this same problem has been experienced in many cities, such as Chicago, Detroit, and Philadelphia, that do not have rent control.)

If we control prices in one segment of the economy without controlling other costs and prices, we shall clearly produce an unstable situation. Landlords, be they public or private, must receive revenue sufficient to meet operating costs. To accomplish this, most low-income families (or their landlords) require subsidies. A city that has a housing shortage but does not have a comprehensive subsidy program must choose between establishing controlled rents and taking the chance that substantial deterioration and abandonment will ensue, or allowing free-market rents to spiral beyond the capacity of low-income families. (Even controlled rents may be too much for low-income families to bear, if increased costs for utilities, taxes and maintenance are passed on to the tenants.) The goals of "reasonable profit" for landlords, protecting the interests of low-income tenants, and adequately maintaining the housing stock appear to be mutually exclusive.

We have regarded rent control as an emergency measure, but the housing crisis faced by the nation's poor, and the inflation that produced it, are probably not temporary phenomena but are instead indicators of a more durable structural defect in the nation's economy. Rent control by no means reaches the underlying problem of how to increase the supply of low- and moderate-income housing; in fact, it may well discourage private investment in new and existing housing because it will encourage investors to place their funds where the return is greater and difficulties fewer. (It should be noted, however, that developers will accept controls on rents voluntarily as a quid pro quo for government assistance in the form of low-interest loans, as they have under the several FHA programs. See chapter 5, "Interest Subsidies and Tax Benefits for Rental Housing.") The only lasting solution lies in more government intervention, not less, through a combination of subsidies, direct construction activity, and controls, to effect a massive increase in the supply of decent lower-rent housing. Without such an increase, rent control will be needed in many if not most American cities to prevent rent levels from climbing beyond the reach of low-income families.

## Reforming the Property Tax

The present property tax system is uniformly damned, on theoretical and experiential grounds, by taxpayers, government officials, and scholars; yet it remains relatively impervious to demands for change, largely because it is so deeply imbedded in our system of local government. The property tax is the cornerstone of local government revenue: it supports public schools, police and fire protection, and other basic public services. Until alternative revenues are available, financially pinched municipal governments simply are not going to let go. Although the proportion of local revenue generated by the property tax has been steadily decreasing, it is still the single largest source of revenue, and it is the "back-up" residual tax: once a locale has calculated its revenue needs and has added up all its other sources of revenue, the remaining amount is what it must raise through the real estate levy. In 1970–71 the property tax accounted for 40 percent of all local government revenue and 60 percent of all local government revenue raised locally (these are aggregate percentages—the actual figure varies considerably among different localities). The term *property tax* can apply to tangible personal property and intangible personal wealth (savings deposits, stocks, bonds) as well as to real property of all types, but we shall concentrate here on the property tax as it applies to housing (which accounts for half of local government property tax revenue), in particular on the impact of the tax on consumers of housing and on housing production and rehabilitation.

Insofar as it affects housing, most economists regard the property tax as a consumption, sales, or excise tax paid by owner-occupants directly and by tenants indirectly, as part of the rent. Absentee owners of residential property tend to avoid the effects of property taxes by passing these costs directly on to tenants. Using data for SMSAs, Dick Netzer concludes that housing bears a 24 percent consumption tax (the figure may be 30 percent and higher for apartment house dwellers in New York City and single-family home owners in the northeast region). This is a startling finding, since tax theory has traditionally held that the necessities of life should be taxed lightly or exempted from taxation altogether. Netzer comments:

> It is simply inconceivable that, if we were starting to develop a tax system from scratch, we would single out housing for extraordinarily high levels of consumption taxation. More likely, we would exempt housing entirely from taxation, just as many states exempt food from the sales tax.

The property tax in its present form is highly regressive—that is, it takes a higher proportion of income as income decreases. This is so partly because housing takes a far larger proportion of the family budget among the poor and partly because the urban poor tend to be located in areas where tax rates are higher. The 1959–1960 data presented by Netzer show that for renters the proportion of total income devoted to the property tax is 8.5 percent for families earning under $2000 a year, 2.5 percent in the $4000–5000 category, and 1.4 percent in the over $15,000 income group. Shannon's 1970 data show that owners of single-family homes paid 16.6 percent of their income for real estate taxes if they earned under $2000, 5.5 percent of their income if they earned $5–6000, and only 2.9 percent of their income if they earned $25,000 or more. Data presented in U.S.Senate hearings in 1969 on the economics of aging disclosed that 3 million households, mainly elderly, paid more than 10 percent of their total income for property taxes in 1968. Federal income tax provisions that permit deduction of local property taxes exacerbate this regressivity, since home ownership rates are positively correlated with income and since there is no upper limit on the amount that may be deducted.

A further source of regressivity may lie in the way the property tax is administered. By law and custom, properties are usually assessed at only a fraction of their true sales value. Oldman and Aaron conducted one of the few comprehensive studies of assessment practices and found that in Boston lower-priced properties tended to have a higher assessment/sales ratio than higher-priced properties, that multifamily homes bore a higher ratio than single-family homes, and that variations by district (holding price and house type constant) ranged from a 41 percent average ratio in the middle-income and more outlying sections of the city to an average ratio of 68 percent in Roxbury, Boston's black ghetto. Using the tax rate prevailing at the time of the study, Oldman and Aaron found that a family living in a $10,000 home in Roxbury was paying $265 more in taxes per year ($22 per month) than a family living in a similarly priced home in an outlying section of the city. Arthur D. Little, in its 1973 study of ten cities for HUD, concluded that "poor-quality housing in blighted neighborhoods, occupied by low-income tenants, pays property taxes at a substantially higher rate than property in other neighborhoods." These systematic variations indicate that the property tax is administered in ways that discriminate markedly against the poor and racial minorities, who tend to occupy lower-priced and multifamily dwellings. Since public services, which are financed primarily by the property tax, are frequently inferior in those areas where relative property taxes are higher, the injustice may be compounded. Infrequent reassessment also means that rapidly developing areas in which values are rising (typically not the domain of the poor) will be systematically underassessed, which also contributes to regressivity.

In addition to its effects on consumption patterns, the property tax also influences housing investment and production, including improvement and repairs. Any tax reduces available consumption income, but the exceedingly high excise tax on housing effectively reduces by a substantial amount the demand for housing that can be met by the private sector, and thereby lowers total production. As Sternlieb shows, owners are often reluctant to improve their properties because they fear reassessment and the resultant tax penalty. In some areas certain types of repairs can be exempted from increased assessment, which serves to encourage rehabilitation.

The property tax also has deleterious effects on metropolitan land use patterns, because the present fractionated system of local government leads each community to attempt to improve its own tax position at the expense of other parts of the metropolitan area and region. The flight of the middle class to the suburbs and many industrial and commercial location decisions are in large part products of the desire for lower property taxes and improved municipal services. The disproportionate number of low-income persons and need to provide a wide variety of services for the entire metropolitan area place a severe financial burden on central cities at a time when they are losing important sources of tax revenue. The results are even higher tax rates and further exodus, while the suburbs, because of their ability to attract desired land-uses and because they have little demand for services relative to property tax payments, increasingly improve their competitive position. One important effect of the severe financial bind of most large cities is a reduction in the quality of public services such as schools, medical care facilities, and garbage collection.

Another defect in the property tax as it is currently administered is the wide disparity in tax-exempt property among different municipalities. All land owned by federal, state, and city governments, and by public authorities, churches, schools, and charitable institutions is exempt from property taxes. Although no definitive estimates have been made of the value of tax-exempt properties, churches alone own several billion dollars worth (in New York City the property owned by religious institutions is worth $700 million). Some tax-exempt institutions make voluntary payments in lieu of taxes, but these are rare and usually amount to only a fraction of the normal tax bill. (However, many tax-exempt institutions —hospitals and private schools, for example—provide services that would otherwise have to be furnished by the public sector, and to the extent that loss of tax exemption would drive them out of business considerable additional governmental costs would be incurred.) A municipality may have to bear the full costs, in terms of foregone tax revenue, of a regional or metropolitan facility that happens to be located within its borders. In Boston (an extreme case) 47 percent of the taxable base is exempt. The tax base is also chipped away through special exemptions and abatements. Large businesses and landholders seem to be most successful in securing reductions in their tax bill through the appeals process. Some types of exemptions (such as provisions for easing the tax burden of elderly homeowners, who are particularly harmed by rising taxes because their incomes are low and fixed) represent progressive social policy (although to the extent that they discriminate against elderly renters, who may need these aids even more, they also have regressive features).

Given the above catalogue of horrors, one may well ask: Is there anything good about the property tax? Why has it survived? Why doesn't someone do something about it? (Four decades ago Jensen noted, "If any tax could have been eliminated by adverse criticism, the general property tax should have been eliminated long ago.") About the most that can be said for it is that it has produced large amounts of sorely needed revenue for cities and towns ($38 billion in 1970, and no alternative source is clamoring to replace it) and has attained a certain stability by virtue of its longevity. But tax rates in many cities have been rising at alarming rates, and as a result tax delinquency and foreclosures also are increasing, as Sternlieb and Burchell demonstrate. New York City now has 30,000 tax-foreclosed properties on its hands, over 90 percent of which are residential. "Taxpayer revolts" are becoming common, even when the solutions offered are irrational. A proposed amendment to the California constitution to limit local property tax to 1.25 percent of market value received 27 percent of the vote in the state's 1972 elections, even though the lion's share of these benefits would have gone to owners of business and income property rather than to homeowners and renters and there would have been a sharp increase in the highly regressive state sales tax. Taxpayers are unwilling to support bond issues for needed public services and facilities because they fear increased tax rates. In a 1972 poll sponsored by the Advisory Commission on Intergovernmental Relations to find out people's views on the least fair tax, over half named the property tax; the federal income tax, which received the next highest number of negative votes, was cited by only 19 percent of the respondents. Clearly the time has come to change the property tax system.

Property tax reform could be instituted on many levels. One approach is to reduce reliance on the property tax by substituting financial aid from the state and federal governments collected through more progressive means, such as income and corporation taxes. The administration's "revenue-sharing" programs embody this approach, although the scale of redistribution is far too small to serve as a substitute for the property tax. A local income tax, such as has been introduced in several large cities, might have similar benefits, though if it is not done throughout the metropolitan area it can serve to accelerate the flight to the suburbs.

Basic changes might also be made in the property tax itself. One such change might be to shift the focus of the tax from improvements to land (either solely or disproportionately), though a tax based solely on land would initially present several practical difficulties. At the moment such a tax is constitutionally prohibited in many states, so it would require lengthy and difficult amendment procedures to make the plan nationwide. The basis for the property tax now is both land *and* improvements, but improvements are considerably more valuable than the land itself, and several studies have shown that land tends to be assessed and taxed at only two-thirds the effective tax rate at which improvements are taxed. The arguments in favor of land value taxation are compelling. Land is a "gift of nature," fixed in quantity and nonreproducible. Its value is not intrinsic (save in the case of agricultural land) but is created by the community and the society through population growth, government action, and general location patterns. Why should an individual or a corporation reap the benefits of increasing land values, rather than the community in general? (Such benefits do not now go completely untaxed: the property tax to an extent begins to reflect increased value, once it is realized, and appreciated land is subject to the capital gains tax upon sale, but these are relatively minor forms of recapture.) The answer to this question is usually couched in terms of "the free enterprise system" and the presumed social benefits from the entrepreneurial activity that attempts to maximize individual profit, but the result has been and will continue to be widespread land speculation and investment in land rather than in improvements, which raises sharply the eventual cost of development. Land speculation has considerable impact on the nation's ability to solve its housing problems since land costs are an increasing portion of total housing costs. The program to build 26 million units of housing called for in the 1968 Housing Act is bound to exacerbate inflationary trends in land prices, which will make achievement of this goal unnecessarily or prohibitively expensive.

If the property tax were to be shifted to land it could provide vast sums of money. In the 1956–1966 decade the market value of privately owned land in the United States rose from $269 billion to $523 billion, an average annual increase of $25 billion (6.9 percent higher than the average annual rate of increase in the GNP, as Manvel points out). Capturing all or part of that increase through the taxing mechanism would substantially increase our capability to deal with urgent social needs, including housing.[5] (A tax to recapture all or part of these values would, of course, retard the upward spiral of land values, but the increase would still be substantial—for the coming decade it will likely exceed the 1956–1966 period.) The social benefits of such a switch—from investing unproductively in land toward maximizing the current potential of land, which would be the incentive effect of high taxes on land value, and low or no taxes on improvements—would of course depend on the use developers made of their land. If we were to abolish the present speculative system and the allocation system the free market provides, we would have to require land-use controls, special incentives, and subsidies in order to insure large-scale construction of low- and moderate-income housing.

Other basic property tax reforms that have been recommended, as explored in the November 1971 newsletter of the Tax Reform Research Group (an offshoot of Ralph Nader's efforts), include ending the local character of the property tax, introducing a progressive rate structure, and improving administration of the tax. If the geographical base for assessment and collection of the property tax were to be enlarged (preferably to a state-wide level), this would go a long way toward eliminating (1) destructive local competition for tax-producing uses; (2) exclusion of lower income residences and other uses which do not "pay their way"; (3) disparities in public services deriving from different local financial capabilities. Enlarging the geographical base would also lessen the vulnerability of local governments to powerful property owners who threaten to move elsewhere if they do not receive preferential treatment. (The 1973 Arthur D. Little study offers evidence that large investors who own a great number of properties and recent purchasers of income properties in blighted neighborhoods appeal high assessments most frequently, and this evidence indicates that the workings of the appeals process add to the regressivity of the property tax.)

Recent successful court challenges to the system of financing education through the local property tax, which results in sharp disparities in school spending among different communities, will have a significant

5. If this were done, there would be something of a problem of equity. The argument for land taxation logically applies to current as well as to future values and owners, yet the expectations of current owners—and the prices they paid, which to an extent reflect these expectations—are possibly in a different class from those of future owners, and differential treatment may be warranted. Decisions about the extent to which the expectations of current owners are to be honored would have to be made in light of arguments that discredit the basis for these expectations, and the degree to which the society wishes to compensate present owners for "losses" suffered by reducing or eliminating these expectations. During the postwar Labour government years, the British introduced a remarkable scheme to capture all increases in land value, as part of a general land planning approach to development. Owners were compensated for the value of their land at that time plus some amount for their expectations of increase. The scheme was dropped when the Conservatives regained control of the government. For a description of the British experience, see Haar, *Land Planning Law in a Free Society.*

impact on the way in which the property tax is levied and allocated, although the exact shape of these reforms is unknown at present. At least four state courts have followed California's lead in 1971 in declaring invalid an educational system that makes school expenditures a function of a school district's taxable wealth. Although the U.S.Supreme Court in 1973 held that no violation of the federal constitution is involved, Long notes that the state courts' finding of a state constitutional violation will probably extend to other parts of the country and that reform legislation is being introduced in many states as well. Given the central role of the property tax in local government revenue and the increasing proportion of local expenditures that go to schools (Oakland's data for the Baltimore metropolitan area show that 39.2 percent of all current expenditures went for schools in 1970, up from 35.7 percent in 1960), it is clear that major changes will have to occur in the property tax to satisfy the equalization principle being laid out by the state courts. Some speculation on the implications of these changes is offered by Hagman.

If the property tax were progressive, as the federal income tax is, there would be a sharp break with the tradition of uniformity that has been fundamental to the property tax, but it would be more in line with current theories of taxation and notions of social justice. Progressive rates might be established (1) on the amount of property a person owns (as is done in Australia), (2) on the value of property, or (3) on income. Among other effects, a taxation system of this type might discourage concentration of property ownership.

The inadequacies of current property tax administration are succinctly described in the following passage from the *Property Tax Newsletter:*

> Throughout the nation—though of course in varying degrees—there is underassessment of large commercial and industrial properties, vacant land, minerals, political favorites, and whole classes of other taxpayers; there are untrained, part-time, politically sensitive local assessors; assessments that have not been revised for decades; obscure and secretive record-keeping systems; complex, expensive appeals procedures; nonfunctioning methods for collecting tax delinquencies; increasing contracting-out of the property tax assessment function to private appraisal firms; and a legion more of infractions and abuses that have made the property tax a major catastrophe in the history of American public administration.

The underassessment of large industries and corporate property owners is one of the more shocking abuses under the current system. The *Newsletter* refers to a Chicago study that shows that the United States Steel Company alone was underpaying $16.5 million in property taxes, a burden shifted to small taxpayers. Ways in which administration of the property tax can and ought to be improved include: eliminate small tax jurisdictions; have the states assume the assessment function (even if rate-setting and collection remain local); upgrade the qualifications and salaries of administrating personnel; remove the assessor position from political influence; reassess annually; improve notification and appeals procedures; modernize record-keeping; and create greater public access to tax records.

The present property tax system is a monument to our inability to bring about necessary social change. Virtually every informed person acknowledges that there are serious defects and inequities in the system, and sound proposals exist for ameliorating or drastically overhauling it. The states are the key to change. Traditionally they have ceded the property tax to local governments. This not only has resulted in the chaos, dysfunction, and inequities already described, it has also increased the reliance of the states on regressive sales and excise taxes. Local resistance to overhaul of the current property tax system will be great, for there are many powerful beneficiaries of current practices, from real estate developers and owners of large commercial, industrial, and mining properties, to upper-income residents of suburban areas with a high level of public services and relatively low taxes. Inertia, failure of public leadership, and the influence of powerful entrenched interests must all be overcome if inequities of the current property tax system are to be eliminated.

## References

ABRAMS, CHARLES
  1966 *Man's Struggle for Shelter in an Urbanizing World.* Cambridge, Mass.: M.I.T. Press.
ACHTENBERG, EMILY
  1973 "The Social Utility of Rent Control," in Jon Pynoos, Robert Schafer, and Chester W. Hartman, eds., *Housing Urban America.* Chicago: Aldine, pp. 434–47.
ACKERMAN, BRUCE
  1971 "Regulating Slum Housing Markets on Behalf of the Poor: Of Housing Codes, Housing Subsidies, and Income Distribution Policy." *Yale Law Journal* 80, 1093–1197.
ADVISORY COMMISSION ON INTERGOVERNMENTAL RELATIONS
  1972 "Public Opinion and Taxes." Washington, D.C.: U.S. Government Printing Office (May).

ARTHUR D. LITTLE, INC.

1971 *Organizing and Managing a Large-Scale Program—Strategies and Techniques.* Report prepared for the U.S. Department of Housing and Urban Development.

———

1973 *A Study of Property Taxes and Urban Blight.* Report prepared for the U.S. Department of Housing and Urban Development (January).

BLUMBERG, RICHARD

1973 "The Landlord Security Deposit Act," *Clearinghouse Review* (November), 411–14.

BOSTON MUNICIPAL RESEARCH BUREAU

1969 *Costs and Other Effects on Owners and Tenants of Repairs Required under Housing Code Enforcement Programs* (July 3).

BURGHARDT, STEPHEN, ED.

1972 *Tenants and the Urban Housing Crisis.* Dexter, Mich.: The New Press.

CARLSON, RICHARD E., RICHARD LANDFIELD, AND JAMES B. LOKEN

1965 "Enforcement of Municipal Housing Codes." *Harvard Law Review* 78 (February), 830–31.

CENTER FOR COMMUNITY CHANGE AND NATIONAL URBAN LEAGUE

1971 *The National Survey of Housing Abandonment.* Washington, D.C.: Center for Community Change and National Urban League (April).

COMMONWEALTH OF MASSACHUSETTS

1965 *Final Report of the Special Commission on Low-Income Housing,* H. 4040.

———

1968 *Report of the Special Commission on a Housing Court for Boston,* H. 4498 (February 5).

COMPTROLLER GENERAL OF THE UNITED STATES

1972 *Enforcement of Housing Codes: How It Can Help to Achieve Nation's Housing Goal.* Report to the Congress (B-118754). Washington, D.C.: General Accounting Office (June 26), p. 12.

DEPARTMENT OF URBAN DEVELOPMENT, CITY OF CINCINNATI

1972 "From Housing Rehabilitation to Neighborhood Development" (September).

FIELDING, BYRON

1967 "Rehabilitation: Philadelphia." *Journal of Housing.* No. 4, pp. 221–25.

FRANK, LAWRENCE
    1963 "To Control Slumlord Abuses—Private Housing Proposed to
         Become Public Utility." *Journal of Housing* (July), 271.

FRANKLIN, HERBERT M.
    1971 "Federal Power and Subsidized Housing." *The Urban Lawyer*
         3, 61–77.

FRIEDMAN, GILBERT B.
    1968 "Uninsurables in the Ghetto." *New Republic* (September 14),
         19–21.

FROSH, LANE, AND EDSON, CONSULTANTS TO ARTHUR D. LITTLE, INC.
    1971 *Analysis of the Tax Shelter.* Report to U.S. Department of Hous-
         ing and Urban Development, C–72753 (November 15), p. 18.

GAFFNEY, M. MASON
    1972 "The Property Tax Is a Progressive Tax." Washington, D.C.:
         Resources for the Future, Reprint No. 104 (October).

GARRITY, PAUL
    1969 "Redesigning Landlord-Tenant Law for an Urban Society."
         *Journal of Urban Law* 46, 695–721. Reprinted in Pynoos,
         Schafer, and Hartman, eds., *Housing Urban America*, pp. 75–86.

GOLDSTON, ELI
    1968 "BURP and Make Money." *Harvard Business Review* 47 (Sep-
         tember-October), 84–99.

GOODMAN, EMILY JANE
    1972 *The Tenant Survival Book.* Indianapolis: The Bobbs-Merrill
         Co., Inc. pp. 193–210, 63–111, 171–91.

GRAD, FRANK P.
    1965 *Legal Remedies in Housing Code Enforcement in New York City.* New
         York: Columbia University Legislative Drafting Research
         Fund, p. 5.

GRIBETZ, JUDAH, AND FRANK GRAD
    1966 "Housing Code Enforcement: Sanctions and Remedies." *Co-
         lumbia Law Review* 66, 1254–90.

GRIGSBY, WILLIAM G.
    1963 *Housing Markets and Public Policies.* Philadelphia: University of
         Pennsylvania Press, pp. 84–110.

GRIGSBY, WILLIAM G., MICHAEL STEGMAN, LOUIS ROSENBURG, AND
GORDON LIECHTY
    1970 "Housing and Poverty in Baltimore, Maryland." Ms., pre-
         pared for the Housing, Real Estate and Urban Land Studies
         Program, Graduate School of Business Administration, Univ.
         of Calif., Los Angeles. Revised form to be published.

HAAR, CHARLES
    1951 *Land Planning Law in a Free Society: A Study of the British Town and Country Planning Act.* Cambridge, Mass.: Harvard University Press.

HAGMAN, DONALD G.
    1972 "Property Tax Reform: Speculations on the Impact of the Serrano Equalization Principle." *Real Estate Law Journal* 1 (Fall), 115–35.

HARTMAN, CHESTER W., ROBERT P. KESSLER, AND RICHARD T. LEGATES
    1974 "Municipal Housing Code Enforcement and Low-Income Tenants." *Journal of the American Institute of Planners* (March), 90–104.

HEILBRUN, JAMES
    1966 *Real Estate Taxes and Urban Housing.* New York: Columbia University Press.

HERZOG, DON A., AND CLARENCE R. BECHTEL
    1969 " 'New Careers' Route to Housing Code Inspector Jobs Tried in Paterson, New Jersey." *Journal of Housing* (July), 356–58.

HOLLISTER, ROB
    1972 "The Politics of Housing: Squatters." *Society* (July–August), 46–52.

INDRITZ, TOVA
    1971 "The Tenants' Rights Movement." *New Mexico Law Review* 1, 1–145.

INSTITUTE OF PUBLIC ADMINISTRATION
    1968 *Rapid Rehabilitation of Old-Law Tenements: An Evaluation* (September), p. 4.

JENSEN, JENS P.
    1931 *Property Tax in the United States.* Chicago: University of Chicago Press, p. 478.

JOHNSON, LEIF
    1970 "Decent Housing for New York's People." Metropolitan Housing Council Community Improvement Fund (April).

KAIN, JOHN F.
    1969 "An Alternative to Rent Control." Unpublished paper, Department of Economics, Harvard University (April).

KATZ, STUART
    1970 "Rent Strikes and the Law—The Ann Arbor Experience." *Yale Review of Law and Social Action* (Spring), 13–18.

KESSLER, RONALD
    1971 "The Second-Mortgage Nightmare." Washington *Post* (October 17).

KEYES, LANGLEY C. JR.
    1970 *The Boston Rehabilitation Program: An Independent Analysis.* Cambridge, Mass.: MIT-Harvard Joint Center for Urban Studies.

KRISTOF, FRANK S.
    1965 "Housing Policy Goals and the Turnover of Housing." *Journal of the American Institute of Planners* 31, No. 3 (August), 232–45.

LANSING, JOHN B., CHARLES WADE CLIFTON, AND JAMES N. MORGAN
    1969 *New Homes and Poor People: A Study of Chains of Moves.* Ann Arbor, Mich.: Institute for Social Research, University of Michigan.

LIPSKY, MICHAEL
    1970 *Protest and City Politics.* Chicago: Rand McNally & Co.

LONG, DAVID C.
    1973 "The Property Tax and the Courts: School Finance after Rodriguez," in George E. Peterson, ed., *Property Tax Reform.* Washington, D.C. John C. Lincoln Institute and Urban Institute, pp. 85–105.

MCFARLAND, M. CARTER, AND WALTER K. VIVRETT, EDS.
    1966 *Residential Rehabilitation.* Minneapolis, Minn.: University of Minnesota Press.

MANVEL, ALLEN D.
    1968 *Local Land and Building Regulation.* National Commission on Urban Problems, Research Report No. 6.

——
    1968 *Three Land Research Studies.* National Commission on Urban Problems, Report No. 12.

MARCUSE, PETER
    1971 "The Rise of Tenant Organizations." *The Nation* (July 19), 50–53. Reprinted in Pynoos, Schafer, and Hartman, eds., *Housing Urban America,* pp. 49–54.

MORTON, WALTER
    1955 *Housing Taxation.* Madison, Wis.: University of Wisconsin Press.

MOSKOVITZ, MYRON
    1972 "Legislative Acceptance of Retaliatory Eviction Doctrine." *Law Project Bulletin* 2, No. 6 (July 15), National Housing and Economic Development Law Project, University of California, Berkeley.

_____ 1970 "Rent Strikes and the Law—The Limitations of the Ann Arbor Experience." *Yale Review of Law and Social Action* (Spring), 19–32.

_____ 1970 "Rent Withholding and the Implied Warranty of Habitability —Some New Breakthroughs." *Clearinghouse Review* (June), pp. 49, 62–67.

_____ 1969 "Retaliatory Eviction—The Law and the Facts." *Clearinghouse Review* (May), 4–6, 10–12.

MOSKOVITZ, MYRON, AND PETER J. HONIGSBERG
1970 "The Tenant Union-Landlord Relations Act: A Proposal." *Georgetown Law Journal* 58 (June), 1013–62.

NASH, WILLIAM W., JR.
1959 *Residential Rehabilitation: Private Profits and Public Purposes.* New York: McGraw-Hill Book Company.

NATIONAL COMMISSION ON URBAN PROBLEMS.
1968 *Building the American City.* Washington, D.C.: U.S. Government Printing Office, p. 287.

NATIONAL URBAN COALITION
1974 *Urban Homesteading.* Washington, D.C.: National Urban Coalition.

NETZER, DICK
1966 *Economics of the Property Tax.* Washington, D.C.: The Brookings Institution, pp. 29–32.

_____ 1968 *Impact of the Property Tax: Its Economic Implications for Urban Problems.* Research Report No. 1, National Commission for Urban Problems, pp. 13–21.

_____ 1973 "Is There Too Much Reliance on the Local Property Tax?" in George E. Peterson, ed., *Property Tax Reform.* Washington, D.C.: John C. Lincoln Institute and Urban Institute.

NEW YORK CITY RAND, INC., AND MCKINSEY AND CO.
1970 *Rental Housing in New York City.* New York City Rand, Inc. and McKinsey and Co. Vol. 6, chapter 2.

NIEBANCK, PAUL L., AND JOHN B. POPE
1968 *Residential Rehabilitation: The Pitfalls of Non-Profit Sponsorship.* University of Pennsylvania Institute for Environmental Studies.

OAKLAND, WILLIAM H.
   1973 "Using the Property Tax to Pay for City Government: A Case Study of Baltimore," in George E. Peterson, ed., *Property Tax Reform.* Washington, D.C.: John C. Lincoln Institute and Urban Institute, pp. 146–47.

OLDMAN, OLIVER, AND HENRY AARON
   1965 "Assessment/Sales Ratio under the Boston Property Tax." *National Tax Journal* 18, 36–49.

OSER, ALAN S.
   1971 "Law on Rents Foreshadows Broad Change." New York *Times* (June 6).

PIVEN, FRANCES FOX, AND RICHARD A. CLOWARD
   1967 "Rent Strike: Disrupting the Slum System." *New Republic* (December 2), 11–15.

RAPKIN, CHESTER
   1966 *The Private Rental Housing Market in New York City.* New York: New York City Rent and Rehabilitation Administration (December).

——————
   1961 *The Washington Park Urban Renewal Area.* Boston: Boston Redevelopment Authority (December).

RONIS, BENJAMIN
   1973 "Abandoned Homes Given for Promises to Renovate." Washington *Post* (September 22).

SAN FRANCISCO DEPARTMENT OF CITY PLANNING AND DEPARTMENT OF PUBLIC WORKS
   1968 "Code Enforcement Feasibility Study of the Alamo Square Neighborhood" (May).

SAX, JOSEPH L., AND FRED J. HIESTAND
   1967 "Slumlordism as a Tort." *Michigan Law Review* 65 (March), 869–922.

SCOTT, ERROL G., AND EDWARD H. RABIN
   1969 *Report of the Low-Income Housing Project: Housing Code Enforcement in the City of Sacramento.* Davis, Calif.: Martin Luther King, Jr. Program, School of Law, University of California (June 30).

SHANNON, JOHN
   1973 "The Property Tax: Reform or Relief?", in George E. Peterson, ed. *Property Tax Reform.* Washington, D.C.: John C. Lincoln Institute and Urban Institute.

SHIPLER, DAVID K.
  1969 "104th Street Walk-Up Offers Profile of Abandoned Building." New York *Times* (January 18).

SLITOR, RICHARD
  1968 *The Federal Income Tax in Relation to Housing.* Research Report No. 5, National Commission on Urban Problems.

SMITH, WALLACE
  1970 *Housing: The Social and Economic Elements.* Berkeley, Calif.: University of California Press.

SOUTH END COMMUNITY DEVELOPMENT, INC.
  1968 *The South End Row House: A Rehabilitation Story.* Summary Report on a Low-Income Housing Demonstration (November).

STEGMAN, MICHAEL A.
  1972 *Housing Investment in the Inner City: The Dynamics of Decline.* Cambridge, Mass.: MIT Press.

STERNLIEB, GEORGE
  1966 *The Tenement Landlord.* New Brunswick, N.J.: Rutgers University Press.

STERNLIEB, GEORGE, AND ROBERT W. BURCHELL
  1973 *Residential Abandonment: The Tenement Landlord Revisited.* New Brunswick, N.J.: Center for Urban Policy Research, Rutgers University.

TAGGART, ROBERT, III
  1970 *Low-Income Housing: A Critique of Federal Aid.* Baltimore, Md.: The Johns Hopkins Press, p. 31.

TAX REFORM RESEARCH GROUP
  1971 *Property Tax Newsletter,* No. 14 (November).

TURNER, JOHN C.
  1968 "Housing Priorities, Settlement Patterns, and Urban Development in Modernizing Countries." *Journal of the American Institute of Planners* (November), 354–63.

URBAN PLANNING AID
  1969 *An Evaluation of the Boston Rehabilitation Program.* Cambridge, Mass.: Urban Planning Aid, Inc. (September).

  _____
  1973 *Less Rent More Control: A Tenants' Guide to Rent Control in Massachusetts.* Cambridge, Mass.: Urban Planning Aid, Inc.

  _____
  1973 *People before Property: A Real Estate Primer and Research Guide.* Cambridge, Mass.: Urban Planning Aid, Inc.

U.S., CONGRESS, SENATE, SPECIAL COMMITTEE ON AGING
  1970 *Economics of Aging: Toward a Full Share in Abundance.* Report No. 91-1548 (December 31), pp. 44–47 and 176–92.
U.S., CONGRESS, SENATE, SUBCOMMITTEE ON ANTITRUST AND MONOPOLY OF THE COMMITTEE ON THE JUDICIARY
  1971 "Competition in Real Estate and Mortgage Lending." Hearings before the Subcommittee on Antitrust and Monopoly, 92nd Congress, 2nd Session, Pursuant to Senate Resolution 32, Section 4, Part I (Boston) (September 13–15).
U.S., CONGRESS, SENATE, SUBCOMMITTEE ON HOUSING FOR THE ELDERLY OF THE SPECIAL COMMITTEE ON AGING
  1969 *Economics of Aging: Toward a Full Share in Abundance.* Hearings before the Subcommittee on Housing for the Elderly, 91st Congress, 1st Session, Part 4, "Homeownership Aspects," (July 31–Aug. 1), p. 818, Table 2.
U.S. DEPARTMENT OF HOUSING AND URBAN DEVELOPMENT
  1970 *City of Chicago Team Preliminary Report on Chicago Housing Supply* (November 19).

——— 1971 *1971 HUD Statistical Yearbook.* Washington, D.C.: U.S. Government Printing Office.
U.S. DEPARTMENT OF HOUSING AND URBAN DEVELOPMENT, FEDERAL INSURANCE ADMINISTRATION
  1972 "Report on FAIR Plan Operations 1971" (January).
U.S. DEPARTMENT OF HOUSING AND URBAN DEVELOPMENT, U.S. DEPARTMENT OF JUSTICE, AND THE OFFICE OF ECONOMIC OPPORTUNITY
  1967 *Tenants' Rights: Legal Tools for Better Housing.* Report on a National Conference on Legal Rights of Tenants.
U.S. PRESIDENT'S COMMITTEE ON URBAN HOUSING
  1968 *A Decent Home.* Washington, D.C.: U.S. Government Printing Office, p. 108.
WILLIS, JOHN W.
  1950 "A Short History of Rent Control." *Cornell Law Quarterly* 36, 54–94.
"American Bar Association National Institute on Housing Code Enforcement"
  1971 *The Urban Lawyer* 3, 525–642.
*Housing Affairs Letter*
  1972 Washington, D.C. (December 1 and December 22).

"National Conference on Uniform State Laws Adopts Uniform Residential Landlord and Tenant Act"

    1972 *Law Project Bulletin,* August 15. National Housing and Economic Development Law Project, University of California, Berkeley, pp. 1–3.

"Residential Rent Control in New York City"

    1967 *Columbia Journal of Law and Social Problems* 3 (June), 30–65.

# Chapter 4

# GOVERNMENT HOUSING PROGRAMS: PART I

The federal government has been in the housing business in a serious way since establishment of the Federal Housing Administration in 1934 and the original public housing program initiated under the National Industrial Recovery Act in 1933. In this section we shall analyze the principal federal programs to see who actually benefits from them, how effectively they provide decent housing, how they are administered, and the salient problems that have arisen in the course of their operation. Most of the direct assistance programs are administered by the Department of Housing and Urban Development, which was established in 1965 to give cabinet status to the Housing and Home Finance Agency.

We have not discussed the Model Cities Program, because it is only marginally a housing program—HUD data indicate that only 8 percent of the funds allocated under Model Cities have gone into the area of housing, mostly for such things as establishing local housing development corporations, assisting tenant organizations, and providing counselling services. The program has undergone a substantial metamorphosis since its introduction in 1966 as part of the Johnson administration's "Great Society," when it was hailed as an all-purpose super-tool to eradicate urban blight and poverty in the most impoverished neighborhoods. The Model Cities Program was to have relied heavily on citizen participation, as the Poverty Program did. The Nixon administration nearly jettisoned the program entirely, then reshaped it into a program to concentrate power in city hall and act as a bellwether for decentralizing federal power to local governments and substituting block grants for the current system of categorical grants for specific programs.

Nor is there discussion of urban renewal, which might more properly be labeled a de-housing program. This program was introduced in the 1949 Housing Act as "slum clearance," but was taken over at the local level by those who wished to reclaim urban land occupied by the poor for commercial, industrial, civic, and upper-income residential uses.[1] Over half a million households, two-thirds of them nonwhite and virtually all in the lower income categories, have been forcibly uprooted. A substantial percentage of these persons were moved to substandard and overcrowded conditions and into areas scheduled for future clearance, at a cost of considerable personal and social disruption. There have been widespread increases in housing costs, often irrespective of improvements in housing conditions or the family's ability to absorb these added costs. The program has clearly exacerbated the shortage of decent low- and moderate-rent housing. In the late 1960s statutory changes in urban renewal law were passed to redirect the program toward meeting the housing needs of low- and moderate-income households, and meaningful citizen participation requirements were introduced. But the recent shift from categorical program grants to comprehensive revenue-sharing grants for community development may nullify these gains and permit localities to return to old style renewal: bulldozing the poor off their land to make way for "higher and better" uses.

The loan guarantee programs of the Federal Housing Administration (which is part of HUD, but for historical and other reasons retains considerable autonomy) are discussed in Chapter 2, "Money Matters," and the federal rehabilitation aids that were introduced as part of the urban renewal program are discussed in Chapter 3, "A Comprehensive Approach to Rehabilitation."

Recently the states have begun to provide various forms of housing assistance, primarily through housing finance agencies that issue tax-exempt bonds and loan money directly, at interest rates a few points below the market rate, to limited- and nonprofit housing developers. Some fifteen states now have such agencies. The housing produced is

1. For general reviews of the problems and accomplishments of urban renewal, see Wilson, ed., *Urban Renewal: The Record and the Controversy;* Bellush and Hausknecht, eds., *Urban Renewal: People, Politics and Planning;* Anderson, *The Federal Bulldozer;* Abrams, *The City is the Frontier;* and Greer, *Urban Renewal and American Cities.* A good description of the program's impact on the black population of New Haven, probably the most "renewed" city in the country for its size, is found in Green and Cheney, "Urban Planning and Urban Revolt: A Case Study." A detailed "anatomy" of a single urban renewal project may be found in Hartman, *Yerba Buena.*

moderate and middle income, because of the limited benefits that a below-market interest rate provides. The law that established the Massachusetts Housing Finance Agency requires recipients of state loans to make at least 25 percent of the units available to low-income families, through leasing arrangements with local public housing authorities, rent supplements, and other devices. A few states are also involved in secondary mortgage market operations and in financing low-rent public housing in a manner similar to the federal program. The Urban Development Corporation is a state agency in New York empowered to issue bonds and directly develop multipurpose urban development projects.

### Income Taxes and Housing

By far the largest subsidy given to housing comes through the workings of the Internal Revenue Code, even though in the peculiar American folk logic "tax breaks" usually are not regarded as subsidies. The savings that result from allowing owners to deduct mortgage interest costs and property taxes from their taxable income and to exempt from taxation the imputed rental income from owned homes are in the neighborhood of $7 billion annually (1966 data), which according to Aaron is "equivalent to a reduction in the price of housing to homeowners that results in benefits to them approximately equal to the tax savings." (The amount of these benefits has risen considerably since the mid-1960s. According to Aaron's 1966 data, $2.9 billion of the total was for interest and property tax deductions. In 1971 the Treasury Department estimated that these two items accounted for $5.1 billion in deductions—see *Housing Affairs Letter,* July 28, 1972. If this rate of increase is true for the entire package of tax benefits, they were worth over $12 billion in 1971.) By contrast, public housing, the largest direct housing subsidy program, received one-tenth the $7 billion amount. (The income tax laws also have important implications for investment in and maintenance of rental housing. See Chapter 5, "Tax Shelters and People Shelters.")

The savings the income tax system provides to homeowners represent a substantial portion of their housing costs: at 1965–1967 tax rates the typical homeowner offset about 12 percent of his housing costs through interest and property tax deductions. But the workings of these tax subsidies are highly regressive and are disadvantageous to renters at all income levels. Because these deductions can only be taken by taxpayers who itemize deductions and the proportion of itemizers increases sharply with increased income, and because there is no upper limit on the amount of interest and property tax expenditures that can be deducted, the lion's share of these benefits goes to upper-income taxpayers. Treasury Department figures for 1971 in the same issue of the *Housing Affairs Newsletter* show that taxpayers in the $3000 to $7000 income class received total benefits of $244 million, while taxpayers in the $15,000 to $50,000 income class received total benefits of $2,538 million, and taxpayers in the over $50,000 income class received total benefits of $594 million. Another way of expressing this, says Aaron, is that property tax and interest deduction were worth a mere one dollar to the average family that earned less than $3000, $45 to the average family that earned $7000 to $10,000, $166 to the average family that earned $15,000 to $25,000, and $1082 to the average family that earned over $100,000. For a home owner with a $50,000 annual income the tax saving is estimated at nearly one-third of his total housing costs. Another inherently regressive feature is that homeownership rates increase with income (see Chapter 3, "Landlord versus Tenant"). This means that higher proportions of upper-income families can take advantage of these tax benefits. A "race tax" is imposed as well, since nonwhites have lower homeownership rates than whites at all income levels, primarily because of discrimination in the sale of housing and difficulties in securing mortgage loans.

The second major feature of the federal income tax system that favors homeowners is exclusion of the implicit rental value of an owner-occupied home from the tax base. That is, the person who invests in stocks and bonds must pay tax on the earnings from that investment; the person who invests the same amount in a home for his family and receives his "return" in the form of housing services does not have to pay taxes on this investment. To illustrate the effect of this differential treatment, assume two persons with annual earned incomes of $10,000 and with $25,000 in investment capital. *A* is a renter and invests his $25,000 equity at a 7 percent return. *B* buys a $25,000 home. He places $15,000 equity in his home and invests $10,000 elsewhere at a 7 percent return. *A* must pay taxes on $11,750 (his $10,000 income plus a return of $1750 on his investment), but *B*'s taxable base is only $9600 (his $10,000 income, plus $700 return on his $10,000 investment, less property taxes—assumed to be $500—and mortgage interest payments—assumed to be $600). The benefits from this feature of the tax laws are also highly regressive: in 1966 $456 million went to homeowners who earned under $5000, $1,079 million went to homeowners who earned $10,000 to $15,000, and $718 million went to homeowners who earned over $25,000. With respect to average benefits per family, Aaron points out that this tax feature was worth $11 to a family with income under $3000, $103 to a family with $10,000 to $15,000 income, $654 to a family with $50,000 to $100,000 income, and $1217 to a family with over $100,000 income.

The homeowner receives yet another form of favorable tax treatment when he sells his home, provided he buys another home within a year of the sale that costs at least as much as he sold his former home for. In this case any appreciation in value of his former residence is not taxable at the time. And if the new home does not cost at least as much, the increase in value on the previous home is taxable only at favorable capital gains rates.

The tax benefits of homeownership originated in some vague but strongly held beliefs that homeownership is in itself desirable and promotes important personal and social values. But many persons who are not able or because of locational and mobility needs do not wish to become owners are denied these financial benefits, and the proportion for whom ownership is neither possible nor desirable is markedly higher among lower-income households and racial minorities. The distribution of these benefits through tax laws designed to foster homeownership clearly provides upper-income families with disproportionate economic gain and makes the tax program in effect the most massive housing subsidy of all.

It is highly desirable to reform the income tax system so that it taxes investment in the household's housing services in the same way that other investments are taxed and eliminates the deductibility of property taxes and interest charges, even though major administrative adjustments would be required. Such reforms are probably not politically feasible, but more modest reforms might be carried out, such as creation of equivalent tax benefits for renters, increasing options for homeownership among low-income families and minorities, and placing upper limits on the amount of ownership expenses that can be deducted. The regressivity and inequities of the present income tax system with regard to housing benefits are firmly rooted, however, and like many obvious injustices and inefficiencies in the housing system they are not likely to be changed in the near future.

## Housing and Public Welfare

Though most public welfare programs are not regarded as housing programs, they provide more direct subsidization for housing low-income families than all other government housing programs combined. Over 14 million persons in the United States receive one of the major categories of welfare assistance. These programs furnish general financial assistance rather than specific housing subsidization, but a 1969 report of the Department of Health, Education, and Welfare estimated that approximately $1.1 billion in welfare funds is spent annually for housing, more than twice the federal outlays for low-rent public housing in that year. In view of the striking increase in the number of welfare recipients over the past few years (8.5 million received welfare in 1968), the amount of welfare money spent for housing may now be close to $2 billion.

Detailed information on the housing conditions of families living on welfare is scant, largely because welfare administrators do not regard housing as one of their concerns (most welfare agencies do not even have standards that define minimum adequacy of housing for welfare recipients); but the data that are available suggest that a very high proportion of welfare recipients are living in substandard conditions. A 1965 survey of recipients of Old Age Assistance showed that 40 percent were living in deficient housing, and the percentage ran as high as 70 percent in rural and southern areas. A Washington, D.C., study showed that 50 percent of all AFDC families lived in poor housing. The 1969 HEW study concluded that "on the basis of available data, it is estimated that at least one-half of all assistance recipients live in housing which is deteriorated or dilapidated, unsafe, insanitary, or overcrowded." According to Podell, two-fifths of the welfare families in New York City were living at densities of 1.5 or more persons per room, and a massive study of welfare housing in that city by Lowry, Guéron, and Eisenstadt concluded "welfare households generally occupy the worst housing in the stock."

The central problem is money. The welfare system does not provide nearly enough assistance for families to secure decent housing. The HEW report notes that "for more than 3 million recipient households [that is, for almost all welfare households at the time] the average allowance for housing is less than $400 per year [$33 per month]" and that "this amount is grossly inadequate for either rental housing or home ownership." A 1969 Massachusetts legislature study commission found that "it is virtually impossible for the welfare recipient, living on a basic subsistence budget, to rent standard housing on the private market for 25 percent of his income. The gap would be much greater if the 18–20 percent figure were used." The financial problem is exacerbated by the fact that a large proportion of welfare recipients are nonwhite, and merely being a welfare recipient—regardless of race—results in discrimination and price-gouging. A 1969 report of the Pennsylvania Governor's Housing Task Force notes of welfare recipients that "discrimination on the part of landlords, utility companies, and others is a widespread . . . practice." (Landlord discrimination against welfare families may be based partly on real or perceived practical problems rather than on sheer prejudice. Grigsby and his colleagues note in their Baltimore study: "By and large, inner-city investors in Baltimore would prefer not to rent to recipients of public assistance . . . [L]arge, fatherless families are shied away from, not because they are on welfare, but because many of them fail to adequately supervise their children, do not pay their rent promptly, use excessive amounts of water and electricity, and cause more than average plumbing and related maintenance problems.") Sternlieb and Idnik found that welfare families also pay more than nonwelfare households for apartments of comparable quality.

Since the entire welfare budget is inadequate, the family that must pay more than the allotted amount for housing does so only by neglecting other necessities. The report of the Massachusetts legislature cited previously noted that "welfare recipients living on the standard welfare budget face a cruel choice between clothing and feeding themselves and their families adequately or paying a very high percentage of their income for standard housing." Most states, in establishing welfare budgets, set an arbitrary shelter maximum, which is usually unrelated to actual housing costs. Few make surveys to establish real housing prices, and the surveys they do make are not regularly updated to account for inflation. Oregon estimates that shelter allowances in rural areas are 33 percent below actual cost, and that in urban areas the allowance is 47 percent below actual cost. Some welfare departments have committed themselves to paying the actual cost of obtaining decent housing (provided the cost is comparable to similar housing obtained by moderate-income families), but they are the exception rather than the rule.

Illinois, Michigan, and New York allow local welfare departments to withhold rents from landlords whose buildings are not in standard condition. But given the tight supply of decent low-rent housing, the unrealistically low shelter allowances, and prevailing prejudices against welfare recipients, these powers offer little real assistance to welfare families. Welfare departments are more apt to accommodate than to harass landlords who are willing to accept welfare tenants. The Baltimore study suggests that " a symbiotic relationship" exists between the welfare department and the coterie of landlords who specialize in renting to welfare clients, and a survey reported in Mogulof by the HUD San Francisco regional office of welfare departments in sixteen Western states concluded that

> public funds will continue to underwrite slum housing unless the low-cost housing market is loose or unless there is a willingness to use the various public fund options that can enlarge the availability of decent low-cost housing. . . . [I]t appears that in many communities we shall continue to use public funds to sustain the residence of poor people in housing that all of our standards point to as indecent or unfit.

Most welfare households that are fortunate enough to get into public housing obtain decent housing at rents they can afford, but the program clearly is not large enough: only 7 percent of these households were living in public housing in 1967. Moreover, conflict often arises between administrators of the two programs about admitting welfare families into public housing. Many local public housing officials are reluctant to have too high a proportion of welfare families in public housing because they assume that welfare families give a "bad image" to public housing and cause too many "social problems." Two-fifths of those who are now public housing residents are welfare recipients. Public housing officials also try to secure the maximum allowable rental from their welfare tenants, so as to shift some of the operating costs of public housing to the welfare program. Welfare officials naturally seek to minimize the amount they have to pay in order to shift some of the costs of providing decent housing for their clients to the public housing program.

In summary, the housing aspect of the welfare system is an income maintenance system that (1) provides totally inadequate amounts for shelter and (2) makes no attempt to insure that shelter funds will be used to provide decent housing. Raising welfare budgets could help to capture some of the existing available stock for welfare recipients from the supply of vacancies, but this would be done only at the expense of the nonwelfare poor, would inflate already high rent levels, and would be an inefficient use of public funds. Given the existing housing market, an increase in welfare budgets sufficient to meet the actual cost of decent housing for each welfare recipient would probably be so costly as to topple the entire welfare system. The housing problems of the welfare and nonwelfare poor must thus be regarded as inseparable.

## Public Housing: Housing for the Poor

The administration's September 1973 announcement on new directions for federal housing policy made clear that the nation's oldest and largest program of direct government housing assistance for the poor is to be terminated, at least with respect to new construction. Signs of its enforced demise had been evident for some time. For decades it had been the one program (aside from the tiny rent supplement program described in footnote 3) with subsidies "deep" enough to produce housing for the low-income group directly. (Massachusetts, New York, Connecticut, and New York City all have their own supplementary low-rent public housing programs. New York City has more units under its combined state and city programs than it has under the federal program.) The public housing program was started in the early 1930s as part of the

also result in lower rents, though the costs of program administration through frequently inefficient LHAs may partially offset this benefit.

This formula in effect means that the local authority must cover all costs once construction is completed through rents, which in public housing are based on ability to pay. Based on these financial needs, local authorities generally establish minimum rents for admission to public housing, and these in turn set an effective minimum income. If a minimum rent of $55 per month is established, based on a 25 percent rent/income ratio families with annual incomes of under $2840 would be excluded from public housing (the minimum income would be $3300 if a 20 percent ratio were used). These are minimum, not average, rents; to cover operating expenses, the average rent required from tenants will be considerably higher than the minimum, which means that only a limited number of families with minimum incomes can be accepted. (See also the related discussion of the welfare program and public housing in "Housing and Public Welfare," this chapter.) A 1966 study by the National Capital Planning Commission showed that 7 percent of the District of Columbia's population at that time was "too poor for public housing." Extrapolation of these data nationally suggests that some 4 million families may not have enough income to be eligible for the government's principal housing program designed to reach the low-income group. To the extent that the new public housing amendments described below are made effective this group will no longer be categorically excluded from the program.

Since ongoing operating costs are a substantial and growing part of the public housing program, the result of the basic public housing subsidy formula has been to increase financial difficulties for local authorities, and this has meant the effective exclusion from public housing of the very poor, those who cannot afford rents sufficient to cover the LHA's ongoing housing costs. A 1970 study of 23 large housing authorities by de Leeuw for The Urban Institute documented the financial crisis of public housing. Price and wage inflation has caused marked increases in the costs of operating public housing, and rent increases have been running 25 percent behind cost increases. The results have been a lower level of maintenance and services by housing authorities and a squeeze on low-income tenants to provide housing authorities with more revenue through higher rents. Many large and small city housing authorities are on the verge of bankruptcy. The former chairman of the New York City Housing Authority, Albert A. Walsh, has indicated that while expenses rose 126 percent from 1952 to 1967, rents rose only 72 percent and tenants' incomes rose only 65 percent. He noted that "public housing dwelling units will soon be priced out of the low-income market and a social crisis of major proportions will develop as low-income tenants face the difficult choice of paying a catastrophic proportion of their income for rent—or returning to the slums." As costs of labor, materials, and utilities steeply rise, the gap between the income of public housing families and the general population steadily widens. In 1963, according to Aaron, median public housing income for nonelderly families was 47 percent of median U.S. family income, and the dollar gap was $3330; in 1970 the figures were 37 percent and $6231. Relative to the population as a whole, the public housing program is obviously serving an ever lower stratum.

Various attempts have been made to deal with the inadequacy of the traditional subsidy formula, through additional grants to certain categories of tenants and through grants to permit renovation of aging housing projects. Thus, local housing authorities received an additional annual subsidy of up to $120 per household for the elderly in 1961, for displacees in 1964, and for the very poor and families with four or more minor dependents in 1968; these supplements were also designed to encourage housing authorities to accept types of families deemed most in need of housing that the authority might prefer not to accept without this additional money. In 1967 HUD announced its "modernization program" for deteriorating housing projects. Grants to renovate older projects were an important innovation, since nothing in the original public housing financial formula took into account the need for major rehabilitation somewhere along the project's assumed forty-year life, Low-income tenants, through their rents, had to foot the bill for excessive maintenance expenditures necessitated by the lack of needed renovation. Many housing projects, particularly those in large cities, are in seriously substandard condition. A newspaper account of a Boston project, completed in 1953, describes "broken windows, fire-burned hallways, overflowing incinerators, glass on the pavement, faulty plumbing, broken locks on doors." St. Louis' huge Pruitt-Igoe project, built in 1954, has been completely abandoned and partially razed.

The growing gap between incomes and housing costs and the financial plight of major housing authorities have led to more basic revisions, in statute and theory, if not in practice. In 1969, 1970, and 1971 there were amendments to the public housing statutes that transformed the program into one of rent supplements in addition to capital cost subsidies. These amendments (known colloquially as the [Senator Edward] Brooke Amendments) and the additional subsidies they made available had three purposes: (1) to place an upper limit of 25 percent on the proportion of family income that could be charged for rent and offset resultant revenue losses to the LHA (HUD data for 1968 published in 1970 show that 15 percent of all nonelderly households and fully 46 percent of all elderly households were paying more than 26 percent of their income for rent in public housing); (2) to provide LHAs with the operating and maintenance subsidies they need on a permanent basis; and (3) to furnish those local housing authorities already in serious financial trouble with additional reserve funds.

Roadblocks to these changes were thrown up, by HUD and later by the Nixon administration's Office of Management and Budget, and the result has been even greater chaos and stress in the public housing system. Recently the OMB, which has been playing an increasingly important albeit behind-the-scenes role in the housing field, has refused to release allocations to LHAs made available under these amendments; consequently more local authorities than ever before are in severe financial crisis. According to *Housing and Urban Affairs Daily* (September 11, 1972) "five major local housing authorities face immediate bankruptcy, twenty more will be there by the end of this calendar year, and within a year's time the number will grow to forty authorities managing 250,000 units—one-fourth of all the public housing in the United States." The National Association of Housing and Redevelopment Officials called an emergency meeting in response to this crisis, and it was revealed there that local housing authorities either have employed or plan to employ one or all of the following measures in response to the administration's withholding of Brooke Amendment funds:

1. Stop further production of low-income housing throughout the community and use development funds for operating costs.
2. Defer payments in lieu of taxes.
3. Cancel leases in leased public housing.
4. Cut off all new applications for units and allow vacancies to occur.
5. Sell equipment.
6. Restrict new occupancy to families in the highest eligible income quartile, and thus eliminate the poorest families from occupancy.
7. Ignore the Brooke amendments, since funds will not be available to cover income losses.
8. Refuse occupancy to all welfare families.
9. Stop utility payments.
10. Declare bankruptcy and ask for federal takeover.
11. Issue program-wide eviction notices and close out operation of LHA.

As a further device to increase local housing authority revenue, HUD has issued a circular entitled "Housing a Cross-Section of Low-Income Families in Low-Rent Public Housing," which calls upon LHAs to admit only tenants who can pay enough rent to maintain the solvency of the program, that is, tenants in the upper ranges if income eligibility limits. The irony of this development, which HUD euphemistically calls "broadening the tenant profile," is that one of the original purposes of the Brooke

Amendments was to end the situation (previously described) wherein families whose incomes were too low to cover operating costs were excluded from public housing.

These recent difficulties in the public housing program stem in part from a belated realization of how costly it would be to implement the Brooke Amendments—that is, to subsidize the true costs of providing decent housing for low-income families—as well as from a more general Nixon administration aversion to the conventional public housing program. The program was designed originally for the "temporary poor" of the Depression, mainly white working-class families, but as Friedman shows, over the years it has evolved into a program that must be regarded as providing long-term, perhaps permanent accommodations for those with truly low incomes, most of whom are black. Substantial long-term (hence costly) assistance to this low-income group is not a very high priority of the Nixon administration, or perhaps of the society as a whole, and it appears that the next few years will see a curtailment of new public housing construction and transformation of many of the existing projects to occupancy primarily by moderate-income families and the upper strata of the poor.

## HOUSING PROJECTS AND BEYOND

Until fairly recently the term *housing projects* was virtually synonymous with public housing. Traditionally the role of the local housing authority has been to develop, own, and manage units specially built for and exclusively occupied by low-income families. "Projects" range in size from ten- to twenty-unit complexes all the way to developments of 1500–2000 units and larger—virtually small towns. The inspiration behind large housing projects was the well-intentioned, if mistaken, idea that a development of sufficient size and distinction could function as a self-contained community, capable of isolating itself from and withstanding the "pernicious influences" of the surrounding slum. While early projects were reasonably well designed and integrated with the surrounding neighborhood, postwar developments tended to massive, high-density, high-rise structures, largely because of the rising costs of land and construction and the difficulty of obtaining suitable sites. (A provision of the 1968 Housing Act forbids construction of high-rise elevator projects for families with children "unless . . . there is no practical alternative.") Such projects are not per se objectionable: New York's Parkchester, for example, a 12,000-unit high-rise development built in 1941 and still one of the city's more desirable places to live, is a project that "works." Large, high-rise developments, poorly designed and located, badly managed, and for the exclusive occupancy of the poor, however, offer a formula

almost guaranteed to produce disaster. The following passage from the
Herbers account of St. Louis' Pruitt-Igoe project in the New York *Times*
gives some of the flavor of conditions in these "brick and concrete
slums":

> Robbers, burglars, narcotics pushers, and street gangs roamed at will
> through the buildings. Anarchy prevailed. Windows were broken faster
> than they could be replaced. . . .
>
> The steam pipes were not covered and children were seriously burned.
> People fell out of windows or walked into elevator shafts to their deaths. . . .
>
> Last winter, with windows out, pipes froze and broke on some of the top
> floors, sending streams of water through the buildings and forming glaciers
> on the stairs. . . .
>
> Tenants moved out as soon as they could find any place at all to go, some
> who were paying the minimum $20 a month rent. The vacancy rate climbed
> even as housing for black families became more scarce.

For many residents and outsiders there is a stigma to living in public
housing; project residents are isolated from the surrounding community,
and existing social problem are exacerbated. (See Steinberg's "Other
People's Battles, Our War" for a description of life in one New York City
project.) The physical isolation of many projects not only heightens the
sense of social isolation, but can impose added costs for transportation
(double transit fares, taxis) and shopping (absence of supermarkets, department stores, and competitive marketing). The dreary locations chosen for most housing projects, the unimaginative architecture, and the
dearth of amenities may in part be attributable to a desire to humiliate
the poor and deprive them of dignity and status, to ensure that they
receive unmistakably less attractive and prestigeful housing than those
who "pay their own way" (even though "paying one's way" in the housing
market is largely a myth, in view of the extensive indirect subsidies upper-
income housing consumers receive via the tax system and other federal
programs such as highways and FHA loan guarantees).

Over the past few years, several new techniques for providing public
housing have been introduced that attempt to avoid the defects of housing projects by abandoning one or more phases of the housing authority's
traditional role of combined developer-owner-manager. Among these
new mechanisms are

1. The "turnkey" technique, whereby a builder arranges to construct or
   rehabilitate a development to housing authority specifications and then
   turns the completed units over to the authority at a prenegotiated price.

2. Leasing new or existing units from private landlords on a short- or long-term basis for occupancy by public housing tenants.
3. Purchase and rehabilitation of substandard buildings by the housing authority.
4. Acquisition by the housing authority of new or existing structures, sometimes foreclosed FHA or VA properties.
5. Home ownership programs.


In many cases these techniques can provide needed housing much more quickly than conventional methods can. Some of the newer methods might also provide public housing more cheaply, though this is a more complex and disputed issue.

Among the newer approaches, the "turnkey" program caught hold most rapidly. The program cedes the development function to the private sector, with the housing authority retaining ownership and management. Most turnkey developments are large projects for the exclusive occupancy of housing authority tenants, and so replicate the least desirable social and design features of traditional housing projects. In political terms, however, the turnkey program converted powerful local opposition—builders, developers, land speculators—into supporters, since it opened up an entire new market for the private sector. Not surprisingly, HUD and the LHAs (whose conservative real estate orientation has already been noted) embraced the turnkey method warmly; and according to the *Fourth Annual Report on National Housing Goals* the proportion of new public housing construction built by conventional means (that is, developed and built by housing authorities) has fallen from 62 percent in 1968 to 31 percent in 1970 to an estimated 24 percent in 1972.

The turnkey approach can speed the development process by avoiding time-consuming bureaucratic procedures and on occasion by using land that a developer already owns and has ready for construction. Turnkey proponents maintain that the private sector's know-how can produce substantial savings over the public sector. Those skeptical of this approach point to the large profits expected by developers and the dangers of lower standards and "cutting corners" as reasons for doubting that there are true savings inherent in turnkey. In a recent action HUD ordered the San Francisco Housing Authority to place 200 planned units under the turnkey process, because it maintained they would cost less. According to a February 12, 1971, account of the incident in the San Francisco *Chronicle*, "San Francisco housing officials have been fearful that by doing so, many of the amenities in the authority's plans would be cut out by developers in order to make their bids acceptable to HUD. In acceding to the government's wishes, the authority loses control over design of the . . . housing." In view of the ample opportunities for profit envisioned by the private sector, one can question whether the turnkey approach best serves the public interest.

The leased housing program has been next after "turnkey" in popularity among the new techniques. Since 1965, when the option was introduced, about one-fourth of all new public housing units have been leased. Under the leasing program the functions of development, ownership, and management all remain in the private sector (the housing authority usually retains some management functions with respect to the tenants). The housing authority serves essentially as a broker and subsidizer in bringing together available units and needy families. Leased public housing has been dubbed "instant public housing," because it amounts only to a redesignation of existing units, a shift in occupancy from nonsubsidized to subsidized families. Leasing does not directly add to the housing supply, but the program may produce efficient use of the existing housing stock in areas with high vacancy rates. Solomon provides evidence that leasing existing units requires considerably smaller federal subsidies than does new construction. Where vacancy rates are not high, however, the program may drive up rent levels throughout the lower-priced housing stock. Leased housing also has social advantages. It looks like any other private housing and therefore avoids the identification and stigmatization associated with living in a project. Leasing also can facilitate the mixing of low-income families with unsubsidized families of higher incomes, and permits tenants to remain in the units once their incomes rise above public housing eligibility limits. (Such limits vary considerably. In large cities, where they are generally higher, maximum entry limits for a family of four are mostly in the $4000–5500 range, with often higher limits for displacees. Income limits for continued occupancy are usually about 25 percent higher than entry limits.) The unit and its tenants revert to the private sector, and the subsidy can be transferred to another unit and another low-income family. This is in contrast to the traditional public housing formula wherein the subsidy is permanently attached to a given unit.[3]

Analyses of the impact of the leasing program have produced mixed conclusions. The most comprehensive study, by de Leeuw and Leaman for the Urban Institute and based on data from over three dozen LHAs,

3. Rent Supplements, a program similar to leased housing, were also introduced in the 1965 Housing Act. These are payments made directly by the FHA to owners of new and newly rehabilitated housing financed under certain moderate-income FHA programs, in order to bring rents for some or all units down to public housing levels. The program thus bypasses local housing authorities. Through the first five years, only 46,000 Rent Supplement units were started, although the program was intended to produce 500,000 units in four years and was described by President Johnson at the time of its introduction as "the most crucial new instrument in our effort to improve the American city." Inadequate federal funding, the need for local government approval, rising interest rates, stringent cost and design limitations, and less than full cooperation from the FHA are all responsible for scant use of the Rent Supplement program. For further discussion see Krier.

indicates that the social benefits of anonymity are important (especially for families with children), that the costs of leasing are appreciably lower than the costs for new construction (via conventional or turnkey methods), and that community acceptance of this form of housing subsidy is decidedly greater. (One reason for this greater acceptance may be that full local property taxes are paid on the privately owned units leased to the LHA.) On the other hand, independent studies, including one carried out by the HUD Office of Audit, have found substantial amounts of substandard housing in the leased stock and payment of inflated rents by LHAs. Other findings are that housing authorities tend to be very selective in choosing tenants for leased housing (often using higher income eligibility limits than for housing project tenancy), "creaming" the waiting lists to select the more middle-class representatives of the poor; that the program seems to have had negligible impact on patterns of racial integration; and that tenants may sometimes be burdened with excessive heating and utility charges. In almost all cities it has been difficult to lease large units, which are generally in short supply.

In the space of a few years, leasing and "turnkey" have come to dominate the public housing program. Based on data in Taggart and in Edson we can say that about four times as many units have annually been added to the public housing supply through these two new techniques as have been added through the traditional means of direct construction, ownership, and management by the local housing authority. According to the administration's September 1973 pronouncement on the future of federal housing, the one form of public housing scheduled for retention is the leasing program. There has been a rapid but covert process of "desocialization" whereby substantial segments of the public housing operation—those involving the greatest opportunity for profit—have been moved from the public to the private sector.

Housing authorities have made but limited use of programs for the purchase and rehabilitation of substandard buildings, for the acquisition of existing or newly built structures, or for homeownership. Like the leased housing program these programs can take advantage of opportunities in the existing housing stock and can offer the social advantages of lesser stigmatization and greater residential heterogeneity.

## Who Lives in Public Housing?

Some 3 million low-income Americans live in public housing, about 1.5 percent of the nation's population. About two-fifths of all public housing households—although a smaller percentage of total residents—are elderly (defined as family head or spouse 62 years or older, or family head disabled according to the Social Security Act). The elderly were first specifically provided for in the Housing Act of 1956. Slightly over half of all public housing starts in recent years were specifically designed for the elderly. The establishment of hundreds of new housing authorities in the 1960s is attributable to the desire to build housing for the elderly among many small cities and towns that have not wanted family public housing. The popularity of this group is probably due, as Friedman suggests, to

> a continued search for the submerged middle class, that lost legion whose ghost still haunts the program. Housing for the elderly taps the only remaining reservoir of poor people who are also white, orderly, middle class in behavior. Neighborhoods which will not tolerate a ten-story tower packed with Negro mothers on AFDC might tolerate a ten-story tower of sweet but impoverished old folks. Old people are never vandals; they do not whore and carouse. Many of them are honest working-class people caught in a trap set by low retirement incomes, small pensions, inadequate savings, and high medical bills. Furthermore, housing for the elderly helps solve a problem all too common for middle-class people—what to do with aged, dependent parents. . . . Moreover, the old people are more likely than the problem poor to be grateful, docile, and unseen.

Moreover, a greater number of units can be produced for the elderly with a given allocation of funds, because they don't need large units. It is notable that housing projects for the elderly have generally been small, well-located, attractive developments that have as their hallmark the highest compliment that can be paid to public housing—they do not look like public housing.

As Friedman implies, racial divisions in public housing are as pronounced as they are in the private sector. The shift from white dominance began in the postwar period and accelerated during the 1950s, when public housing became the "receptacle" for urban renewal and highway project displacees who were overwhelmingly nonwhite and who by law had priority for admission to public housing. Rising white incomes, the flight of white families from the central city, and restricted housing choices for nonwhites in the private market abetted this shift. Project after project "tipped," as nonwhite occupancy rose sharply and triggered a rapid exodus of whites. Seventy percent of all households in public housing now are nonwhite, and the proportion is higher in the family (as opposed to elderly) program. In Atlanta and Chicago, for example, 95 percent of all households in non-elderly projects are black.

Segregation in individual projects is blatant, largely as a result of site location decisions. Public housers, following the prevailing pattern in the housing market, have located projects for whites in white areas, projects for blacks in black areas.[4] Segregation by race may also be furthered by tenant assignment policies: white applicants have generally been sent only to white projects, black applicants to black projects, though HUD has made attempts to end this practice. (The independence of tenant assignment procedures from site selection policies was dramatically revealed by the NAACP and Boston CORE in a 1963 case against the Boston Housing Authority brought before the Massachusetts Commission Against Discrimination. In support of their contention that the Authority was intentionally maintaining a segregated system, the civil rights groups pointed to the existence of two projects separated by a single roadway, one of which was 90 percent black, while the other had not a single black tenant.) Of the 4458 housing projects in the HUD 1971 *Low-Rent Project Directory* for which data on racial composition are given, 56 percent are either all-white or all nonwhite, and another 11 percent are segregated within the project site. (The definition that HUD uses for "integrated"—that a project contain at least two members of the "other" race—is so broad that the figures greatly understate the actual degree of segregation. A 300-unit project with two black families would be listed as integrated.)

Other characteristics of the public housing population may be noted briefly. Two-fifths of all nonelderly and elderly families of this population are welfare recipients. Nearly three-fifths of all nonelderly families have only one adult, and over one-third of these have four or more minors. (A good deal of officially unrecognized overcrowding exists in public housing, as shown in the study by Smart, Rybeck, and Shuman. Few apartments are built with more than three bedrooms because of HUD limits on per-unit construction cost, set in large part to avoid the political flak that might result from spending the $30,000 or more it costs in most cities to construct a large unit. Turnover in large units is low, too, because of the difficulty in finding large quarters on the private market. Calculations made from a HUD report that cross-tabulates family size and unit

4. The issues and conflicts generated by the location of new public housing in Chicago are well documented in Meyerson and Banfield's case-study of the Chicago Housing Authority in the post-War period and early 1950s. A recent Federal District Court decision ordered the Chicago Housing Authority to integrate its present and future projects and to cease the practice (doubtless not confined to Chicago) of "clearing" proposed sites with ward aldermen, which has the effect of keeping public housing out of white neighborhoods. The Court laid out a detailed integration plan, analogous to court-ordered school desegregation plans, that requires specific numbers of units in given areas of the city, with limitations on the size and height of future projects. The ability of Chicago officials to ignore and evade the Court order over the past three years has been striking. See "Public Housing and Urban Policy: *Gautreaux* v. *Chicago Housing Authority*," and Terry P. Brown, "How Not to Handle Public Housing."

size suggest that some 15 percent of all families in public housing are
living at densities greater than 1.0 persons per room, which is the Census
definition of overcrowding. Among the 27,000 seven-person families
living in public housing in 1967, nearly three-fourths had only two or
three bedrooms.) These are aggregate figures, based on data from "Families in Low-Rent Projects"; individual projects will differ widely in population composition, as tenant assignment procedures and applicant
preferences may tend to reinforce dominant social and racial characteristics of a project.

Who Doesn't Live in Public Housing?

Although the public housing program was established to provide
decent housing for persons unable to afford standard housing on the
private market, the workings of the program categorically exclude the
majority of the nation's poor—apart from the fact that even within the
category of eligible beneficiaries the program is far too small to meet
existing needs. In addition to all those who do not live in a jurisdiction
served by a public housing authority, the following are excluded:

1. Federal public housing law requires that "a gap of at least 20 per centum
   has been left between the upper limits for admission to the proposed
   low-rent housing and the lowest rents at which private enterprise unaided
   by public subsidy is providing (through new construction and available
   existing structures) a substantial supply of decent, safe, and sanitary housing." This ensures that there will be a segment of the low-income market
   with incomes too high for public housing but insufficient to obtain decent
   housing on the private market. The Washington study previously referred
   to indicated that 11 percent of that city's population falls into this "20
   percent gap." If the Washington figures are representative, 6.5 million
   households are in need of housing subsidies but are ineligible for public
   housing because their incomes are slightly too high for admission.
2. Individuals who are neither elderly nor handicapped are not eligible for
   public housing; roughly 2.7 million low-income Americans fall into this
   category.
3. Poor families who live in standard housing but who pay too high a proportion of their rent for standard housing will generally not be accepted by a
   local authority (although they are not excluded by law).
4. Families who do not meet the local residency requirements established by
   the housing authority may also be denied admission to public housing.
   These residency requirements have been struck down by the courts in
   several jurisdictions as a violation of the equal protection clause and constitutionally protected freedom to travel, but they are still widely used. Some

communities have established residency requirements of as long as ten or fifteen years.

5. Families that in the housing authority's eyes may be destructive of property, make poor neighbors, or prove troublesome to the project manager may also be excluded for "social ineligibility" under the authority's power within general guidelines established by federal (and in some cases state) law to control tenant selection. These rules and standards apply to continued occupancy of public housing as well, and violations can lead to eviction. In recent years some advances toward more equitable management practices have been made via lawsuits and organized tenant action.

### DISSATISFACTIONS WITH PUBLIC HOUSING

Criticism of the public housing program is widespread, even among those who generally approve of the idea of publicly subsidized housing. Perhaps the most important criticism comes from the poor themselves, in the form of action rather than words.

While most housing authorities have long waiting lists, the number of people eligible for and in need of housing assistance, even with the exclusions catalogued above, is usually many times the number who actually apply to the housing authority. Public housing evokes images of overregulation, stigmatization, isolation, and rampant social problems, and such images—at least partially grounded in reality—are responsible for the self-exclusion of a substantial portion of families in need of decent subsidized housing. Hartman found that nearly four-fifths of the familes of a white working-class population about to be displaced for an urban renewal project would not consider living in public housing. Racial factors are probably an important and increasing cause among whites for rejecting the program. High vacancy rates at some projects—particularly large projects in big cities—are another indication of rejection.

Probably the strongest index of dissatisfaction is the extraordinarily high turnover rate in the system as a whole and in many projects. About one-fifth of all families living in public housing in any given year leave, only a small minority of whom are forced to leave because of eviction or income ineligibility. The vast majority are people who voluntarily move out, even though they presumably are not able to afford decent alternative housing. Public housing moveout rates are no higher than general mobility rates among Americans, but given the superior physical quality of most public housing relative to slum alternatives, the low rents, and the fact that external employment "pulls" that frequently motivate geographic mobility among the middle class are probably rare among the public housing group, these turnover figures are distressingly high and would seem to be *prima facie* evidence of strong dissatisfaction. Data on individual project moveout rates in "Move-Out Rates in Low-Rent Housing" indicate that over 12 percent of all projects had annual moveout rates of 48 percent or more. So high a degree of transiency has serious impact on community and family stability. Evidence from the Philadelphia Housing Authority's "used house program" suggests that turnover may decrease in types of public housing other than projects: turnover figures for families who moved to homes purchased and rehabilitated by the Authority average only five percent annually, compared with 18 percent among residents of a nearby high-rise project.

Tenant dissatisfaction is high within public housing, particularly in the larger projects and cities. Protracted and bitter rent strikes have taken place in St. Louis, Washington, and other cities. A city-wide rent strike in Newark has entered its fifth year, involving thousands of families and nearly $7 million in withheld rents. Complaints focus on the poor physical condition of apartments and common areas; arbitrary and unnecessary rules, which tend to reflect more concern for physical property than for the people who inhabit it; disrespectful management attitudes and hostile treatment of tenants; and the imposition of arbitrary fines and charges. As a result of pressure from tenant groups and their advocates, HUD recently issued regulations requiring all housing authorities to adopt a lease form and grievance procedures that meet minimum HUD standards. Clauses abrogating tenants' legal rights are now prohibited; housing projects must conform to local housing code standards; tenants will be entitled to rent abatements if they have to live in hazardous quarters; fines and other charges must be collected separately from the rents; inspection of a tenant's unit now requires advance written notice; and leases are now perpetual rather than monthly, and can be terminated only for cause. In addition, a detailed grievance procedure is mandated, which includes hearings before an impartial body and adequate notice provisions. Of critical importance in this shift toward protection of tenants' rights in public housing is the rise of the National Tenants Organization, which now serves as a countervailing force to the National Association of Housing and Redevelopment Officials, the established organization of agency personnel. (The NTO publication *Tenants Outlook* gives a monthly review of developments in this area. The NAHRO monthly publication is called the *Journal of Housing.*) More broadly, tenants are demanding a greater say in project affairs, from the formation of tenant associations and unions to proposals for full-scale tenant management and even ownership. Such proposals are bound to meet with great resistance from those who run the program and the general public, which feels that these families ought to be nothing but grateful for what they are receiving.[5]

In sum, the public housing program has been characterized by serious quantitative and qualitative shortcomings. After 35 years of operation it provides housing for less than 4 percent of all U.S. families with incomes under $6000. The qualitative shortcomings of the program are such that even the most ardent supporters of decent housing for the poor are reluctant to advocate continuation of the program in its present form. The social, financial, and administrative problems that have plagued the program can, however, provide important lessons and guidelines with respect to the design of a better way to meet the nation's housing needs.

## References

AARON, HENRY

    1970 "Income Taxes and Housing." *American Economic Review* (December), 789–806.

_____

    1972 *Shelter and Subsidies: Who Benefits from Federal Housing Policies?* Washington, D.C.: The Brookings Institution, pp. 58–59, 115, 116, 223–24.

ABRAMS, CHARLES

    1965 *The City Is the Frontier.* New York: Harper & Row, Publishers.

ALEXANDER, ROBERT C.

    1972 "Fifteen State Housing Finance Agencies in Review." *Journal of Housing* (January), 9–17.

5. For a discussion of the accomplishments and advantages of the tenants' new role in public housing see Hirshen and Brown, "Public Housing's Neglected Resource: The Tenants." A description of the successful experimental Tenant Management Corporation in Boston's Bromley-Heath Project is in Gallese, "Light in the Hallway." A proposal for giving tenants ownership of the public housing they occupy, based upon the principles and example of the Nineteenth-Century Homestead Act, is found in Stone, "Needed: An Urban Homestead Act." Discussion of the views of management is in George Schermer Associates and Kenneth C. Jones, *Public Housing Is the Tenants,* Peattie, "Public Housing: Urban Slums Under Public Management," and Hartman and Levi, "Public Housing Managers: An Appraisal."

1973 "State Housing Finance Agencies Face Difficult Problems during Housing 'Freeze' and Pending Federal Housing Re-Evaluation." *Journal of Housing* (March), 20–23.

ANDERSON, MARTIN
1964 *The Federal Bulldozer.* Cambridge, Mass.: M.I.T. Press.

BELLUSH, JEWEL, AND MURRAY HAUSKNECHT, EDS.
1967 *Urban Renewal: People, Politics, and Planning.* New York: Doubleday & Company.

BRANDON, D. DAVID, AND BESSIE C. ECONOMOU
1973 "State Housing Programs," in Donald J. Reeb and James T. Kirk, eds., *Housing the Poor.* New York: Praeger Publishers.

BROWN, TERRY P.
1971 "How Not to Handle Public Housing." *Wall Street Journal* (April 16).

CLIFF, URSULA
1972 "UDC Scorecard." *Design & Environment* (Summer), 54–63.

DAVID, HARRIS, AND J. MICHAEL CALLAN
1974 "Newark's Public Housing Rent Strike: The High Rise Ghetto Goes to Court." *Clearinghouse Review* (February), 581–87.

DE LEEUW, FRANK
1970 *Operating Costs in Public Housing: A Financial Crisis.* Washington, D.C.: The Urban Institute.

DE LEEUW, FRANK, AND SAM H. LEAMAN
1972 "The Section 23 Leasing Program," in *The Economics of Federal Subsidy Programs,* Part 5 of a Compendium of Papers Submitted to the Joint Economic Committee, U.S. Congress (October 9), pp. 642–59.

DOLBEARE, CUSHING N.
1972 "Federal Rip-Offs: Housing Subsidies for the Rich." Washington, D.C.: Rural Housing Alliance.

EDSON, CHARLES
1969 *Homeownership for Low-Income Families.* Chicago: National Legal Aid and Defender Association.

EDSON, CHARLES L., AND BRUCE S. LANE
1972 *A Practical Guide to Low- and Moderate-Income Housing.* Washington, D.C.: Bureau of National Affairs.

FISHER, ROBERT M.
1959 *Twenty Years of Public Housing.* New York: Harper & Row, Publishers.

FREEDMAN, LEONARD
    1969 *Public Housing: The Politics of Poverty.* New York: Holt, Rinehart and Winston.

FRIEDMAN, LAWRENCE M.
    1966 "Public Housing and the Poor: An Overview." *California Law Review* 54 (May), 642–69.

GALLESE, LIZ ROMAN
    1973 "Light in the Hallway." *Wall Street Journal* (April 18).

GEORGE SCHERMER ASSOCIATES AND KENNETH C. JONES
    1967 *Public Housing Is the Tenants.* Report prepared for the National Association of Housing and Redevelopment Officials (February).

GREEN, PETER M., AND RUTH CHENEY
    1968 "Urban Planning and Urban Revolt: A Case Study." *Progressive Architecture* (January), 134–56.

GREER, SCOTT
    1965 *Urban Renewal and American Cities.* Indianapolis, Ind.: The Bobbs-Merrill Co.

GRIGSBY, WILLIAM G., ET AL.
    1970 "Housing and Poverty in Baltimore, Maryland." Ms., prepared for Housing, Real Estate and Urban Land Studies Program, Graduate School of Business Administration, Univ. of Calif., Los Angeles. Revised form to be published. (pp. 40, 41)

HARTMAN, CHESTER
    1967 "The Housing of Relocated Families," in Jewel Bellush and Murray Hausknecht, eds., *Urban Renewal: People, Politics, and Planning.* New York: Doubleday & Company, pp. 315–53.

    ———
    1963 "The Limitations of Public Housing: Relocation Choices in a Working-Class Community." *Journal of the American Institute of Planners.* (November), 283–96.

    ———
    1971 "Relocation: Illusory Promises and No Relief." *Virginia Law Review* 57, 745–817.

    ———
    1974 *Yerba Buena: Land Grab and Community Resistance in San Francisco.* San Francisco: Glide Publications.

HARTMAN, CHESTER W., AND GREGG CARR
    1969 "Housing Authorities Reconsidered." *Journal of the American Institute of Planners* (January), 10–21.

———
    1969 "Rejoinder" (to comment by Beatrice Cohen on "Housing Authorities Reconsidered.") *Journal of the American Institute of Planners* (November), 434–36.

HARTMAN, CHESTER W., AND MARGARET LEVI
    1973 "Public Housing Managers: An Appraisal." *Journal of the American Institute of Planners* (March), 125–37.

HERBERS, JOHN
    1970 "The Case History of a Housing Failure." New York *Times* (November 2).

HIRSHEN, AL, AND VIVIAN BROWN
    1972 "Public Housing's Neglected Resource: The Tenants." *City* (Fall).

———
    1972 "Too Poor for Public Housing: Roger Starr's Poverty Preferences." *Social Policy* (May/June), 28–32.

HIRSHEN, AL, AND CHRISTOPHER N. VISHER
    1972 "HUD Lease and Grievance Circulars Upheld." *Clearinghouse Review* (November).

KRIER, JAMES E.
    1967 "The Rent Supplement Program of 1965: Out of the Ghetto, into the . . .? " *Stanford Law Review* 19, 555–78.

LILLEY, WILLIAM, III
    1970 "Urban Report/Model Cities Program Faces Uncertain Future Despite Romney Overhaul." *National Journal* 2, No. 28 (July 11), 1467–80.

LOWRY, IRA S., JUDITH M. GUÉRON, AND KAREN M. EISENSTADT
    1972 *Welfare Housing in New York City.* New York: Rand Institute (November), pp. viii, 65–67.

MACEY, JOHN
    1972 "Publicly Provided and Assisted Housing in the U.S.A." Washington, D.C.: The Urban Institute (May).

MASSACHUSETTS GENERAL COURT
    1969 *Report of the Special Commission on Housing for Welfare and Low-Income Families.* H. 4893 (December 19), p. 22.

MEYERSON, MARTIN, AND EDWARD BANFIELD
    1955 *Politics, Planning, and the Public Interest.* New York: The Free Press.

MOGULOF, MELVIN B.
    1967 "Subsidizing Substandard Housing Through Public Welfare Payments." *Journal of Housing* No. 10, pp. 560–63.

NATIONAL CAPITAL PLANNING COMMISSION
    1966 *Problems of Housing People in Washington, D.C.:* National Capital
    Planning Commission, pp. 1–7.

NATIONAL COMMISSION ON URBAN PROBLEMS
    1968 *Building the American City.* Washington, D.C.: U.S. Government
    Printing Office, p. 400.

NATIONAL HOUSING AND ECONOMIC DEVELOPMENT LAW PROJECT
    1972 *Law Project Bulletin* 2, Issue 8 (September 15).

OTT, DAVID J., AND ATTIAT F. OTT
    1972 "The Tax Subsidy Through Exemption of State and Local
    Bond Interest," in *The Economics of Federal Subsidy Programs,*
    Part 3 of a Compendium of Papers Submitted to the Joint
    Economic Committee, U.S. Congress (July 15), pp. 305–16.

PALMER, ROBERT G.
    1970 "Section 23 Housing: Low Rent Housing in Private Accom-
    modations." *Journal of Urban Law* 48, 255–78.

PEARLMAN, DANIEL D.
    1974 "State Housing Finance Agencies and the Myth of Low In-
    come Housing." *Clearinghouse Review* (March), 649–55.

PEATTIE, LISA R.
    1971 "Public Housing: Urban Slums under Public Management,"
    in Peter Orleans and William R. Ellis, eds., *Race, Change, and
    Urban Society.* Beverly Hills, Calif.: Sage Publications, pp. 285–
    310.

PENNSYLVANIA GOVERNOR'S HOUSING TASK FORCE
    1969 *Better Housing: A Social Priority for Pennsylvania.* Harrisburg, Pa.

PHILADELPHIA HOUSING ASSOCIATION
    1963 *Issues* (April).

PODELL, LAWRENCE
    1969 *Families on Welfare in New York City.* New York: City University
    of New York Center for the Study of Urban Problems.

RURAL HOUSING ALLIANCE AND HOUSING ASSISTANCE COUNCIL
    1973 *Public Housing: Where It Is and Isn't.* Washington, D.C.: Rural
    Housing Alliance and Housing Assistance Council.

SCHECHTER, HENRY B.
    1971 "Federally Subsidized Housing Program Benefits." Washing-
    ton, D.C.: Library of Congress, Congressional Research Ser-
    vice (October 15).

SMART, WALTER, WALTER RYBECK, AND HOWARD E. SHUMAN
    1968 *The Large Poor Family—A Housing Gap.* Research Report No. 4,
    National Commission on Urban Problems.

SOLOMON, ARTHUR P.
    1973 "Housing and Public Policy Analysis," in Jon Pynoos, Robert
    Schafer, and Chester Hartman, eds., *Housing Urban America.*
    Chicago: Aldine, p. 567.

STARR, ROGER
    1971 "Which of the Poor Shall Live in Public Housing?" *The Public
    Interest* (Spring), 116–24.

STEINBERG, JON
    1973 "Other People's Battles, Our War." *Social Policy* (July/Au-
    gust), 71–75.

STEINER, GILBERT Y.
    1971 *The State of Welfare.* Washington, D.C.: The Brookings Institu-
    tion, pp. 122–153.

STERNLIEB, GEORGE S., AND BERNARD P. IDNIK
    1973 *The Ecology of Welfare: Housing and the Welfare Crisis in New York
    City.* New Brunswick, N.J.: Transaction Books, pp. 163–99.

STONE, LEWIS B.
    1973 "Needed: An Urban Homestead Act." *Ripon Forum* (January
    15).

TAGGART, ROBERT III
    1970 *Low-Income Housing: A Critique of Federal Aid.* Baltimore, Md.:
    The Johns Hopkins Press.

U.S., CONGRESS, HOUSE
    1972 *Fourth Annual Report on National Housing Goals* (June 29).
    House Document 92–319, 92nd Congress, 2nd Session, p. 46.

U.S. DEPARTMENT OF HEALTH, EDUCATION, AND WELFARE
    1969 *The Role of Public Welfare in Housing.* Washington, D.C.: U.S.
    Government Printing Office (January).

U.S. DEPARTMENT OF HOUSING AND URBAN DEVELOPMENT
    1971 Low-Rent Project Directory, S-101. Washington, D.C.: U.S.
    Government Printing Office.

——— 1973 *Report of the Task Force on Improving the Operation of Federally
    Insured or Financed Housing Programs,* II ("Public Housing").
    Washington, D.C.: National Center for Housing Manage-
    ment.

U.S. DEPARTMENT OF HOUSING AND URBAN DEVELOPMENT, HOUSING
ASSISTANCE ADMINISTRATION
    1968 "Move-Out Rates in Low-Rent Housing." Publication 228.0
    (December 31).

U.S. DEPARTMENT OF HOUSING AND URBAN DEVELOPMENT, OFFICE OF AUDIT
  1972 "HUD Monitoring of Local Authority Management of Section 23—Leased Housing Program," Region I (July 20).

U.S. DEPARTMENT OF HOUSING AND URBAN DEVELOPMENT, STATISTICS BRANCH, HOUSING ASSISTANCE ADMINISTRATION
  1970 "Families in Low-Rent Projects," Publication RHS-225.1 (February), pp. 32 and 53.

U.S. DEPARTMENT OF HOUSING AND URBAN DEVELOPMENT, STATISTICS BRANCH, OFFICE OF PROGRAM DEVELOPMENT
  1971 "Families in Low-Rent Projects," Publication HMS 225.1 (September), pp. 32, 53.

U.S. PRESIDENT'S TASK FORCE ON MODEL CITIES
  1970 *Model Cities: A Step toward the New Federalism.* Washington, D.C.: U.S. Government Printing Office.

WALSH, ALBERT A.
  1969 "Is Public Housing Headed for a Fiscal Crisis?" *Journal of Housing,* No. 2, pp. 64–71.

WILSON, JAMES Q., ED.
1966 *Urban Renewal: The Record and the Controversy.* Cambridge, Mass.: M.I.T. Press.

Housing Affairs Letter
  1972 Washington, D.C. (July 28, December 1, and December 22).

"No Room for Singles; A Gap in the Housing Law"
  1970 *Yale Law Journal* 80, 395–432.

"Procedural Due Process in Government-Subsidized Housing"
  1973 *Harvard Law Review* 86, 880–913.

"Public Housing and Urban Policy: *Gautreaux* v. *Chicago Housing Authority*"
  1970 *Yale Law Journal* 80, 712–23. Reprinted in Pynoos, Schafer, and Hartman, eds., *Housing Urban America* pp. 108–13.

"S.F. Housing Authority Gives in on U.S. Demand"
  1971 San Francisco *Chronicle* (February 12).

# Chapter 5

# GOVERNMENT HOUSING PROGRAMS: PART II

## Subsidized Home Ownership

In Section 235 of the 1968 Housing Act, Congress introduced a program of direct homeownership subsidies for families unable to purchase a decent home on the private market. In a few short years the program became the largest single subsidized housing program, and the most controversial. In fiscal 1971 Section 235 accounted for 138,000 (29 percent) of the 480,000 total units produced under all federal subsidy programs, and even higher amounts were projected for fiscal 1972 and 1973. The program also accounted for an equal proportion of the existing units subsidized under various federal programs.

The form of the subsidy is as follows. Eligible families (income limits are generally set 35 percent higher than those for public housing) are required to pay 20 percent of their income for mortgage payments, taxes, and insurance; the federal government insures the mortgage through FHA and pays a subsidy directly to the mortgage lender to make up the difference between the family's contribution and actual mortgage payment requirements, not including insurance and taxes. The maximum subsidy payment is the difference between the actual amount of mortgage payments and the borrower's obligation if the mortgage were to bear a one percent interest rate. For convenience we can regard the program as direct subsidy of the mortgage interest down to the point where the homeowner may have to pay only a one percent interest rate. Ownership is facilitated by reducing down payment requirements to $200. The nature of the subsidy makes it a moderate-income rather than a low-income program. Median income of families entering the program in 1971 was $6150.

The Section 235 program and its companion Section 236 interest subsidy program for rental housing (see "Interest Subsidies and Tax Benefits for Rental Housing," this chapter) reflected the emphasis on housing production in the 1968 Housing Act and its stipulation of specific numerical goals and annual assessment of progress toward meeting these goals. These programs and the specification of goals were largely the work of the most powerful Washington lobbying group in the housing and urban development field, the National Association of Home Builders, a broadly based organization of large and small homebuilders, mortgage bankers, and some land speculators and realtors (who also have enormous influence on state and local levels). According to one knowledgeable analyst, in the 1968 Housing Act

> the home builders extracted important concessions for their industry from the Johnson administration and Congress. . . . Staff members for the two [Congressional] Banking Committees said that [the Section 235 and 236] programs were drafted so as to be acceptable to NAHB. . . . NAHB provided major inputs to both efforts, said homebuilder lobbyists and committee staffers. "That's why they are builder programs," said a House Banking Committee staff member. "They are oriented toward housing production—units, starts, and property—with people being a secondary consideration." [1]

The interest-rate subsidy programs proved to be the salvation of the building industry during the 1969–1970 tight money period, and the homebuilders' political power was demonstrated by their ability to secure federal appropriations for the full amounts authorized and to defeat the

---

1. See Lilley, "Washington Pressures/Home Builders' Lobbying Skills Result in Successes, 'Good-Guy' Image." In the article Lilley describes the intimate interrelationship of the homebuilders with congressmen and their staffs, HUD (in particular, FHA), and the executive branch, especially the regular flow of personnel back and forth. Sections 235 and 236 of the 1968 Housing Act, for example, were drafted by a HUD official who shortly thereafter went on the NAHB staff as their No. 2 lobbyist, in which position he is considerably aided by the fact that his father is staff director for the Senate Housing and Urban Affairs Subcommittee. Similarly, in 1969 President Nixon appointed the president of NAHB as FHA commissioner. Further discussion of the political background to the 1968 Housing Act may be found in Carnegie, "Homeownership for the Poor: Running the Washington Gauntlet."

attempt by their rival lobbying group, the National Association of Real Estate Boards (recently renamed the National Association of Realtors), to divert Section 235 funds from new production into existing housing.

The Section 235 program has run into enormous difficulties and has been the subject of well-publicized investigations by several congressional committees, HUD, the General Accounting Office, and the U.S. Commission on Civil Rights. The principal problems have been the high but hidden cost of the long-term interest subsidy commitment, scandalous abuses perpetrated by realtors, and the failure of the FHA to supervise the program properly. Commitments made for Section 235 mortgages extend thirty to forty years, in amounts that are unknown because they depend on changes in recipients' incomes over time, which in turn determine the amount of the subsidy. The amount appropriated in any one year does not appear very large, but commitments are cumulative, and Congress and the public are just beginning to wake up to the vast amounts of money that may be involved in the long run. (The General Accounting Office has recommended that direct government lending be substituted for interest subsidies.) According to Wright Patman, chairman of the House Banking and Currency Committee, the full cost of Section 235 mortgages entered into through 1971 may run as high as $40 billion. High interest rates, of course, increase the costs of the Section 235 program, since the government is committed to paying (sometimes indirectly, through the tandem plan described in Chapter 2, "Money Matters") the difference between a one percent interest rate and the market interest rate, however high that may be.

Abuses under the Section 235 program have been widespread and have shocked even those who expect the worst from programs that rely on subsidizing the private sector to produce housing for low- and moderate-income households. A study by the House Banking and Currency Committee concluded that the program was a "bonanza to fast-buck real estate speculators." The FHA approved shoddy structures that would not last the life of the mortgage and prices that exceeded fair market values by substantial margins. In some cases homes approved by the FHA were condemned by local code enforcement officials within months after purchase. Families that purchased Section 235 homes were found to be "paying suburban prices for slum housing." Real estate brokers and developers sold homes in deteriorating areas, often to minority group families in neighborhoods characterized by rapid racial transition, at outrageous prices. Among the examples cited in the Banking and Currency Committee report were a home sold for $13,500 that had been bought by a speculator for $9000 just two months previously and a home sold for $16,000 that had been bought for $6500 four months prior to the sale. Cheap cosmetic repairs were made to "upgrade" the housing. Extensive abuses of this type have been found in Detroit, Philadelphia,

Oakland, Washington, Baltimore, Chicago, St. Louis, and many other cities. According to the U.S. Commission on Civil Rights, existing housing sold under the Section 235 program was the source of most abuses (through 1970 about one-third of all Section 235 units were existing rather than new units). In 1970 HUD temporarily suspended the program for existing housing, and Congress added to the Housing Act a narrowly drawn provision designed to compensate defrauded homebuyers and to provide funds to repair defective homes; the FHA has administered the provision so stringently, however, that it has been of little use.

The problem has been that unsophisticated buyers, greatly limited in their choice of housing, and with little experience in and knowledge of the housing market, become the prey of unscrupulous real estate speculators. Homes with structural problems and defective heating, plumbing, and electrical systems are sold to unwary buyers who have stretched their budgets to the limit to make the payments necessary under the Section 235 program. Because of excessive maintenance and repair costs purchasers often default on their mortgage payments and leave the house in the hands of the mortgage insurer, the U.S. Department of Housing and Urban Development. In city after city the secretary of HUD appears as the owner of record of thousands of substandard buildings abandoned by their owners under the Section 235 and 236 programs. In Detroit alone, says Wallace, the government took title to 5000 single-family homes, and the loss could amount to $200 million.

The U.S. Commission on Civil Rights has charged the FHA with using the Section 235 program to perpetuate racially segregated residential patterns in metropolitan areas. The Commission found that the agency had delegated its legal responsibilities under the 1968 Fair Housing Law and the Civil Rights Act of 1964 to bar discrimination in any federally supported housing to the private housing and home finance industry, which has largely ignored the intent of the civil rights legislation. The investigation, which covered the Philadelphia, Denver, Little Rock, and St. Louis metropolitan areas, revealed that the Section 235 program followed the pattern of the private market by providing mostly new suburban homes for whites and older, often dilapidated central-city homes for nonwhites. The report stated that white and minority group buyers were offered Section 235 housing on a segregated basis and that "minority buyers received cheaper, inferior housing and smaller government subsidies than white buyers." According to the Commission, "we found, in fact, a dual marketing system so pervasive, so entrenched and so commonplace that most real estate brokers described it openly to the Commission staff without any sense of wrongdoing."

Some of the program's defects are built in. The subsidy formula requires families to pay 20 percent of their income for mortgage payments, insurance, and taxes, but Schafer and Field found that the added costs of maintenance, utilities, and heat have meant that many families were paying one-third and more of their income for housing, particularly in areas with severe winters. Families with marginal incomes and few savings are especially vulnerable to economic setback from unemployment, illness, and other crises, and the tenuous financial position of many families living in Section 235 housing will do little to enhance their sense of security, ability to rise out of poverty, and other virtues popularly associated with home ownership. If home ownership is not to be illusory and burdensome, lower-income owners need some kind of insurance, comparable to unemployment benefits, to permit them to weather short-term, sudden adversity.

Another defect relates to the operation and abuse of the tandem plan. The tandem plan was designed to deal with the problem of excessive discount points in FHA mortgages. Since the FHA insures for the face value of the mortgage, even though the mortgage has been given and traded at a discounted price, the holder of a foreclosed mortgage will receive a substantial profit. In fact, the more often the lender can turn over his money in the mortgage discount market through repeated lending and foreclosures, the more profit he can make. According to Hood and Kushner:

> Since it is in the interest of lenders to loan money on uninhabitable homes, the multiplier effect of the discount point system is staggering. Such loans provide the same if not higher point charges as standard homes, plus they promise early defaults and the rapid return of capital for further loans, discounts, and defaults. . . . The discount point system can thus be seen as a substantial contributing force to the perpetuation of substandard housing in our cities. This is certainly a sad commentary on our national priorities and the existing insurance legislation . . . The practices of playing discount point money into rapid profits by quick foreclosures on FHA-insured mortgages on inner-city slum property is the ultimate perversion of our attempt to improve the housing standards in America.

Much of the blame for the failings of the Section 235 program must be laid at the doors of the Federal Housing Administration. The FHA has traditionally operated much in the way that a conservative private real estate business operates with a middle-class clientele. Over the years the agency has built up a reserve fund (essentially the excess of insurance premiums over losses) of nearly $2 billion. As the National Commission on Urban Problems noted:

> The main weakness of FHA from a social point of view has not been in what it has done, but in what it has failed to do—in its relative neglect of the inner cities and of the poor, and especially Negro poor. Believing firmly that the poor were bad credit risks and that the presence of Negroes tended to lower

real estate values, FHA has generally regarded loans to such groups as "economically unsound." Until recently, therefore, FHA benefits have been confined almost exclusively to the middle class, and primarily only to the middle section of the middle class . . . FHA was not merely neutral with respect to the incidence of decay and blight; its policies actually aided, abetted, and encouraged it.

In 1968 Congress moved to halt FHA's acknowledged practice of "redlining" whole areas of central cities, usually those occupied by the poor and nonwhites, by authorizing the agency to insure mortgages for construction, rehabilitation, and purchase of properties in "declining urban areas" in which normal eligibility requirements cannot be met; but the past and present orientation of the agency makes it unlikely that a switch of emphasis and clientele can be effectuated. It is thus not surprising that the FHA mishandled its new assignment—to run a subsidy program for lower-income families—in favor of a property orientation and concessions to realty interests. According to Herbers in the New York *Times:*

> In some cities, the problems [with Section 235 and 236 defaults] are compounded by the fact that FHA, a former independent agency brought against its will under HUD, has had a cozy relationship with the local private interests, including the "suede shoe" operators, who proliferate in the central cities.

The directors of almost all local FHA insuring offices and many upper-echelon FHA Washington officials are drawn directly from the real estate field. One FHA appraiser cited in the House Banking and Currency Committee report acknowledged that the regional FHA office is "heavily influenced by the mortgage and real estate industries." Most positions as FHA appraisers are patronage jobs, and many appraisers feel that their future is a good job in a real estate firm or with a mortgage-lending institution. Specific abuses by local FHA offices include failure to make adequate inspections and reinspections, inflated appraisals, FHA appraisers who moonlight as real estate speculators, and other forms of malfeasance that in several instances have led to criminal indictments.

The Section 235 program has brought decent housing to thousands of families, despite this catalogue of horrors.[2] But it would appear that programs of this type, which heavily subsidize the private sector and rely on its sense of social responsibility, are inherently defective and wasteful. The scandals associated with the FHA Section 608 program of the 1940s

2. For a recent HUD-sponsored report supporting the Section 235 program and recommending changes to improve its effectiveness, see Department of Housing and Urban Development *Report of the Task Force on Improving the Operation of Federally Insured or Financed Housing Programs,* Vol. I, "Single-Family Housing."

and 1950s are similar to what has happened under the Section 235 program. Under Section 608, the FHA granted extraordinarily liberal concessions to lackadaisically supervised private developers to induce them to produce rental housing rapidly in the postwar period. Nearly a half million units were in fact constructed until a series of scandals and congressional hearings put an end to the program in 1954. As Abrams described the system:

> A whole web of deception was spun which made it possible for the knowledgeable to build projects with costs running into the millions without investing a dime. Some made dummy leases between themselves and wholly-owned subsidiary corporations at a spurious rent for ninety-nine years. FHA would then insure a mortgage on the leasehold and upon default would have to pay the fictitious rent for the duration of the lease. The mortgages insured by FHA so far exceeded investment that builders withdrew millions above what the projects cost. The builders' costs were in many cases 30 percent less than FHA estimates, while land values as filed with FHA were as much as five and six times the actual cost. The huge bailouts, the fantastically inflated land prices and building costs, and the lease-backs at fictitious rentals were long an open secret. In some cases, FHA even allowed builders who had already "mortgaged out" (gotten all their money back from the insured mortgage) to increase their mortgages and draw out more than they had done already.

The Housing Act of 1968, which President Johnson trumpeted as "a Magna Carta to liberate our cities," apparently served also to liberate some of the more venal profit-making drives of the private sector. As Congressman Wright Patman, Chairman of the House Banking and Currency Committee, put it:

> Many of these programs start out with high-sounding purposes and what appear to be really outstanding concepts. Then someone comes along and insists that we add in the profit margin for each real estate interest as the program moves forward. There's a little bit for the land speculator, the builder, the lender, the closing attorney, the title company, the insurance company, and on down the line. By the time the project reaches the end of the line it is so top heavy that you can't be sure who just did get the subsidy.

### Interest Subsidies and Tax Benefits for Rental Housing

Programs to provide mortgage money at below-market interest rates originated in 1959. This kind of subsidy results in housing for moderate-income rather than low-income families, unless it is combined with further subsidies, such as rent supplements (see Chapter 4, footnote 3) or public housing leasing funds (see Chapter 4, "Housing

Projects and Beyond"). The low-rent public housing program subsidizes full capital costs, rather than just lowering the interest rate, and even this subsidy has proved inadequate to the real needs of low-income families.

The initial approach for providing low-interest mortgage money was direct federal lending, under the Section 202 program for the elderly, introduced in the 1959 Housing Act, and the Section 221(d)(3) program, introduced in the 1961 Housing Act, which was designed originally to provide replacement housing for displacees from urban renewal projects but was later developed into a more general rental housing program for moderate-income families. Under both of these programs, long-term (fifty years under the Section 202 program) FHA-guaranteed loans for up to 100 percent of value were made at a 3 percent interest rate to limited-dividend and nonprofit developers.[3] Income limits were set somewhat above public housing levels, and rents were regulated by the FHA. Under the Section 221(d)(3) program, average family income in 1968 was just under $5700, according to Aaron. Until both programs were effectively superseded by the 1968 Housing Act, they produced a total of about 165,000 units, mostly under the 221(d)(3) program.

The Section 236 rental housing program of the 1968 Housing Act signalled a switch from direct government loans to government interest subsidies on privately originated loans. The reasons for this had to do with the technicalities and political implications of government budgetary procedures. When the government lends money directly, the entire amount of the loan appears on the debit side of the budget (although over time the loan is repaid to the government with interest). If private capital is used, the federal government appropriates only what is needed to cover a portion of the interest rate, and this amount is all that appears on the federal budget. Although this method results in higher government payments to private lending institutions (assuming a 2 percent difference between the long-term federal borrowing rate and the market rate, according to data in Taggart and in Schechter, the government would have to pay an additional $7200 over the life of a thirty-year, $15,000 mortgage, one-third more in subsidy costs), an administration may feel it can benefit politically by lowering the apparent, but not the real, level of government expenditures. Another difference between direct government loans and interest subsidy programs is that under the

3. Technically Section 221(d)(3) loans were not regarded as direct government loans; instead a complex indirect procedure was worked out whereby the loan was made by a private lender and then bought at par by the Federal National Mortgage Association, which until 1968 was a government secondary mortgage market, under its special assistance program. The interest rate under the 221(d)(3) program was originally pegged at the federal government's own borrowing rate, but was fixed in 1965 at 3 percent. Cooperatives as well as rental housing could be built under both programs, and units could be produced through rehabilitation as well as through new construction.

latter homeowners build up equity far more slowly, which is disadvantageous to the consumer and has been shown to lead to higher rates of default. Taggart calculates that on a thirty-year, $15,000 loan, for example, the borrower has built only $3200 equity after fifteen years under a privately originated, FHA-insured 8.5 percent loan with interest subsidized down to one percent, whereas after fifteen years with a direct one percent government loan he would have an equity of $6950.

Production under the Section 236 program has been much higher than under the previous below-market interest rate programs. In fiscal 1970, 51,000 units were produced, in fiscal 1971, 107,000 units, and estimates for fiscal 1972 and 1973 combined are 322,000 units. Over 90 percent of Section 236 production is new construction; the remainder is rehabilitation. Maximum income limits for eligibility are set at 135 percent of local public housing income limits, with the provision that 20 percent of authorized Section 236 funds may be used for families with somewhat higher incomes. Median family income in Section 236 projects, according to Aaron, is approximately $5100 (1971 data). Families are required to pay at least 25 percent of their income for rent, and the FHA regulates rent levels, although approvals for rent increases are usually given to enable limited-profit sponsors to earn the 6 percent maximum return allowed on their equity. Lower-income families can be accommodated in the program via additional subsidies under the rent supplement program or by leasing units to the local public housing authority, although there are limitations on the proportion of units that may be given to such families. There is, however, no requirement that Section 236 sponsors make units available to low-income families under these supplementary subsidy programs; Taggart estimates that less than 5 percent of Section 236 units receive rent supplements, and three-fourths of all such developments have made no such provision.

As with the Section 235 homeownership program, numerous problems of financing and quality have characterized the first few years of production under Section 236. Shoddy construction, poor site selection, and irresponsible management have been the primary causes of these difficulties, and the results have been high rates of foreclosure and default. As of late 1971, one in every fifteen Section 236 projects completed was in default. Herbers in early 1972 noted:

> The department [HUD] was contracting for the management of 45,000 to 50,000 apartment units that had been foreclosed. ... The foreclosures, however, show only a tip of the iceberg. Below the surface are the units in default—no longer making mortgage payments—and the units in trouble that the government is helping on a temporary basis in a number of ways. This includes extension of the mortgage or suspension of payments.

Rehabilitation projects carried out under interest-subsidy programs are in even more serious trouble. Management attempts to pass on these unforeseen added costs to the tenants through increased rents have led to much resistance and occasional lawsuits. By early 1974, defaults in the Section 236 and 235 programs combined were costing HUD $2 billion annually, a figure administration officials predicted would keep rising in the years to come.

### Tax Shelters and People Shelters

As noted, profit-oriented developers of Section 236 housing are limited to a cash return of 6 percent on their equity. Since real estate investment generally is not considered attractive unless the investor can be fairly certain of receiving a 15 percent return after taxes, the reasons for the popularity of the Section 236 program must lie somewhere else. That somewhere else is the income tax system and the benefits it gives to high-income investors in rental housing. (Most of these benefits apply to all rental housing, subsidized and unsubsidized, but for convenience they will be described within the context of the Section 236 program.)

As Slitor and Netzer point out, the two provisions of the tax system that directly benefit investors in rental housing are what is called accelerated depreciation and the favorable capital gains treatment given to proceeds from the sale of rental property. Accelerated depreciation in essence is a fictitious construct by which the owner of rental property, which is a capital good, is allowed to assume a far more rapid "book" depreciation of his asset (on improvements only; land does not depreciate in value and therefore cannot be depreciated for tax purposes) than depreciation determined on a "straight-line" basis. It is important to note that even "straight-line" depreciation (2.5 percent annually over a presumed forty-year life of a new building) benefits landlords enormously, since most buildings last longer than forty years and tend actually to appreciate in value over time because of inflation and the housing shortage. Value depends on income-producing capacity, and as long as a housing shortage exists even poorly maintained housing will usually produce considerable amounts of income.

Using one of several formulas,[4] the taxpayer is permitted to deduct from his income tax the assumed accelerated depreciation, which may be

4. The three commonly used formulas for accelerated depreciation are the 200 percent declining balance (twice the normal rate of depreciation); the 150 percent declining balance (one and one-half times the normal rate of depreciation); and the sum-of-the-years-digits methods, a rate of depreciation for any year represented by a fraction of which the numerator is the remaining useful life at the beginning of the year and the denominator is the sum of the digits representing the remaining useful life (if the useful life is four years the numerator for the first year would be four and the denominator ten—1 + 2 + 3 + 4). See Ritter and Sunley, "Real Estate and Tax Reform: An Analysis and Evaluation of the Real Estate Provisions of the Tax Reform Act of 1969."

as high as two-fifths of the depreciable cost over the first quarter of the building's useful life and two-thirds to three-fourths of the cost over the first half of the building's useful life. Furthermore, the tax system allows each new owner of a property to depreciate it all over again (although over a lesser presumed life span), based on the amount paid for the building. This allows a total depreciation over the life of a structure that may be many times its value, and also encourages sale and resale of buildings to maximize depreciation advantages, which are more favorable in the early years of ownership. Other tax deductible expenses (mortgage interest, state and local property taxes, other actual operating expenses) involve actual cash outflow, but depreciation does not, so depreciation in excess of any real loss of value can be used to create a "tax shelter," a tax-exempt cover for other income to shield it from normal income tax. The availability of this shelter has enormous value to the developer, because it allows him to offset taxes he would otherwise have to pay on other income, and this lies at the heart of most real estate investment decisions. Depreciation allowances may be taken on the total value of the property, regardless of the amount of equity the owner has in the property. Thus, an owner may have only 20 percent equity in a particular property (often much less), but he is allowed to reap the tax benefits from the entire value of the property, that which is mortgaged and that which is represented by his equity investment, and thus take advantage of the real estate principle known as leverage. An example of how the tax shelter system operates is as follows (from Slitor):

> The property is a $400,000 new apartment building ($300,000 of which represents the value of the building, $100,000 the value of the land), bought using a twenty-year $300,000 mortgage at 6 percent interest rate. Net operating income (before interest, depreciation and income tax) is assumed to be $33,000 (8 percent). Income tax deductions amount to the interest paid on mortgage loan ($18,000 the first year) plus accelerated depreciation of $15,000, using the 200 percent declining balance formula (twice the straight-line rate of 2.5 percent, as applied to the remaining undepreciated balance—the full $300,000 for the first year of operation). Since the operating income of $33,000 exactly equals the amount that can be deducted from income tax (interest plus accelerated depreciation) there is no taxable income from owning the property. On the other hand, since financing costs (interest plus amortization) amount to only $26,000 on such a mortgage, there is a net cash flow to the owner (net operating income minus mortgage costs) of $7000, which is completely untaxable. Since $8000 of the mortgage repayment cost went to pay off principal, the owner (assuming realistically that the property after one year can be sold for $400,000, the same amount that it cost to construct it) has a net return of $15,000 ($7000 net cash flow plus the $8000 amortization payment) on his original $100,000 investment (the sum above the mortgage amount the owner had to furnish), or 15 percent after taxes—equal to a 30 percent before-taxes return for someone in the 50 percent bracket.

One of the major criticisms of accelerated depreciation is that a great deal of "leakage" is caused in the tax system through the tax shelter device that is extremely regressive in impact, since high-income investors benefit most from tax-free income. Some $250 million in taxes is lost annually from the accelerated depreciation allowance applied to residential properties. Stern cites one taxpayer with $1,433,000 income, another with $738,000 income, neither of whom paid a penny in federal income taxes, primarily as a result of deductions related to real estate investments.

The 1969 Tax Reform Act altered and limited the depreciation allowance so as to provide more direction for real estate investment, and to add a touch of social policy priorities to these incentives. Prior to 1969 the 200 percent depreciation formula could be used for any new real estate, the 150 percent formula for any existing real estate, regardless of the use to which the property was put. Commercial and industrial property received the same tax advantages as residential property. As a result, commercial and industrial facilities and luxury housing were generally favored over low- and moderate-income housing because of their greater profitability and value appreciation. The 1969 legislation placed the tax system on the side of housing by restricting use of the most favorable depreciation formulas (200 percent declining balance and sum-of-the-years-digits) to new residential rental property, and also attempted to make dealing in existing properties less attractive by allowing new owners of existing residential property to depreciate at only a 125 percent rate, although retaining a comparative advantage over existing nonresidential properties, which are now permitted only straight-line depreciation.

In recent years the real estate tax shelter has become even more profitable through a process known as equity syndication, by which investors develop sophisticated schemes for marketing these shelters. Equity syndication reaches its maximum potential when it is done in conjunction with FHA rental housing programs, particularly Section 236. In this process the builder-developer forms a limited partnership (in which he is the general partner) and then contracts with the partnership to build the project. Investors are brought in as limited partners to share in the tax loss shelter. According to Lane and Edson, the going price in 1971 for a 95 percent interest in a new Section 236 project was 11 to 15 percent of the mortgage amount. The reason the sale is so profitable for the builder-sponsor lies in the extraordinary leverage allowed under the Section 236 program, through another fiction known as the Builders and Sponsors Profit and Risk Allowance (BSPRA). When the BSPRA, which amounts to 10 percent of the project's replacement cost (land, construction cost, landscaping, architect's fees, legal and other organizational expenses, overhead and financing fees, and the like), is left in the project and counted toward the equity requirement, the FHA-insured mortgage is effectively increased from 90 percent to 97 or 98 percent. Breckenfeld describes the way it works:

> Thus in a typical deal, a group of professionals and businessmen might lay out about $600,000 for a 95 percent interest in a $4.7 million Section 236 apartment project being built with a $4 million FHA-insured mortgage. The builder-sponsor would pocket most of the $600,000 as his construction profit. Over the next eleven years, provided that the project is built at the estimated cost and can be kept reasonably full of tenants, the limited partners should be able to recoup $1,055,000 on their investment, almost entirely in taxes avoided on the members' other income. At the end of that time, if all goes well, the owners might donate the project to charity and acquire a further $1 million in tax deductions.

The builder-developer, who because of the BSPRA feature has had to put in less than $100,000 in cash on the $4.7 million project, is able to profit enormously by converting the tax shelter into immediate cash. Substantial additional profits are available to the builder-sponsor, depending on the capacity of his organization, from management fees, architectural and engineering work, legal and organizational work, and as a general contractor; and all partners may receive further benefits from the cash distribution available through the 6 percent allowable cash return on equity and the residual value of the project upon eventual sale. The investment banking and financial community has become actively involved in finding buyers and sellers for these equity syndicates, and the trend is toward public offerings to enable these tax losses to be passed on to small investors.[5]

Another recent development in the tax shelter game involves nonprofit organizations, such as churches and community groups, that act as cosponsors with builder-developers of FHA rental housing projects, and that may handle some of the social management and community-relations aspects of the development. Since such organizations pay no income tax and therefore cannot benefit from the tax shelter, they will sell their share of the project to upper-income investors who can utilize the

---

5. According to Lane and Edson, "Recently, a public offering of limited partnership interest was made by the American Housing Partners. The first of its kind, this offering has created a publicly held limited partnership . . . which will . . . invest in many HUD projects around the country and pass the tax losses back to its investors. . . . [The former] Deputy Assistant Secretary for Housing Production and Mortgage Credit and Deputy Commissioner of FHA, HUD, is president of [the general partner in the partnership]." The National Corporation for Housing Partnerships, created by Title IX of the 1968 Housing Act, attempts to foster housing investment by corporations, utilities, financial institutions, and labor organizations by passing on tax losses as dividends from accelerated depreciation—in effect an entity sponsored by the government to foster avoidance of its own tax system. See *Third Annual Report of National Corporation for Housing Partnerships and The National Housing Partnership,* January 1, 1971 to December 31, 1971.

tax loss and who will use the profits to support the organization and its activities.

The other major federal income tax benefit to investors in rental housing is the depreciation "recapture" provisions upon sale of the property. Any gain upon disposition of personal property that is the result of prior depreciation is taxed as ordinary income. (This, of course, does not cancel the benefits of depreciation allowances, since it still permits taxes to be postponed and "timed.") For real property the recapture is based not on the total depreciation previously taken but only on the difference between the depreciation actually claimed and what the depreciation would have been had the straight-line method been used, and attractive provisions exist for phasing out even this limited form of recapture, so that all receipts are treated as long-term capital gains rather than as ordinary income and are taxed at half the taxpayer's normal rate, with a maximum of 25 percent. The system is succinctly described by Richard Slitor:

> Book profits reflecting the artificial write-down of the depreciable invest-
> ment by accelerated depreciation represent deductions previously taken
> against ordinary income, so that the whole process represents a conversion
> of ordinary income into capital gains for tax purposes.

Prior to 1969, after real property had been held for twenty months the amount recaptured was permitted to phase out at the rate of one percent per month, until at the end of ten years (120 months) there was no recapture at all. Under the Tax Reform Act of 1969 all phase-out provisions for nonresidential real estate were eliminated. Residential real estate is favored under the new tax laws by retaining phase-out provisions, although at a less attractive rate: the one percent per month phase-out does not begin until the property has been owned 100 months, and the time the property must be held until complete phase-out occurs is therefore extended to sixteen and two-thirds years (200 months). Section 236 and 221(d)(3) housing and housing similarly aided under state and local programs receive favored treatment because they are allowed to retain the pre-1969 recapture rules. (Housing that has been rehabilitated under the five-year rapid depreciation permitted by the 1969 Tax Reform Act is governed by the 100-month, sixteen-and-two-thirds years rule though, even if it has been rehabilitated with a Section 236 loan.) These favorable recapture rules for Sections 236 and 221(d)(3) housing are scheduled to terminate at the end of 1974 by terms of the 1969 Act, but Congress can and may decide to extend them. It is clear that some complex juggling and computation are required to optimize both the advantages of accelerated depreciation and capital gains treatment. Correct timing of property turnover is the key to skillful real estate management, inasmuch as high-income investors are primarily concerned with minimizing the effects of the federal tax system on their incomes.

The tax reforms of 1969 thus served to give housing an edge over other forms of real estate investment, although specific policy directions still are poorly defined: luxury as well as low- and moderate-income housing still receives the benefits of the most attractive accelerated depreciation formulas. But the larger issue is the wisdom of relying on the tax system to implement social policy objectives in the housing field and other areas. Tax incentives prove to be a less equitable way of accomplishing desired ends than direct subsidies because the benefits of tax incentives are far more available to high-income taxpayers. The system provides windfalls to those who would do anyway what the tax incentives are trying to encourage them to do; and it keeps the tax rate high by constricting the tax base and reducing revenues. As Stanley Surrey, former assistant secretary of treasury for tax policy, has written: "We thus have the paradox of cutting a tax escape path through our income tax system, through which the tax millionaire and others well off may pass, in the hope of building more rental housing. We should do better." Damage is done both to the tax system and to the administration of housing policy. As Surrey put it in a speech:

> [The progressive income] tax system stands as a moderating influence that keeps the rewards of our private enterprise system within acceptable levels by channelling an appropriate part of those rewards into tax payments to maintain our government. But when the rewards are cast in terms of tax benefits and subsidies, then the tax system is itself asked to stand aside. There is no longer any moderating force.

The outcome and beneficiaries of the tax system are very different from housing priorities as expressed in direct aid programs. Surrey well describes the upside-down world of tax subsidies, using the homeowner's tax deductions (see Chapter 4, "Income Taxes and Housing") as his example:

> If cast in direct expenditure language, the present assistance under the itemized deductions for interest and taxes would look as follows:
>
> —for a married couple with more than $200,000 in income, HUD would, for each $100 of mortgage interest on the couple's home, pay $70 to the bank holding the mortgage, leaving the couple to pay $30. It would also pay a similar portion of the couple's property tax to the state or city levying the tax.

—for a married couple with income of $10,000, HUD would pay the bank on the couple's mortgage $19 per each $100 interest unit, with the couple paying $81. It would also pay a similar portion of the couple's property tax to the state or city levying the tax.

—for a married couple too poor to pay an income tax, HUD would pay nothing to the bank, leaving the couple to pay the entire interest cost. The couple would also have to pay the entire property tax.

It is clear that we would never do with direct subsidies what we do with indirect ones through the tax system. There would seem to be no reason to retain existing tax incentives for investors in rental housing, other than the nation's desire or willingness to allow enormous profits and benefits to those who need them least. As McKee demonstrates, direct subsidies are more equitable, cheaper, and more effective.

## Rural Housing: The Forgotten Area

Despite the fact that housing conditions in rural areas are generally worse than in urban areas, comparatively little attention is paid to nonurban housing problems. In large part this may be explainable by the absence of concentration of rural housing problems; such areas lack even the minimal visibility, organizing ability, and potential for disruptive behavior that exist among the poor and nonwhites in urban areas. HUD, as its name implies, concentrates on urban areas, and its various housing subsidy programs—under FHA, urban renewal, rehabilitation, and public housing—are little used in rural areas. In 1970 only 10 percent of all places with less than 10,000 population had local public housing authorities. Rural housing needs are greater not only because current housing conditions are worse, but also because incomes are generally lower, credit scarcer, and homebuilding capacity smaller. Although the population movement from rural to urbanized areas tends to relieve pressure somewhat, improved housing opportunities in rural areas and small towns would provide more viable options for people to remain in or return to such places.

Special rural housing programs are administered by the Farmers Home Administration (FmHA) in the Department of Agriculture. FmHA is confined to places with less than 10,000 population (before 1970 the limit was 5500). Despite its name, FmHA operates primarily in nonfarm rural areas.

Unlike the Federal Housing Administration, which insures and subsidizes loans made by private lenders, the Farmers Home Administration makes direct loans, because of the unavailability of private credit in rural areas and the poor terms (much shorter loan periods, lower loan-to-value ratios, higher interest rates) for the credit that is available. (FmHA subsequently sells a large part of its portfolio to private lenders, however, to whom it furnishes a repayment guarantee similar to FHA and VA insurance.) The principal FmHA program is Section 502, which provides homeowners with variable interest rate loans for home construction, purchase, or rehabilitation that may be as low as one percent, depending on the income of the borrower. According to data from Aaron and the *Fourth Annual Report on National Housing Goals,* the median income of recipients of these loans was $6100 in 1969; 14 percent had incomes under $4000. The average loan is for less than $10,000. Through 1970 a total of 313,000 Section 502 loans were made, and the pace of lending is scheduled to increase in the future. FHA Section 235 homeownership loans are also available in rural areas, where FmHA administers the program, but relatively few such loans are made because of the lack of private credit.

FmHA also makes direct and subsidized loans for rental housing under its newer Section 515 and 521 programs, but only a few thousand units have been funded nationally, and the rental programs have served families that by rural standards are essentially middle income. (See *Three Studies of Rural Rental Housing.*) A variety of other programs are offered by the Farmers Home Administration—disaster loans and technical assistance grants for self-help housing, so-called shelter-type rehabilitation loans to remove health and safety hazards, farm labor housing loans and grants, and site loans—but they are all pathetically small in absolute terms and relative to need. (See *Low-Income Housing Programs for Rural America.*)

Apart from inadequate funding levels, rural programs are inherently difficult to administer, because of low population densities and a lack of awareness of available aids. FmHA has 1700 county offices, of which many are poorly staffed, and many persons live in areas far removed from a center. More widespread use of FmHA programs can come about only through aggressive information and outreach campaigns on the part of local administrators and from sympathetic personnel who are willing to spend the time it takes to assist rural residents, many of whom may be poorly educated, in filling out forms and the other paper work involved in loan transactions. But as a recent report on one FmHA county office, entitled *Abuse of Power,* points out, "historically Farmers Home Administration has had firm ties with farm owners and growers." Staffs generally are unsympathetic with poor applicants and nonwhites and oppose such "irregular" programs as self-help and cooperative housing. *Abuse of Power,* prepared by the American Friends Service Committee, concludes that builders were served to the detriment of clients. Attempts were made to discourage clients by quoting high interest rates and high down payments. Moral judgments on the life style of applicants were made to deny access to the program. Maximum interest rates and highest possible down payments were extracted from the clients rather than attempting to get the poor clients the best possible deal under the regulations. Lack of sympathy with the poor and racial bias was a general pattern in dealing with the client population.

Local administrators inevitably have a high degree of discretion over the highly decentralized FmHA programs, a potential advantage in view of the red tape and bureaucratic delays in the housing area. However, as the AFSC report points out, "this same discretionary power can totally undermine the purpose of the program when in the hands of one not sympathetic to the poor, the black, or those needing special consideration." Rural black families are greatly discriminated against in FmHA programs, and according to Bryce one key reason is the existence of local loan committees, composed of successful farmers, who make the loan decisions.

It is clear that rural housing is an undeservedly forgotten area. Much more attention needs to be paid to programs designed to meet the needs of low-income rural households, and serious restructuring of the government's delivery mechanism for helping the rural poor is also necessary. (See Cochran and Rucker for a set of suggestions for changing the FmHA and its programs.)

## Housing Allowances: The Grand Delusion

Housing allowances are the "in" idea of the 1970s. The essence of the proposal is to provide direct subsidies, in cash or some kind of "funny money" like rent certificates, to low-income housing consumers and allow them to seek their own housing on the private market, rather than to subsidize the production of housing and an elaborate administrative network to allocate these units to the poor. Virtually all middle- and upper-income people live in good housing, because the market—aided by various tax breaks discussed (which might legitimately be termed housing allowances for the rich)—provides for those with adequate incomes. If poor people have enough money to spend on housing so that as housing consumers they are no longer poor, many feel they could solve their own housing problems. (Ideally, general income maintenance programs could also make people no longer poor as consumers of other nonluxury goods, such as food, medical care, transportation, and the like. But the costs of such a program would be immense—according to the Bureau of Labor Statistics, the average lower budget for an urban family of four to achieve a decent standard of living in 1972 was $7386—and well beyond what appears politically feasible at this time. So-called categorical grant programs have been advocated as a viable alternative, despite many acknowledged defects.)[6]

The idea of such allowances dates back to the 1930s and 1940s, when the U.S. Chamber of Commerce and conservative real estate interests urged similar proposals in an effort to undercut "socialistic" public housing. In 1968 the President's Committee on Urban Housing recommended an experimental housing allowance program, and the following year HUD initiated two small-scale pilot projects in Wilmington and Kansas City, under the Model Cities program. The 1970 Housing Act included authorization for large-scale experiments with the allowance approach. An elaborate series of experimental projects, involving 15,000 to 20,000 families, directed by HUD, the Urban Institute, and several of the nation's leading urban research groups, is currently underway in a dozen areas; it will last two to five years and cost an estimated $150 million. In 1973, the secretary of HUD directed an extensive half-year study of federal policy in conjunction with the moratorium of federal housing aids announced at the beginning of that year. In late 1973, the Nixon administration, jumping the gun on these feasibility tests, proposed in a message to Congress that housing allowances be adopted on a wide scale in the near future. The idea has received enthusiastic support from important elements of the business community, including the National Association of Realtors and the Committee for Economic Development.

The renascence of the idea and its firm embrace by the Nixon administration are to be seen against the background of widespread disenchantment and difficulties with existing federal programs, most notably low-rent public housing, and the administration's "New Federalism" approach of decentralizing administrative responsibility from the federal level to state and local governments. (In announcing the federal housing allowance plan, President Nixon stated, "This plan would give the poor the freedom and responsibility to make their own choices about housing, and it would eventually get the federal government out of the housing business.") Housing allowances also are touted as a less costly approach to housing the poor. Estimates of the cost of a housing allowance program vary according to different estimators and the type of

6. Gans makes a good case for a series of categorical grants in "Three Ways to Solve the Welfare Problem." Lee Rainwater, in "The Lessons of Pruitt-Igoe," argues that housing and other categorical grant programs divert attention and energies from more basic income redistribution approaches. Netzer, in *Economics and Urban Problems*, makes the point that the complex nature of housing production and the workings of the housing market render specific housing-directed subsidies necessary.

coverage envisioned. Henry Aaron has put forth the figure of $4.9 billion as the annual cost of a program to cover all eligible beneficiaries, using 1967 cost data, but the calculation pays little attention to possible inflationary effects on rent levels and the need to increase the supply of housing. The administration's September 1973 announcement noted that full implementation of a housing allowance program would cost $8–11 billion annually and asserts that to reach all eligible families under current programs would cost $34 billion annually. Fried and his colleagues at the Brookings Institution posit an annual cost of anywhere from $2.5 billion to $15.5 billion depending on what assumptions are used regarding the level of housing benefits, the percentage of family income the recipient is required to pay, and the proportion of eligible families that receive benefits.

As the president's announcement notes, the principal advantage to the consumer is expanded choice: instead of being limited to housing projects, FHA developments, and other units subsidized by a government agency, the recipient of a housing allowance would be free to live in any unit he chooses that is within his rent limitations. (The experimental programs are confined to rental units, but there is no reason the allowance approach could not be expanded to cover homeownership.) This has the same kind of personal and social advantages that characterize the leased public housing program, without the intermediary of a public housing authority as the middleman landlord (though some kind of public agency would still be needed to administer the housing allowance). What is more, concentration of low-income "multi-problem" families in large housing projects can be avoided.

Housing allowances will allegedly provide landlords with sufficient rent revenue to maintain their buildings properly and remove housing code violations. As such, they would go a long way toward solving the abandonment problem. Administratively, housing allowances would require a far simpler bureaucratic mechanism than the present housing authority-FHA structure. (Administrative costs for a housing allowance program would depend on how rigorously the system was structured and monitored. Leaman estimates that it would range from $15–20 to $100–130 per family annually.) It would also enable persons who live in areas not now served by local housing authorities to receive housing subsidies.

The problem with the housing allowance approach as it is presently conceived is that making the poor "free-market" consumers leaves unchanged the numerous defects of that market, which will severely hamper, if not totally undermine, efforts on the part of recipients to find and keep decent housing. The elaborate social science experiments that are being undertaken will, to be sure, produce much important information about the mechanics and results of the housing allowance approach. But we already know from experience a great deal about what the poor and near-poor get for their housing dollars, how much their housing costs, how landlords behave, and how well housing codes are enforced; and we know enough about the housing market to explain the results we see.

The housing allowance approach assumes that the sole cause of housing problems is inadequate incomes. It pays insufficient attention to the vast shortage of decent, moderate-rent housing in most urban and suburban areas, particularly for groups the market now serves poorly, such as large families. Only in those few areas where there is a high vacancy rate for such housing will allowances be successful (the Kansas City experiment that HUD touted so widely was undertaken in an area with a 6.2 percent metropolitan vacancy rate, 8.7 percent in the county where most of the participants found housing). While allowances by law will be available only for standard housing, few doubt that the introduction of housing allowances into a static supply of housing will lead to rent inflation (on a short-term basis at least), not only for recipients but also for other low- and moderate-income households competing for the same units. Rents are spiralling across the country even without an allowance program, and as a result many cities have introduced or plan to introduce rent control (see Chapter 3, "Should Rents Be Controlled?"). Yet the design of the housing allowance experiments does not call for any form of rent control, and it is highly improbable that an administration-introduced program will include regulation of rents to be charged in the private sector. Without such measures, housing allowances will benefit landlords far more than they will benefit low-income families.

The housing allowance approach also ignores pervasive housing discrimination with respect to acceptance of tenants, eviction, and rents charged—on the basis of race, welfare status, number of children, family composition, age, and life style, which are all grounds for systematic discrimination on the part of landlords and others who control the allocation of private housing. Extensive racial discrimination was reported in the Kansas City housing allowance pilot project. The mere ability to pay the rent by no means guarantees that the housing consumer will get what he or she wants. Landlords may charge to housing allowance recipients a covert premium for the privilege of being accepted as tenants. Nor will lending institutions and insurance companies cease to "redline" areas occupied by nonwhites and the poor. A sellers' market prevails, and just as housing code enforcement has been a failure, so strict attempts to police a quality standard requirement will also be ineffective. Allowances may induce some owners to upgrade their units, but wherever possible landlords will attempt to capture the additional consumers' income made available through allowances without doing renovation, or by making minimal, nondurable repairs.

New York City's experience under its revised rent control system is instructive. Based on Rand Institute studies of New York's housing market, a Maximum Base Rent was established for each rental unit, taking into account the actual costs of maintaining a rental unit and a permitted 8.5 percent return on the landlord's investment. Landlords are permitted to increase rents 7.5 percent annually until the MBR is reached. There is no government subsidy involved, and so tenants must bear the full brunt of these rent increases, but it is revealing to see what has happened as a result of this new system. The theory was that landlords previously were unable to afford to keep their properties up to code standards, but that with adequate rental revenue they could and would maintain their buildings properly. Although they had no choice in the matter, tenants would at least receive better housing for their higher rents. In order to qualify for the MBR rent increases, the landlord had to certify by June 30, 1971, that he had corrected all of the "rent-impairing" violations that were outstanding as of January 1, 1971. By October 1971 the landlord had to certify that he was maintaining all "essential services" for the building. However, since there was no mechanism for pre-inspection of the more than one million rent-controlled units in New York City eligible for MBR rent increases, the city relied on the honesty of landlords (and tenant protests of housing code violations or inadequate services) to ensure that MBR rent increases would indeed provide improved housing. An analysis of the impact of MBR by the New York State Study Commission for New York City revealed the following:

> HDA [The New York City Housing and Development Administration] inspected buildings with violations on the books [as of January 1, 1971]; of the 36,000 certifications which landlords reported as free of violations, 17,000 were found upon inspection to be false. . . .
>
> If HDA inspections of violations showed that almost *half* of the certifications were false, it could well be imagined what an inquiry into "essential services" might produce. . . .
>
> Given the final form of the MBR program and its subsequent administration, it is obvious that it has become primarily a mechanism for increasing rents paid.

The New York City experience gives no support to the hypothesis put forth by housing allowance advocates that landlords will correct code violations upon receiving increased rent revenues. New York City's MBR system provided for tenant protests of continuing poor maintenance, benefited from a sophisticated automated data processing system, and was run by an extensive administrative bureaucracy with over twenty years' experience in the area of controls over rental housing. If under such a system almost half of the landlords who reported no substantial code violations lied, one can hardly believe that landlords in other major cities without these safeguards will be any more honest or anxious to invest their windfall profits from a housing allowance program in increased maintenance.

Finally, the state of most landlord-tenant legal relationships throughout the country will severely limit the ability of housing allowance recipients to get a fair shake in the housing market. (See chapter 3, "Landlord Versus Tenant.") Without good lease protections, warranty of habitability rights, rent withholding provisions, and protection against retaliatory evictions and other forms of intimidation, the low-income tenant is at the mercy of the landlord. If a federal model lease that incorporated most or all of these protections were made a mandatory part of the housing allowance program, this would be a substantial step toward creating a set of balanced legal relationships between landlord and tenant—and toward reform of landlord-tenant law nationwide—but there is virtually no likelihood of this, in light of the program's announced emphasis on the "free market" and minimal government intervention.

These, then, are the characteristics of the housing market in which housing allowance recipients will be permitted to exercise their "free choice." If the nature of the market does not raise severe doubts about the fate of housing allowance recipients, the results of two very similar programs—public welfare and the public housing leasing program—should. While families receive a lump sum under the public welfare program, a specified portion of this amount, based on standard budgets, is earmarked for housing. As Martin Rein notes, "If the federal government were seriously to consider developing a housing allowance to low-income households, the experience of those on welfare could serve as a useful guide in anticipating some of the strains and difficulties that such a program might encounter." Those strains and difficulties are outlined in chapter 4, "Housing and Public Welfare": just about the worst housing conditions of any group in the society, inadequate government supervision and intervention, and widespread discrimination and maltreatment by landlords. Leased public housing is also similar to housing allowances, the principal difference (other than administrative arrangements for handling the subsidy) being that the housing authority instead of the family itself locates the unit. In some communities the local housing authority permits or encourages eligible tenants to find units on their own and bring them to the housing authority, which virtually obliterates the distinction between the two programs. According to an Urban Institute study, "because the leasing program uses the private real estate market to a much greater degree than other housing programs, it can be viewed as a test of what the market can deliver in the way of decent but not luxurious housing services when the effective demand is increased." As noted in "Housing Projects and Beyond," chapter 4, studies by HUD's Office of Audit and other independent researchers found widespread incidence of substandard housing and inflated rents. (The Urban Institute study was based on interviews with local housing authorities; while it put forth more positive conclusions about the leasing program than those of the independent studies, this may have stemmed from the desire of housing authorities to furnish overly roseate reports about their own work.) The presence of a public agency as intermediary should, if anything, produce results more beneficial to the low-income tenant than the proposed housing allowance system, which would leave the poor and powerless tenant to bargain directly with the landlord.

The housing allowance is only part of a good idea. It fosters the principle of individual choice in the housing market, which is a critical component of housing satisfaction, but it takes no steps to ensure that market conditions will be such that the low-income consumer can truly have free choice or satisfaction. With the present realities of housing conditions and the housing market, freedom of choice can only be enhanced by more government intervention, not less. As Miles Mahoney, former Commissioner of Community Affairs of Massachusetts, noted, "unless the government is, in fact, willing to intervene forcefully in the workings of the private market, the housing allowance program will prove to be no more than yet another subsidy program for the private sphere—the poor will benefit only marginally and the near poor will likely be harmed." Housing allowances are a backward step, as they are being developed, for they will not improve the housing conditions of the poor and will postpone the basic changes that are needed in the housing system if all Americans are to be decently housed.

## The Lessons Learned

There is much to be learned from this review of the major federal housing programs. The most salient points are the overall regressivity of federal aids and the small number of lower-income households assisted by government programs compared with the need for such help. Table 1 lists the amount of federal aid by income class under the major programs, based on 1971 data in Cochran and Rucker.

Table 1

Federal Housing Assistance by Income Class (1971)

| | INCOME LEVEL | | |
| --- | --- | --- | --- |
| | Under $3500 | $3500–$10,000 | $10,000 and above |
| Public Housing | $413 million | $233 million | – |
| FHA Sections 235 and 236 | $34 million | $108 million | $1 million |
| Farmers Home Administration Sections 312 and 115— | $2 million | $18 million | $16 million |
| Rehabilitation Loans and Grants | $25 million | $18 million | – |
| Federal income tax deductions for mortgage interest, property taxes, and depreciation | $58 million | $2,552 million | $3,190 million |
| TOTAL | $532 million | $2,929 million | $3,207 million |

Incredibly, the truly poor (those with less than $3500 annual income)
receive only one-sixth as much benefit from federal housing aids as do
moderate- or middle- to high-income families, only 9 percent of the
combined amount received by these higher-income groups. The inadequacy of government housing aid, particular to low-income households,
is revealed, via the data in von Furstenberg, in the fact that the public
housing program—in essence the only government program that directly
provides housing to the poor—has over its 35-year life produced less than
five units for every 100 low-income households, and the total output is
not much more than a single year's production goal for low- and moderate-income housing under the 1968 Housing Act.

What we need is both a new scale of government housing assistance
and a restructuring of present aids and delivery systems so as to provide
assistance to those who need it and take it away from those who don't.
A first step is to eliminate or reform the totally upside-down nature of the
housing subsidies distributed to homeowners through the income tax
system. This will not only introduce greater equity into the tax system,
but could also provide the government with substantial revenue to transfer to lower-income groups in the form of direct subsidies.

Useful guidelines for how such a subsidy system ought and ought
not to be structured can also be gleaned from an analysis of the strengths
and weaknesses of present and past programs. The principle of consumer
sovereignty should to the greatest extent possible be an intrinsic part of
any housing program: people ought to be able to choose the area and the
type of structure they want to live in, whom they want to live near, and

whether to own or rent. The theory of housing allowances embodies this freedom, but the nature of the housing market does not permit the housing consumer to exercise this freedom. For the short-term future, at least, government programs must intervene in the housing market to create an adequate supply of decent housing available to lower-income households so that consumers in fact can have choice, through housing allowances or any other system. The various forms of government aid should have as a primary aim expanding the number and type of decent dwellings available to the ill-housed, in various parts of the central city as well as throughout the suburbs and rural areas, in single- and multifamily structures, and for sale as well as for rent. This expansion of the supply should be carried out through large-scale rehabilitation (of the type outlined in Chapter 3, "A Comprehensive Approach to Rehabilitation") as well as through new construction.

The key issues in developing programs to expand the supply of decent housing are deciding what tools will be most effective and who should implement them. Both the private sector and public agencies have demonstrated numerous defects in the past. The widespread abuses in the Section 235 and 236 programs and the FHA Section 608 program before that indicate clearly that if private developers are to be a component of this effort they will have to be strictly regulated. The problems with public agencies have been different. In the case of the FHA and its administration of the Section 235 and 236 programs, the principal problem has been an attitude lying somewhere between indifference and hostility to the housing problems of the poor and near poor. Many local public housing authorities also have this problem to some degree, and most can operate only within their municipal boundaries and make use of only the public housing program. What we need is a delivery mechanism with broader jurisdiction and powers and greater motivation, backed up by the federal government's commitment to act directly where the local agency is not meeting the need.

There has never been an effective delivery mechanism for the federal housing programs. This may be no accident. Since there never has been a federal commitment to mount a comprehensive attack on substandard housing, a really good delivery system at the local level not only has been unnecessary, it might have been risky, for an agglomeration of such agencies might have created irresistible pressures on the federal government to expand its housing effort vastly. We need agencies with metropolitan-wide jurisdiction (county-wide jurisdiction in rural areas) to plan and implement a comprehensive, short-term program to provide everyone in that jurisdiction with decent housing of the type they desire at rents they can afford, making use of all available federal programs and administering and coordinating the participation of private developers under those federal programs that call for private sector participation. In those instances where the public agency cannot or will not put forth and carry out a comprehensive housing plan, the federal government itself must step in as "houser of last resort." (This might be a role for the states as well: a bill submitted to the Massachusetts legislature called for communities without local housing authorities to establish such bodies and for all communities to build annually enough units to meet 10 percent of the local housing need, as determined by surveys, or 10 percent of the housing authority's waiting list; where localities did not meet their obligations, the State Department of Community Affairs would be empowered to act directly.) Administration of the federal housing system, as Herbert Franklin has described it, represents "institutionalized discrimination against the poor." Programs for middle- and moderate-income families work primarily through underwriting the home finance system; only those programs that aid the poor—public housing and rent supplements—require local approvals, and "in the absence of strong national policy, localities can confine the poor and minority groups to the central city or refuse to aid those who are residents." This system of responsibility must be turned around if the poor and near poor are to get decent housing.

A comprehensive program of this type would be available to all who need housing assistance. The enormous categories of persons now excluded from the public housing program would become eligible beneficiaries: nonelderly, nondisabled individuals; those who do not meet local residency requirements; those with incomes too high for public housing but too low for the private market; those with incomes too low to meet minimum rent requirements; those who fail to meet "social eligibility" standards; and those who live in decent housing only by paying an excessive portion of their income (such persons would need housing allowances only). To whatever extent it is possible to draw on the existing housing stock without causing shortages and price inflation for nonsubsidized families, this would be done, through leasing arrangements. But in most areas there will likely be a need to expand the supply of decent, moderate-priced housing.

Much of the housing under such a comprehensive plan might be developed by the private sector. Limited-profit and nonprofit developers might receive low-interest loans—but directly from the Treasury, as was the case under the Section 202 program for the elderly and the earlier FHA Sec. 221(d)(3) program, not the Section 235–236 interest-subsidy-type loans that have proved so wasteful and such a boon for the lending institutions. Or there might be assistance in assembling building and rehabilitation sites by writing down the cost of land or using eminent domain powers to assemble large parcels as is done under urban renewal. Developments produced in this fashion would initially be for the exclusive occupancy of those living in substandard conditions, and provision would be made for admission of a wide range of eligible occupants, so as to avoid the concentration of the poor and consequent stigmatization that have characterized low-rent public housing projects. Subsidy arrangements would be such that families who no longer were eligible for a housing subsidy could continue to live in the same unit by paying an unsubsidized rent. Rents and occupancy conditions would be controlled so as to protect tenants. A development program of this type might well interlock with a system of housing allowances pegged to this new production. Large-scale production under this system would soon produce a wide range of housing options with respect to location and housing type, and if housing allowances were issued *pari passu* with this production, developers would be guaranteed full occupancy and allowance recipients would be guaranteed decent and satisfactory housing. (See Hartman for more on this proposal.) Homeownership of single-family homes or apartments in multiunit buildings, on a cooperative on condominium basis, would also be available, although adequate back-up mechanisms as outlined by Abrams would have to be established to protect homeowners with marginal incomes against short-term and unexpected adversity owing to sickness or unemployment.

To the extent that private developers are willing to operate under these controls, to meet the area-wide housing goals, their expertise and entrepreneurial talent would be welcome. (Inequitable and inefficient tax shelter arrangements ought, however, to be substantially modified or done away with altogether, and this might substantially reduce the private sector's willingness to participate.) Direct construction, rehabilitation and management by the area-wide housing agency would be used to meet that portion of the area's housing need not being met by the private sector. A combination of direct government financing of construction and subsidization of operating expenditures to lower rents to an appropriate level, similar to a local public housing authority's mode of operation, would be used. Management and perhaps ownership of new and rehabilitated developments should be given to resident cooperatives wherever possible. The public agency would also plan and administer a full range of rehabilitation aids to lower-income owners and on behalf of lower-income tenants: low-interest loans, outright grants, rent subsidies and other forms of assistance.

## References

AARON, HENRY J.
    1972 *Shelter and Subsidies: Who Benefits from Federal Housing Policies?*
    Washington, D.C.: The Brookings Institution, pp. 129–31,
    137, 149, 167–73.
ABRAMS, CHARLES
    1965 *The City is the Frontier.* New York: Harper & Row, p. 88.

———
    1970 *Homeownership for the Poor: A Program for Philadelphia.* New York:
    Praeger Publishers.
AMERICAN FRIENDS SERVICE COMMITTEE
    1971 *Abuse of Power: A Case Study of the Rural Housing Program of the
    Farmers Home Administration by a County Supervisor in Two Florida
    Counties.* Washington, D.C.: Rural Housing Alliance (Octo-
    ber).
BECKHAM, ROBERT
    1973 "The Experimental Housing Allowance Program: An Old
    Idea Will Get a New Kind of Test in 1973." *Journal of Housing*
    (January), 12–17.
BOYER, BRIAN D.
    1973 *Cities Destroyed for Cash: The FHA Scandal at HUD.* Chicago:
    Follett Publishing Co.
BRECKENFELD, GURNEY
    1972 "Housing Subsidies Are a Grand Delusion." *Fortune* (Febru-
    ary), p. 139.
BRYCE, HERRINGTON J.
    1973 "The Farmers Home Administration's Program," in Donald
    J. Reeb and James T. Kirk, Jr., eds., *Housing the Poor.* New
    York: Praeger Publishers, p. 190.
CARNEGIE, CHRISTA LEW
    1970 "Homeownership for the Poor: Running the Washington
    Gauntlet." *Journal of the American Institute of Planners* 36 (May),
    160–67.
COCHRAN, CLAY, AND GEORGE RUCKER
    1973 "Every American Family: Housing Need and Nonresponse,"
    in Donald J. Reeb and James T. Kirk, Jr., eds., *Housing the Poor.*
    New York: Praeger Publishers, pp. 149–79.
COMMITTEE FOR ECONOMIC DEVELOPMENT
    1973 *Financing the Nation's Housing Needs.* Washington, D.C.: Com-
    mittee for Economic Development (April), pp. 20–22, 45–
    55.

COMMONWEALTH OF MASSACHUSETTS
1970 *Report of the Joint Committee on Urban Affairs Relative to Public Housing,* Appendix C. H. 5000 (February 2).

COMPTROLLER GENERAL OF THE UNITED STATES
1972 "Opportunities to Improve Effectiveness and Reduce Costs of Homeownership Assistance Programs." B–171630 (December 29).

DOWNS, ANTHONY
1973 *Federal Housing Subsidies: How Are They Working?* Lexington, Mass.: Lexington Books.

FRANKLIN, HERBERT M.
1972 "The Federal Government as 'Houser of Last Resort': A Policy for Democratic Urban Growth." *Urban Law Annual,* pp. 23–44.

———
1971 "Federal Power and Subsidized Housing." *The Urban Lawyer* 3, 61–77.

FRIED, EDWARD R., ET AL.
1973 *Setting National Priorities: The 1974 Budget.* Washington, D.C.: The Brookings Institution, pp. 138–45.

FROSH, LANE, AND EDSON, CONSULTANTS TO ARTHUR D. LITTLE, INC.
1972 *Utilization of Tax Incentives by Non-Profit Organizations to Foster Rehabilitation of Low- and Moderate-Income Housing.* Report to the U.S. Department of Housing and Urban Development, C-72753 (April 28).

GANS, HERBERT J.
1971 "Three Ways to Solve the Welfare Problem." New York *Times Magazine* (March 7), pp. 26–27, 94–100.

HARTMAN, CHESTER W.
1973 "The Private Sector and Community Development: A Cautious Proposal," in Jon Pynoos, Robert Schafer, and Chester W. Hartman, eds., *Housing Urban America.* Chicago: Aldine, pp. 536–42.

HARTMAN, CHESTER W., AND DENNIS KEATING
1974 "The Housing Allowance Delusion." *Social Policy* (January/February), 31–37.

HERBERS, JOHN
1973 "President Urges U.S. Allowances to Spur Housing." New York *Times* (September 20).

———
1971 "Rights Panel Says U.S. Housing Plan Aids Segregation." New York *Times* (June 11).

———
1972 "U.S. Now Big Landlord in Decaying Inner City." New York *Times* (January 2).

HOOD, EDWIN T., AND JAMES A. KUSHNER
1971 "Real Estate Finance: The Discount Point System and Its Effects on Federally Insured Home Loans." *University of Missouri—Kansas City Law Review* 40, 18–19, 23.

LANE, BRUCE S., AND CHARLES L. EDSON
1972 *A Practical Guide to Low- and Moderate-Income Housing.* Washington, D.C.: Bureau of National Affairs, Ch. 11.

LEAMAN, SAM H.
1970 "Estimated Administrative Cost of a National Housing Allowance." Working Paper 112–7. Washington, D.C.: The Urban Institute (May 22).

LILLEY, WILLIAM III
1971 "Washington Pressures/Home Builders' Lobbying Skills Result in Successes, 'Good-Guy' Image." *National Journal* (February 27), 431–44. Reprinted in Jon Pynoos, Robert Schafer, and Chester Hartman, eds; *Housing Urban America,* pp. 30–48.

LILLEY, WILLIAM III, AND TIMOTHY B. CLARK
1972 "Urban Report/Federal Programs Spur Abandonment of Housing in Major Cities." *National Journal* (January 1), 26–33.

MCKEE, WILLIAM S.
1971 "The Real Estate Tax Shelter—A Computerized Exposé." *Virginia Law Review* 57, 521–73.

MAHONEY, MILES
1972 "Housing Myths." Second National Rural Housing Conference, Rural Housing Alliance, Washington, D.C. (November 28–30).

NATIONAL COMMISSION ON URBAN PROBLEMS
1968 *Building the American City.* Washington, D.C.: U.S. Government Printing Office, pp. 100, 178, 31.

NETZER, DICK
1970 *Economics and Urban Problems: Diagnoses and Prescriptions.* New York: Basic Books, pp. 73–79.

———
1969 *Impact of the Property Tax.* Research Report No. 1, National Commission on Urban Problems.

NEW YORK STATE STUDY COMMISSION
1972 *The Management of the Maximum Base Rent (MBR) Program by the Housing and Development Administration of New York City—from June 1970 to October 1972,* pp. 37, 70, 81.

OFFICE OF THE WHITE HOUSE PRESS SECRETARY
    1973 "Housing Policy Recommendations, Fact Sheet" (September 19).

PATMAN, WRIGHT
    1972 Address before the Forty-First Annual Convention of the National Housing Conference (March 5).

PEABODY, MALCOLM JR.
    1972 "Housing Allowances, A New Way to House the Poor." *HUD Challenge* (July), 10–14.

    _____

    1974 "Housing Allowances: A New Way to House the Poor." *New Republic* (March 9), 20–23.

RAINWATER, LEE
    1967 "The Lessons of Pruitt-Igoe." *The Public Interest* (Summer), pp. 116–26. Reprinted in Jon Pynoos, Robert Schafer, and Chester Hartman, eds., *Housing Urban America*, pp. 548–55.

REIN, MARTIN
    1972 "Welfare and Housing." Working Paper No. 4, M.I.T.-Harvard Joint Center for Urban Studies (February).

RITTER, C. WILLIS, AND EMIL M. SUNLEY, JR.
    1970 "Real Estate and Tax Reform: An Analysis and Evaluation of the Real Estate Provisions of the Tax Reform Act of 1969." *Maryland Law Review* 30, 5–48.

RURAL HOUSING ALLIANCE
    1971 *Low-Income Housing Programs for Rural America*, 3rd ed. Washington, D.C.: Rural Housing Alliance (August).

    _____

    1971 *Three Studies of Rural Rental Housing.* Washington, D.C.: Rural Housing Alliance (November).

SCHAFER, ROBERT, AND CHARLES FIELD
    1969 "Section 235 of the National Housing Act: Homeownership for Low-Income Families?" *Journal of Urban Law* 46, 667–85. Reprinted in Jon Pynoos, Robert Schafer, and Chester Hartman, eds., *Housing Urban America*, pp. 460–71.

SCHECHTER, HENRY B.
    1972 "Federal Housing Subsidy Programs," in *The Economics of Federal Subsidy Programs*, Part 5 of a Compendium of Papers Submitted to the Joint Economic Committee, U.S. Congress (October 9), pp. 597–630.

SENGSTOCK, FRANK S., AND MARY C. SENGSTOCK
    1969 "Homeownership: A Goal for All Americans." *Journal of Urban Law* 46, 317–602.

SLITOR, RICHARD E.
    1969 *The Federal Income Tax in Relation to Housing.* Research Report
         No. 5, National Commission on Urban Problems, p. 114, 15.
STERN, PHILIP M.
    1973 *The Rape of the Taxpayer.* New York: Random House, p. 165.
SURREY, STANLEY S.
    1970 "Federal Income Tax Reform: The Varied Approaches Nec-
         essary to Replace Tax Expenditures with Direct Govern-
         mental Assistance." *Harvard Law Review* 84, 397, 403.

    _____

    1970 "Tax Incentives as a Device for Implementing Government
         Policy: A Comparison with Direct Government Expendi-
         tures." *Harvard Law Review* 83, 705–38.

    _____

    1968 "Taxes and the Federal Budget." Address before the Finan-
         cial Executives Institute, Dallas (February 13).
TAGGART, ROBERT III
    1970 *Low-Income Housing: A Critique of Federal Aid.* Baltimore, Md.:
         The Johns Hopkins Press, pp. 71, 82, 67.
THE URBAN INSTITUTE
    1971 *The Section 23 Leasing Program.* Washington, D.C.: The Urban
         Institute.
U.S. COMMISSION ON CIVIL RIGHTS
    1971 *Home Ownership for Lower-Income Families: A Report on the Racial
         and Ethnic Impact of the Section 235 Program,* Appendices A and
         B. Washington, D.C.: U.S. Government Printing Office
         (June).
U.S., CONGRESS, HOUSE
    1972 *Fourth Annual Report on National Housing Goals* (June 29).
         House Document 92–319, 92nd Congress, 2nd Session, pp.
         44–45, 47.
U.S., CONGRESS, HOUSE, COMMITTEE ON BANKING AND CURRENCY
    1970 *Investigation and Hearings of Abuses in Federal Low- and Moderate-
         Income Housing Programs: Staff Report and Recommendations.* 91st
         Congress, 2nd Session (December).
U.S., CONGRESS, HOUSE, COMMITTEE ON GOVERNMENT OPERATIONS
    1972 *Defaults on FHA-Insured Home Mortgages—Detroit, Michigan,*
         15th Report. 92nd Congress, 2nd Session, House Report No.
         92–1152 (June 20).
U.S. DEPARTMENT OF HOUSING AND URBAN DEVELOPMENT
    1971 *1970 HUD Statistical Yearbook,* Tables 145 and 328.

1973 *Report of the Task Force on Improving the Operation of Federally Insured or Financed Housing Programs,* I ("Single-Family Housing"). Washington, D.C.: National Center for Housing Management.

U.S. DEPARTMENT OF HOUSING AND URBAN DEVELOPMENT, OFFICE OF POLICY DEVELOPMENT AND RESEARCH
1973 *First Annual Report of the Experimental Housing Program* (May).

U.S. DEPARTMENT OF LABOR, BUREAU OF LABOR STATISTICS
1973 "Autumn 1972 Urban Family Budgets and Comparative Indexes for Selected Urban Areas" (June 15).

VON FURSTENBERG, GEORGE M.
1972 "The Distribution of Federally Assisted Rental Housing Services by Regions and States," in *The Economics of Federal Subsidy Programs,* Part 5 of a Compendium of Papers Submitted to the Joint Economic Committee, U.S. Congress (October 9), pp. 633–34.

WALLACE, LAURA
1972 "Now Owner of Thousands of Slum Dwellings, FHA Cuts Back on Loans, Tries to Rebuild." *Wall Street Journal* (September 12).

"Mortgage Defaults Costing $2 Billion."
1974 San Francisco *Chronicle* (March 16).

# Chapter 6

# THE FUTURE PROSPECT FOR HOUSING

The country never has had anything that might be called an overall housing policy. (The absence of a national housing policy is strikingly illustrated by a 1970 report of the Comptroller General showing that in 324 cities HUD's urban renewal program had demolished 88,000 more units than had been constructed under all other HUD programs in these cities, that in all there was 70 percent more demolition than construction as a result of HUD activities in these cities.) Until 1968 there was no quantified estimate of how much housing this country would need to provide everyone with a decent place to live, and even the 1968 figure was incomplete. Nor was there any breakdown of where units would be needed, what kinds they should be (other than an indication as to how many should be subsidized), and whom they were to be for. Resource planning to implement this goal was totally absent, and there is still nothing that resembles a true *housing plan* to implement the National Housing Goal of "a decent home and a suitable living environment for every American family." We do not have studies of the housing needs for each metropolitan area and rural region in the country, and without these a national plan of the necessary specificity cannot be developed. We also lack a comprehensive set of standards for defining decent housing and a suitable living environment. Census criteria are of little use. What we need is a national housing and residential environment code, to specify and make operational what we mean by the terms dwelling quality, space standards, ability-to-pay standards, standards for a decent neighborhood environment (including necessary community facilities, municipal services, open space, and transportation), and locational criteria (including access to employment opportunities).

The absence of a national housing policy and plan may stem from the simple fact that implementing such a plan would be exceedingly costly. The Third Annual Report on National Housing Goals (1971) noted that as many as 25 million families—40 percent of the population—may be eligible for federal subsidies under current programs.

> If all eligible families were subsidized, the cost could be astronomical. . . . Since it is doubtful that the public, and hence the Congress, will be prepared to accept the staggering budgetary cost of a more global coverage toward which present housing subsidy programs may be forced to head, the time to make needed changes is rapidly approaching.

The recent redirection of federal housing policy—away from public housing and toward housing allowances—may be seen as an example of these "needed changes." For all of its defects, public housing is (was) the one program that directly added to the supply of decent housing for the poor. The financial difficulties of local housing authorities and the federal government's resistance to implementing the Brooke amendments (which were designed to increase subsidies to house the poor) may be both a representation of the full costs of housing the poor decently and indication of our reluctance to pay those costs. In reference primarily to the staggering long-term costs of the Section 235 and 236 interest-subsidy programs, the Third Annual Report also warned: "Clearly, the public interest demands that the federal government not stand impassively at the cash register and continue to pay whatever is necessary to feed runaway inflation of housing costs." The implication is that the federal government is spending too much for housing, but the truth is that if the housing problem is to be solved, government expenditures will have to be increased substantially. The "needed changes" apparently are not seen as government action to counter this housing cost inflation by exercising government controls to end land speculation and providing direct government loans for housing development.

The report emphasized the concept of "equity" in federal housing aid, and noted how much was spent on a per-household basis for those receiving aid under existing programs, stating "it will be difficult to continue favoring a select few in the population while the rest of the nation is left to seek decent housing completely on its own." Equity, as put forward in this report, apparently requires that existing housing subsidies be thinned out and given to a larger number of people—something for nearly everyone, even though the "something" will not give people enough for decent housing. The goal of equity is laudable, and it is by no means inconsistent with providing decent housing conditions; but the price of meeting both goals comes high.

The real problem is that the nation has never faced, or even calculated, the costs of providing all its people with decent homes and suitable living environments. Compared with present outlays, the costs would indeed be "staggering"—although not so staggering with respect to the nation's $1 trillion-plus GNP and other "needs" such as armaments and space exploration. Cost estimates vary according to housing standards and assumptions about who would be eligible for subsidies. Based on average annual shelter costs ranging from $720 for a single person, $1255 for a family of four, and $2140 for a family of six or more, with the household contributing 15 percent of the first $300 per member from its own income and 25 percent of all its income beyond that, Clay Cochran and George Rucker calculate that an annual subsidy of $9.5 billion would be needed nationally to bridge the housing cost gap (based on 1968 income distribution figures). But if instead we assume shelter costs of $900 a year for single persons and $1800 a year for a family of four, and lower the required contribution from the family's own income to exclude $600 for each household member and demand 25 percent of the remaining income, the national subsidy rises sharply to $25 billion. These latter assumptions are by no means extreme, given the rising costs of housing production, the shortage of decent existing units, and the need for low-income families to pay a minimal proportion of their income for housing, so as to have enough left over for food, medical care, and other requirements.

In the absence of a national housing policy based on rational planning to satisfy social needs, special-interest groups in finance, construction, and real estate have virtually taken over the housing system at all legislative and administrative levels, locally and nationally. According to Herbers:

> Unusually close ties [exist] between the commercial interests which want to see the [housing] programs continue essentially unchanged, and members of Congress responsible for drafting legislation. . . .
>
> [A] common background [exists among] . . . many of the housing experts on the legislative committee staffs, in the Department of Housing and Urban Development and in the industry. The move from one job to another . . . form[s] a closed circle of expertise. . . .
>
> Whenever Senator Sparkman [chairman of the Senate Banking Committee] runs for re-election, the interests his committee regulates pour thousands of dollars into his campaign coffers. . . .
>
> [H]ousing has become an insider's game, with the Banking and Currency Committees of Congress giving lobbying interests pretty much what they wanted in one omnibus housing act after another, with little contributed by

consumers and little public notice of what was going on. . . . The [congressional] subcommittees that write the housing laws have had little public scrutiny. Because the subject is complex and frequently dull, the national press has given little attention to housing.[1]

There is virtually no interest group that represents the housing consumer, no national leaders who are primarily identified with decent housing as a national goal,[2] and no longer a strong "housing movement" of the type that brought about and nurtured the public housing program in the 1930s and 1940s.

A detailed plan to attain "a decent home and a suitable living environment for every American family," backed by the resource commitment and institutional changes necessary to implement this plan, probably can come about only if there is acceptance of the goal as a *right* that can be demanded politically if not legally. But the notion of a right to decent housing conflicts with deeply rooted feelings about the meaning of housing and about race and class in America. Securing a good and satisfying place to live, in an area of one's choice, is generally regarded as something that must be "earned," and not without some struggle— particularly if it is a home the person owns. This ethic is a barrier to achieving these same goals through comprehensive planning and widespread government subsidies. Thus, the Section 235 homeownership program for moderate-income households engendered opposition

> from the lower-middle-class homeowners, who are going to be writing their Congressmen about how they worked and saved to buy a house, and now some guy, with none of that blood and sweat, has gotten a subsidy for an even newer house. These subsidies are going to get resented, especially by the guy at the end of the line who is just a little bit too rich to qualify for the program.[3]

1. The power of the National Association of Home Builders and National Association of Realtors is particularly potent at the state and local levels. On the former, see Lilley, "Washington Pressures/Home Builders' Lobbying Skills Result in Successes, 'Good Guy' Image"; on the latter, see Denton, *Apartheid American Style*. The power nexus among banking interests, large landowners, and government officials at the local level is well described for one city (Cambridge, Massachusetts) in Mollenkopf and Pynoos, "Boardwalk and Park Place: Property Ownership, Political Structure, and Housing Policy at the Local Level."

2. "We also desperately need leadership. There is nobody in America, who is nationally known, who is a crusader for a slumless America. He doesn't exist. I'm thinking of a Martin Luther King, or a Bayard Rustin, or a Whitney Young, or a John Lindsay, or a Governor Rockefeller, or a Hubert Humphrey, or a Gene McCarthy, who says: 'My goal, my plan is a slumless America within the next fifteen years. We have the blueprint, and I am going all out to bring that into being. . . . I'm going to organize a march on Washington on its behalf. I'm going to fight this thing right down to the end, because the basic thing that the cities need is housing.' " Conversation with Timothy Cooney, in "Housing and Education," An Occasional Paper by the Center for Urban Education, New York, April, 1971. While the specific figures mentioned by Cooney may be dated or questionable, his point is extremely valid.

3. Statement of an aide to Senator William Proxmire, quoted in Lilley, "Washington Pressures/Home Builders' Lobbying Skills Result in Successes, 'Good-Guy' Image." See also Welfeld, "Toward a New Federal Housing Policy."

(Interestingly, there was little resentment of this type under the public housing program, which, while expensive, did not provide the kind of housing or housing situation that even approached the American ideal.) One way to eliminate this resentment and opposition might be to expand the group of beneficiaries to cover all those who cannot obtain a decent place to live without government assistance. Another way to develop support for a national housing plan is to clarify to the community as a whole the indirect benefits everyone would receive through the elimination of slum conditions by providing all people with decent living conditions. But the dangers of overemphasizing possible benefits should be avoided: what is referred to as "the urban problem," and its counterpart in rural areas, can only be met with a full range of programs to provide jobs, public services, general income support, and other forms of assistance.

The issues of race and class that underlie any discussion of residential patterns in America will probably be an even greater barrier. Any program that gives people real choice about where they will live and access to newly developed housing over a wide area will mean a substantial degree of racial and socioeconomic heterogeneity as lower-income people move to take advantage of job opportunities[4] and amenities in areas formerly closed to them. It is not clear what form this dispersion would take. Gans points out that segregation among social class lines is based on different class values and patterns with respect to child-rearing, schooling, neighboring and spatial orientations, and other aspects of life-style. To the extent that these are real and insoluble conflicts or true preferences for homogeneity, metropolitan heterogeniety might come about on a "coarse-grained" (relatively homogeneous enclaves scattered throughout the metropolitan area) rather than a "fine-grained" (heterogeneity within each neighborhood) basis.

The extent to which blacks and other racial minorities, given real choices (including the options outlined in chapter 3, "A Comprehensive Approach to Rehabilitation," for renewing the blighted areas they now live in), would leave central city ghetto areas is also unknown. Increasing nonwhite dominance and control of central cities can produce concrete political and economic gains for blacks and other minority groups (as of 1970 blacks represented over 40 percent of the population in Detroit, Washington, Baltimore, New Orleans, Atlanta, St. Louis, Newark, Birmingham, Richmond, Gary, Savannah, East St. Louis, and many smaller cities). But a large proportion of nonwhite families would doubtless prefer to join the suburban exodus, in order to obtain improved housing,

4. On the suburbanization of jobs see *The Impact of Housing Patterns on Job Opportunities,* and Kain, "Housing Segregation, Negro Employment, and Metropolitan Decentralization."

open space, homeownership, better schools and public services, lower taxes, greater access to jobs, and all the other real and presumed benefits that have motivated metropolitan decentralization over the past three decades. An end to the "black neck in a white noose" character of our metropolitan areas would provide substantial benefits to the entire society, not the least of which might be to terminate the inefficient and somewhat absurd system of bussing schoolchildren all around to bring about the kind of integration that could and should be achieved by more direct means.

An additional source of support for a national housing plan might come via the job-creation potential of such an effort. Jobs as well as housing are critical needs for low- and moderate-income people, and a program that fostered both goals in tandem would be a perfect marriage. The present situation in the construction labor force is one of restrictiveness and fear: entry into unions is severely constricted, according to Dubinsky, for nonwhites in particular, and union leaders fear levels of construction that don't provide their members with full-time work and short-term "crash programs" that require expansion of the labor force but then leave union members high and dry after the program ends. The psychology isn't very complicated, as Cooney points out:

> If I'm in the union now, I know that if we can just keep construction at the present level, I'm going to work for the rest of my life. On the other hand, if we suddenly expand the industry, and take in twice as many men in the carpenter's union, and then go into the bust period everything becomes uncertain, seniority does not prevail, maybe I lose my job to a younger carpenter. So my basic position is only build enough, only expand the union to the level of construction on which we've been operating. And this construction [that] happens now in New York City to be mostly office buildings, and a few luxury apartments, is fine with me because I can see that teased out for the next ten years easily.

A massive long-term building program, with provision for ongoing housing maintenance, continuous replacement of the obsolete housing stock, and adequate levels of new construction to house an increasing population, would provide the job stability construction workers rightly demand, particularly if it were part of a broader program to deal with unmet social needs in the areas of schools, hospitals, parks, and other facilities. According to *Economic News Notes,* each new home provides about two person-years of employment, one on site and one off site. Twenty-six million new units means 52 million person-years of employment, and rehabilitation and ongoing maintenance add substantially to this figure. Construction is an ideal field for on-the-job training and could provide jobs and economic mobility for low-income unemployed men and women, white and black. On the community level, programs controlled by the local community to tie in neighborhood renewal with jobs for local residents could effectively solve several problems simultaneously. On a national level, a movement for a slumless America in five to ten years would be much more likely to develop if it were joined with a movement for a job for everyone over that same period.

Ada Louis Huxtable has written: "The hard truth is that there is absolutely no way, with current tools, procedures, and appropriations, of solving America's basic shelter problems." That truth at least should be clearly comprehended. At the government level expenditure levels are miniscule compared with need, and the required degree of public intervention in and control over the housing system has not been accepted. The private sector's need for profit from new housing production—in land speculation, money lending, materials production, and development —as well as from the ownership and operation of existing housing conflicts frequently and drastically with the human right to live decently. Establishment and implementation of a right to decent housing is essentially a political question. It is not a matter of further studies and commissions. The reports of the President's Committee on Urban Housing, the National Advisory Commission on Civil Disorders, and especially the National Commission on Urban Problems laid out the basic nature of the housing problem and many of the steps needed to attain the national housing goal, but as Shuman points out, these reports have mostly been ignored. Failure to face the fundamental issues of resource distribution and political control will consign millions of American families to substandard living conditions and excessive housing costs for decades to come.

## References

CENTER FOR URBAN EDUCATION
    1971  Conversation with Tim Cooney, in *Housing and Education.* Occasional paper, New York (April).
COCHRAN, CLAY, AND GEORGE RUCKER
    1973  "Every American Family: Housing Need and Nonresponse," in Donald J. Reeb and James T. Kirk, Jr., eds., *Housing the Poor.* New York: Praeger Publishers, pp. 167–69.

COMPTROLLER GENERAL OF THE UNITED STATES
1970 *Opportunity to Improve Allocation of Program Funds to Better Meet the National Housing Goal.* Report to Congress, B-118754 (October 2).

DENTON, JOHN
1967 *Apartheid American Style.* Berkeley, Calif.: Diablo Press.

DOWNS, ANTHONY
1970 "Alternative Futures for the American Ghetto," in *Urban Problems and Prospects.* Chicago, Ill.: Markham Publishing Company, pp. 27–74.

DUBINSKY, IRWIN
1971 "Trade Union Discrimination in the Pittsburgh Construction Industry: How and Why It Operates." *Urban Affairs Quarterly* (March), 297–318. Reprinted in Jon Pynoos, Robert Schafer, and Chester W. Hartman, eds., *Housing Urban America.* Chicago, Ill.: Aldine, pp. 376–91.

GANS, HERBERT J.
1961 "The Balanced Community: Homogeneity or Heterogeneity in Residential Areas." *Journal of the American Institute of Planners* 27 (August), 176–84. Reprinted in Pynoos, Schafer, and Hartman, eds., *Housing Urban America,* pp. 135–46.

HERBERS, JOHN
1972 "Federal Housing Aid Stirs Widening Debate." New York *Times* (January 3).

_____
1972 "Federal Housing Reform Unlikely Despite Scandal." New York *Times* (September 20).

_____
1972 "Housing and Government: Official Criticism of Subsidy Program Is Growing." New York *Times* (February 1).

HUXTABLE, ADA LOUISE
1969 "Housing: The American Myth." New York *Times* (April 21).

KAIN, JOHN F.
1968 "Housing Segregation, Negro Employment, and Metropolitan Decentralization." *Quarterly Journal of Economics* 82 (May), 175–97.

LILLEY, WILLIAM III
1971 "Washington Pressures/Home Builders' Lobbying Skills Result in Successes, 'Good-Guy' Image." *National Journal* (Feb-

ruary 27), 431–44. Reprinted in Pynoos, Schafer, and Hartman, eds., *Housing Urban America,* pp. 30–48.

MOLLENKOPF, JOHN, AND JON PYNOOS
    1973 "Boardwalk and Park Place: Property Ownership, Political Structure, and Housing Policy at the Local Level," in Pynoos, Schafer, and Hartman, eds., *Housing Urban America,* pp. 55–74.

NATIONAL ASSOCIATION OF HOME BUILDERS
    1970 "Significance of Home Building in the American Economy," special supplement, *Economic News Notes.* Washington, D.C.: National Association of Home Builders (April).

NATIONAL COMMITTEE AGAINST DISCRIMINATION IN HOUSING
    1968 *The Impact of Housing Patterns on Job Opportunities.* New York: National Committee Against Discrimination in Housing.

PIVEN, FRANCES, AND RICHARD CLOWARD
    1967 "The Case Against Urban Desegregation." *Social Work* (January), 12–21. Reprinted in Pynoos, Schafer, and Hartman, eds., *Housing Urban America.* Chicago, Ill.: Aldine, pp. 97–107.

SHUMAN, HOWARD E.
    1969 "Behind the Scenes ... and under the Rug." *Washington Monthly* (July), 14–22.

U.S., CONGRESS, HOUSE
    1971 *Third Annual Report on National Housing Goals* (June 29). House Document 92–136, 92nd Congress, 1st Session, pp. 22–24.

WELFELD, IRVING H.
    1970 "Toward a New Federal Housing Policy." *The Public Interest* (Spring), 31–43.

# INDEX